Cornish Cases

Essays in Eighteenth and
Nineteenth Century Social History

John Rule

Foreword by Professor Roger Burt

CORNISH CASES

Essays in Eighteenth and Nineteenth Century Social History

First published in 2006 by Clio Publishing, Southampton, England.

www.cliopublishing.co.uk

A full CIP record for this book is available from the British Library.

ISBN: 0-9542650-8-4

Designed & typeset by Steve Messer, Southampton.
Printed by Antony Rowe, Eastbourne.

For my family, past and present.

The Experience of Labour in Eighteenth-Century Industry (1981)

'A well-written book which all teachers of modern industrial change should read'
(Teaching History)

The Labouring Classes in Early Industrial England c. 1750 to 1850 (1986)

'This is a magnificent accomplishment…his knowledge of the secondary literature is astounding, his guidance through it masterful…perusing it as a whole is an enormously enriching experience' (Callum Brown)

'…a work to be cherished by all serious students of modern social history…in many ways a classic…a quality of detail allied to unremitting analysis makes this an immensely educative read…a major achievement' (Teaching History)

'Tout a fait excellent. C'est a coup sur le meilleur ouvrage que nous possedions sur la question' (Annales)

'…rich in factual detail and judicious in its syntheses…it will be welcomed by all who recognise the importance of expanding our understanding of the economic bases of this watershed period in English history' (Albion)

The Vital Century: England's Developing Economy 1714-1815 (1992)

'…general readers and university students alike have been done a great service by the publication of this fine pair of historical surveys…succeeds with elegance and facility…should enjoy a wide readership for years to come' (History)

Albion's People: English Society, 1714-1815 (1992)

'His work sparkles with insights…there is certainly nothing better available' (Higher)

(with Roger Wells) Crime, Protest and Popular Politics in Southern England 1740-1840 (1970)

'This valuable collection gathering essays that two distinguished social have written over two decades, sets out to rescue the English rural south from historical neglect' (Victorian Studies)

'…both illuminates and challenges standard historiographical assumptions and offers a first rate model for those whose interest in popular politics leans towards local analysis (Albion)

Contents

Acknowledgements

Chapters 1, 2 and 12 appear here for the first time.

Chapters 4, 8 and 10 are reprinted from John Rule and Roger Wells, *Crime, Protest and Popular Politics in Southern England 1740 to1850*, (1997), pp. 53-66; 67-80, 81-90 with the permission of Hambledon Press.

Chapter 7 first appeared in R. D. Storch, (ed.), *Popular Culture and Custom in Nineteenth Century England*, (Croom Helm, 1982) pp. 48-70.

Chapter 3 originated in a paper given to a conference on the Archaeology and Anthropology of Mining held at Bellagio and funded by the Rockefeller Foundation. It was subsequently printed in A. Bernard Knapp, Vincent C. Pigott and Eugenia W. Herbert, (eds.), *Social Approaches to an Industrial Past*, (1998), pp. 155-173 and appears with the permission of Routledge.

Chapters 6 and 11 are reprinted from *Southern History*, Vol. 20/21, 1999, pp. 168-188 and Vol. 22, 2000, pp. 168-188 and appear with the permission of the Southern History Society.

Chapter 10 originated at a Conference on the regional implantation of Labour Movements held at Gronnigen in 1990. It was published in *Tijdschrift voor Sociale geschiedenis*, 18e jaargang, No. 2/3 July, 1992, pp. 248-262.

Chapter 5 is reprinted from *Cornish Studies*, 9, 2001, pp. 127-144 with the permission of the editor.

Public Record Office (PRO) material appears by permission of the Controller of H.M. Stationery Office.

Thanks are offered to the several funding bodies who in part supported research for this project: The British Academy, the Nuffield Foundation, the Rockefeller Foundation and the Research Fund of the University of Southampton.

Special thanks are due to Dr Susan England and Steve Messer of Clio Publishing.

Illustrations and Abbreviations

Chapter 1 Introduction
Elizabeth ('Bessie') Simmons and her daughters, Agnes and Maud. Author's personal collection.
Richard and Margaret Rule and family. Author's personal collection.
Frederick John ('Fred-John') Simmons, South Africa, c. 1897.
Author's personal collection.
Tom Rowse and family members. Author's personal collection.

Chapter 2
Handbill: 'Cato', circulated at Stratton in 1801. Public Record Office, Home Office, HO, 42/61.
Broadsheet: endorsed: 'Starving - Bonaparte and Bread before Oppression'. Public Record Office, Home Office, HO 42/61.

Chapter 3 and Front cover
Engraving of working miners. Source unknown. Author's personal collection.
Botallack Mine, St Just. C. Redding, *An Illustrated Itinerary of Cornwall*.
Cartoons by Oswald Pryor. Reproduced with kind permission of the artist's family.

Chapter 5
Miners at Redruth, *Western Morning News*.
Miner in mine shaft. C. Redding, *An Illustrated Itinerary of Cornwall*.

Chapter 7
'Primitive Methodists at Prayer', St Ives. W. H. Y. Titcomb, 1889. Reproduced with kind permission of the Dudley Museum and Art Gallery.
Hurling at St Colomb, www.kernowcottages.co.uk
Billy Bray. Frontispiece to F. W. Bourne, *The King's Son, or a Memoir of Billy Bray*, 1898 edition.

Chapter 9

The island and harbour, St Ives. H. Besley, *Cornwall*, n.d.

Vignette of William Lovett by W. Langstaffe, R. Tawney, (ed.,) *Life and Struggles of William Lovett*, MacGibbon & Kee, 1967.

Chapter 10

'The Gentleman and the Miner', John Opie, 1786. The painting shows Thomas Daniell who profited greatly from investment in mines like Wheal Towan (in the background). The miner is probably Thomas Morcom, a captain at the mine.

Reproduced with the kind permission of the Royal Institution of Cornwall, Royal Cornwall Museum.

Chapter 11

Fish sellers. *Western Morning News.*

'Jowsters' with baskets in 1842. C. Redding, *An Illustrated Itinerary of Cornwall.*

Mounts Bay luggers. C. Redding, *An Illustrated Itinerary of Cornwall.*

Trawlers. C. Redding, *An Illustrated Itinerary of Cornwall.*

Chapter 12

Woman collecting 'furze and turf': the main source of fuel in St Just cottage. *Early Photographs. The West Cornwall Peninsula.*

Abbreviations

BL	British Library
BM Add Mss	British Museum Additional Manuscripts
BPP	British Parliamentary Papers
SC	Select Committee
RC	Royal Commission
CRO	Cornwall Record Office
CL	Courtney Library, County Museum, Truro
Jenkin Mss	Letter books of William Jenkin
PRO	Public Record Office
HO	Home Office
SP Dom	State Papers Domestic
WO	War Office

Foreword

John Rule is not the most well-known of Cornish historians but he is the most important and influential of his generation. While many others have provided a bounty of glossy popular publications for locals, tourists and a compliant overseas Diaspora, John has focussed on producing his research in a range of highly specialised academic journals. It shows. Much of what is presented here is not an easy read – there are no diverting anecdotes and pictures to speak of – and it is frequently couched in the sometimes complex and impenetrable language of the academic historian – but it is none the worse for that. The issues he deals with are complex and often require recourse to a wide range of other scientific literature. Readers will have to think hard to derive the full benefit of his work, but it will repay their labour. While many others have been content to rework an essentially imagined historical tradition of the county, embroidering upon it with every retelling, John has laboured in many archives, piecing together and interpreting the social dynamics of the county in a lost age. His research has undoubtedly moved us further forward; has added significantly to our knowledge and understanding of the past; and has provided invaluable signposts for future work. He has laid down many of the essential building blocks that I, and others, have used in constructing and extending our own research and will no doubt help and inspire others in the future. Most importantly, John has projected Cornish history in its wider national and international context. He does not simply claim that the experience was somehow different and special – he shows us how it was different, how much it was different, and investigates carefully and methodically what may have produced the difference.

As he tells us, John's contribution may have been conceived during a childhood in Cornwall but was intellectually delivered during his undergraduate and graduate years in Cambridge and Warwick. This time exposed him to the great debates and intellects in social and economic history that blossomed during the third quarter of the twentieth century. He was particularly fortunate to encounter E. P. Thompson, the most influential social historian of his age. It was from him that he learnt the techniques and skills of the professional historian and, more importantly, the penetrating analytical approaches that have remained a distinguishing mark of his life's work. Rule became the heir to Thompson and carried and progressed that tradition more effectively than any of his other now eminent students. From Thompson, John acquired two vital historiographical truths – the importance of careful micro-history, and the essential need to interpret findings in the wider context of general intellectual debate. The material reproduced here clearly reflects both strands. The masterful knowledge of primary and secondary sources, the careful analysis of their content, and the painstaking presentation of conclusion. The whole conducted in the context of wide understanding of old and emerging issues across the social sciences. Working almost alone in eighteenth and early nineteenth century Cornish history during the 1970s and 1980s, he was very much the progenitor of what is now seen as the 'new' Cornish historiography'. Thus, the work presented here encompasses what today would be regarded as aspects of ethnographic history, gender history, maritime and mining history, as well as the history of religion, and industrial relations and management. Modern practitioners in all of those and other specialized fields – not just in Cornish history – would commonly find it useful to reference work produced by John three decades ago and more.

John's career focuses attention on an issue that has long been a conundrum for those who have promoted, and indeed admirably succeeded, in establishing a broad based higher education institution in Cornwall. On the one hand the new Combined Universities in Cornwall provides facilities for those who live and work in the county and means that they no longer need to leave in order to complete their education. Similarly, it provides an admirable vehicle to foster the study of Cornish culture and identity. But John's experience clearly shows the even greater benefits that can be derived from the very act of stepping beyond the county into the great national and international centres of learning. To acquire the skills of and inspiration to go back to the county and to see and study it within the broader context. To see it more clearly for what it is but to understand it much the better through the perspective of every 'special' locality. That new institution must take care to balance its attention with an eye to both traditions if it is to produce a new generation of historians comparable to John Rule. What is clear is this collection will greatly assist in resolving that conundrum. Setting the Cornish social experience in the wider context of academic debate it will provide an essential basic text for any course on modern Cornish history developed for students in further and higher education – a clear methodological model for others to follow. A path that can be further clarified by reference to his more widely known and admired books on the social history of Britain as a whole. Here the particular Cornish context can be clearly portrayed against the national picture. Cornwall has been fortunate to produce an historian of national stature who has still found the time and enthusiasm to turn his skills to a sustained study of his home county – few others have done so. His work has served the county well and its real impact is yet to come.

Roger Burt
Exeter
October 2006.

1 Introduction

Contexts

I am a Cornish Historian in both senses. I am a Cornishman who has had a more than thirty year career researching and teaching history at a university, and an historian of Cornwall in that a quarter of my fifty publications have been wholly concerned with the history of that county and several more partly so. [1] So far as 'being Cornish' is concerned I was born in Redruth of Cornish parents, moving at the age of eleven to Truro. Until I went to Cambridge in 1962 to read history, I had apart from a few trips to Plymouth only once been out of the county, for a short holiday at Torquay. My decision to seek a career as an academic historian was quite a sudden one. Halfway through my degree at Cambridge in 1963, I read Edward Thompson's newly published *The Making of the English Working Class* and even at the then astonishing price of 63 shillings dug deeply into my student pocket to buy it. The impact of the book on my generation was huge. Thompson's 'socialist humanism', drawing on a British Marxist cultural tradition and moving away from the economic determinism of Marxist orthodoxy, brought a new subtlety and inter-rogative power to the emerging discipline of social history. He opened previously closed doors, famously, to use his own phrase, rescuing his-tory's forgotten groups, including casualties of technological change like the Luddites and handloom weavers from the 'enormous condescension of posterity'. [2] Finding out that Thompson would be moving to the brand new University of Warwick to direct a Centre for the Study of Social His-tory, I made contact and with his encouragement succeeded in obtaining a postgraduate scholarship to undertake a Ph.D at the Centre. [3]

I arrived at Warwick in October 1965 armed with little more in the way of a defined project than a stubborn determination that Cornwall should figure large in my researches. Thompson had misgivings at first, wanting a broader concern with the South West. I needed to convince him that there was scope enough. I recall pointing out that Hamilton Jenkin's classic history of the miners was even then 40 years old, while John Rowe's excellent *Cornwall in the Age of the Industrial Revolution* was primarily an economic history. I presented two long research papers one on food rioting in Cornwall, his own interest at the time, and a second on Methodist influence on the miners. Methodism had been discussed in an extremely critical and controversial chapter in *The Making of the English Working Class*. The Cornish do not easily give ground and the outcome was the registration of a thesis under the title 'The Labouring Miner in Cornwall c. 1740 to 1870: a Study in Social History'. The matter had been settled by the end of the first term when I returned to Cornwall to begin my first stint in the County's archives.

Did it make sense to be working on a thesis on Cornish miners at a university on the outskirts of Coventry? In 1965 it did. There was then no appropriate university presence in Cornwall. So far as spending research time there, my family home was in Truro so I incurred neither expense nor discomfort! London's essential places, the Public Record Office, the British Museum and its Newspaper Collections at Collingdale were reachable for 29 shillings on a day return and as far as expenses were concerned, the grant authorities were rather more forthcoming than they later became. There was no University library in Cornwall, while at Warwick essential resources like the British Parliamentary Papers were directly available. [4] The networking of historians now working in Cornwall did not then exist. I do not remember meeting any other postgraduate researchers of Cornish history during my doctorate period. Of course like so many others over the years I benefited from the assistance and guidance of Henry Douch, and Peter Hull, the main 'keepers' of Cornwall's archives and from time to time met with an older generation, John Rowe, Norman Pounds, and F. L. Harris, mainly through the seminars run at Dartington Hall by Exeter's Department of Economic history where I also met Roger Burt, now Professor of Mining history and an historian of Cornish mining of my own generation. I also benefited by the growth in serious history publishing not only of histories of lasting value such as Thomas Shaw's *History of Cornish Methodism*, but also of reprinted sources. At the same time there was an encouraging stirring of activity in some specialist areas, notably in industrial archaeology and in the local history of Methodism, exampled by the permanently useful data collected and processed by John Probert. At Warwick I did not work in isolation. Seminars at Warwick were enormously stimulating. Thompson's reputation was such that few turned down invitations to come to them. It was not hard for a young scholar at Warwick then to feel close to where things were happening.

My postgraduate years ended in 1968 and I was appointed to a lectureship at Southampton University where I spent the rest of my academic career. I was required to teach a course on the international economy since 1780 as well as an advanced course on eighteenth century industrial labour. It took me a couple of years to complete my thesis, which was submitted in 1971. With completion I had to make a decision. I had at first some not well thought out ideas of rushing into immediate publication, but I had no real enthusiasm. These days when the Research Assessment Exercise has become the main driver of publication, doubtless I would be denied the luxury of working to my own timetable, then I was able to put the thesis aside. I had every intention of returning to it, but had the conceit that I would be able to so as a more mature and developed historian. I did, however, begin to write-up two projects. Working on Cornwall had given me an interest in the fishing industry sufficient to begin researching its national development. After publishing an overview of its modern development, I produced an article on the harsh lives of the North Sea trawler men. This was followed by one, included in this collection, on the role of the market in the nineteenth century expansion of the deep-sea fisheries of the South West. [5] My second project was to involve me in a publishing venture, which attracted a great deal of attention. When searching the public records for information on wreckers, I came across a set of printed questionnaires returned to the Home Office in 1839 from every coastguard district. For the moment I noted the evidence from Cornwall, but once the thesis was finished, I turned to write an account of wrecking around the coastline of England and Wales. This article was to appear in 1975 in a volume of essays on crime and society in Hanoverian England in the company of contributions from Thompson and three others from the Centre. Entitled *Albion's Fatal Tree* it helped set the agenda for the history of crime and the criminal justice system, sold in large numbers, especially in the USA and provoked much critical response. For a while it gave currency to the idea that a 'Warwick School' was overturning the received historiography of eighteenth century England. [6]

I had not done with crime and wrote two further pieces, one on defining 'social crime', and the other using sheep stealing as a way into an investigation of rural crime. The former in particular has had some influence. [7] At this time too I was making progress on a book on eighteenth century industrial labour. This was published in 1981 and led the way for a series of articles on aspects of protest and early trade unionism. I was then commissioned to contribute a book on the English working class to a well-regarded series. *The Labouring Classes in Early Industrial England c. 1750 to 1850* appeared in 1986. It was generally well-received, being described by one reviewer as a 'magnificent accomplishment' and by another as 'in many ways a classic'. [8] My thoughts then began to turn again to my thesis, by now fifteen years old! But one more project was to prove too tempting to refuse; that was Lord Briggs's project to cover the eighteenth century for his well-established economic and social history of England. I completed this over the next five years and it came out in 1992 in two volumes: *The Vital Century. England's Developing Economy 1714-1815* and its companion, *Albion's People: English Society 1714-1815*.

It might appear that all this research and writing activity together with a full teaching programme would have precluded my doing much Cornish history. In fact I continued to mine a Cornish lode. I did not set out to submit completed articles to the journals. Rather I responded to invitations to contribute to symposia, especially those related to thematic conferences. Several of the essays in this book went through this process. Accordingly they saw the light of day in a variety of places, abroad in some cases: Gronnigen, Maastricht. The Hague, Bellagio and Prato as well as Dartington, Liverpool, Oxford, London, Leicester and Cornwall itself. What I planned eventually was an over-arching monograph, which would embrace the fishing as well as the mining communities. By 2000 I was ready to begin. I had secured funding and had negotiated an early retirement from my chair at Southampton. Circumstances changed.

They did so without warning in the shape of a diagnosis of Parkinson's Disease. The physical research effort needed to write a new ethnographic micro-history was not now sustainable, but over the last three years I have been sufficiently well to edit and complete this present collection. There is, I admit, an element of self indulgence in this, but it has cost no one's time but mine and need cost no one money, unless they volunteer a purchase! In particular I would be delighted if this collection were to prove useful to the increasing numbers involved in teaching Cornish history. The essays present argument and seek to provoke discussion. With this in mind I have had to accept a degree of overlap to allow the essays to be read independently. Thus the 'Configuration of Quietism' for example stands as a polemic. Were I to revise it too heavily it would not slip so well into its particular slot in Cornish historiography.

While most of us have our moments of the mind when we think we sparkle with intellectual brilliance, what characterises the work of historians generally, certainly to a greater extent than in other disciplines in the humanities, is the sense of following a skilled craft. The key perhaps is the relationship to evidence. History demands an engagement with evidence of all kinds and is therefore rather harder than some post-modernists think. There are some similarities to the legal process in the notion of historical 'proof'. The jury must be convinced by sound argument based on hard evidence. That evidence involves both the application of forensic skills and the evaluation of concurrent or contesting testimony. It is easy enough to effect a scorn for empiricism, but the grand approach and the 'big question' proceed the better, the stronger their foundation in knowledge. There is, it is said, 'no safety in numbers', but statistics if they cannot always be as robust as social investigators would want, can at least help to indicate upper and lower limits. There is much to think about in the post-modernist position. But good social historians anyway have always read texts with a proper concern for their authorship and intended audience, reading them at times with an 'attentive disbelief'. Sharpness in the scrutiny and evaluation of sources has always been part of the logic of historical practice, more so, perhaps than in much sociology. As important for good historical practice is a sense of historical context. This is needed to avoid the inapt comparison, if the understanding of history is to be advanced through analogy. Even the most local of histories contain at least an implicit comparison, after all 'peculiarities' and 'particularities' are not self-defining, while 'differences' are obviously from something. The deployment of the possessioning adjective 'Cornish' is sometimes stretched to the limit by those who market the county, without an appropriate sense of whether it is actually describing uniqueness, significant difference or a minor variation. For example, Cornish smuggling, real and important enough in its own location was so far as government was concerned, less of a problem than smuggling in Kent and Sussex where the narrowness of the sea crossing was aided by the nearness of the enormous market for contraband provided by London. These counties were responsible in the 1770s for an estimated loss to national revenue five times as large as that contributed by Cornwall. However, from the local perspective it could be noted that at that time, St Ives seizures were almost treble the value of the Port's legal trade, while, it appears that the Cornish vessels though smaller tended to be more heavily armed. 'Cornish wrecking' too was hardly unique, wrecking took place around the coasts and in places, for example the Wirral Peninsula, was a way of life. But partly because of the nearness of the mining districts to the coast, the size of the crowds involved was larger in Cornwall than those that assembled elsewhere. Cornish wrecking was a crowd activity in which by weight of numbers, with a sufficient sense of determination, wreckers could secure their object despite attempts to prevent them. [9]

The proclivity of Cornish miners for food rioting has been often stressed. Thompson's striking description of them as 'notoriously' having an 'irascible consumer consciousness and a readiness to turn out in force' has perhaps been seen as marking the miners as a very special case, but as is shown in Chapter Two of this book, many communities of mining or manufacturing workers, including the textile workers of Devonshire shared the proclivity. Indeed this tradition of protesting against rising corn and flour prices lasted longest in Devon. The last Cornish episodes were in 1847, parts of Devon experienced rioting in 1858 and 1867. [10] While food riots took place on hundreds of sites, they did so in ways which were responsive to local conditions, as were the particular choices from the forms of action offered in the repertoire of contention. Food riots were national in the sense that in several years they were extremely widespread, i.e. 'countrywide'. Their specific targets however depended on the local patterns of food production and distribution while if the deficiencies of government were blamed, then it was local not national governance which was failing to protect the poor. That is not to deny any particularity to food rioting in Cornwall. Cornish food riots were larger than most others; and they were certainly peculiar in only missing out in a single year, and with at one time or another all the known forms being used, they exhibited the most variety. One of these forms, the visiting of grain hoarding farmers, with a noose and threatening a hanging unless they signed an agreement to bring their corn to market for sale at a reasonable price, seems to be found only in Cornwall or Devon. [11]

Much is currently being written on 'Cornish identity' and how it is related to 'differences'. I have no problem in thinking of myself as Cornish, being born in Redruth of Cornish parents. I don't speak the Cornish language, but it is nevertheless a source of pride to me that we have one! I am reminded also that in my time of growing up to hear someone described as 'proper Cornish' meant that they spoke with a heavy dialect. Dialect matters in culture perhaps as much as does language. It seems to me for example that there is a distinctive Cornish humour, which depends on the rhythms and patterns of everyday Cornish speech. It can be found in the captions to Oswald Pryor's cartoons and in a large number of locally produced slim books. In his memories of forty years previously J. S. Flynn writing in 1917 observed that while the Cornishman was very sensitive to the criticism of strangers:

He could rock with laughter, while his foibles and blunders and quaint dialect were set forth with even outrageous exaggeration, by a native, born and bred. I have seen a room full of rustics convulsed with merriment, girls stuffing handkerchiefs into their mouths while tears streamed from their eyes, men excitingly ejaculating words of appreciation, as one of their number read a Cornish tale of some Jan or Lisbeth, out for a first time ride on a railway train, or a steam-boat excursion, or a visit to grandfather. [12]

This observation is useful as it presents dialect as a cohesive force, not in a socially vertical sense but rather in a horizontal one. It is a linguistic frontier, although perhaps not a high one. It at least excludes most 'foreigners' except for the odd ethnographer.

Elites might learn it and indeed parade this knowledge in print. But in general, dialect offers some possibilities of hearing the voices of the ordinary Cornish. There are also the 'voices' responding to the prompting questions of members of Parliamentary enquiries such as those of 1842 and 1867. [13] They can tell us something, as can a few autobiographies or autobiographical fragments. Dialects like languages have a history. What the later nineteenth century might defend as a natural, but quaint feature of the local populace, might at one time have been viewed differently. There were claims that the tinners spoke and even appeared as a different race distinguished not only from higher social classes, but even from the lower ranks of local urban society. James Silk Buckingham recalled of a body of food rioters 300 to 400 strong entering Flushing in the 1790s, that they were all armed with clubs and dressed in the mud-stained frocks and trousers in which they worked, and were 'speaking an uncouth jargon, which none but themselves could understand'. [14]

With the exception of the one on the fishing industry, all the essays in this volume are concerned with the period from the early eighteenth century to the mid-Victorian years. It seems to me that by the 1870s, and in part driven by cultural forces as well as by the changing economy and the great emigration, an older Cornwall was already well into a period of irreversible change. The late A.L Rowse began his *A Cornish Childhood* sixty years ago:

There is the village in my mind's eye, as it was in those years before the last war, the age-long routine of Cornish life still unbroken, though perhaps like an old grandfather clock it was winding down slowly, imperceptibly, to a stop. [15]

For Rowse the War brought 'all that life of habit' to a stop. It ended the old calendar customs, although he already relied on his father for an account of many of these as he did for the more spontaneous displays of popular theatre such as the 'shivaree', the public teasing of couples on their bridal night with much noise and bawdy humour. Curiously Rowse could 'throw no light' on this custom, not knowing even if it was general or peculiar to his home village of Tregonisssey. In fact it is clear from his description that 'shivaree' is a corruption of 'charivari' a widespread form of public display, sometimes known as 'Skimmington' or 'rough music' and not always as benign as it is described by Rowse. Not all had passed away, he could remember for himself St Austell feast, lasting for almost a week with its games, processions and donkey races, During it the Wesleyans, Baptists, Primitives, Bible Christians, and Wesleyan Reformers had their tea treats in different fields though on the same day - the 'church people' however 'held rather aloof' choosing a different day. [16]

There is a passage near the beginning of Thomas Hardy's *Tess of the d'Urbervilles*, which on a recent re-reading seemed to me to capture well the sense of what was happening:

Between the mother, with her fast-perishing lumber of superstitions, folk-lore, dialect and orally transmitted ballads, and the daughter, with her trained National teachings and Standard knowledge under an infinitely Revised Code, there was a gap of two hundred years as ordinarily understood. When they were together the Jacobean and the Victorian ages were juxtaposed. [17]

The Revised Code with its conditional financial support for schools came in 1862. Dorset is not Cornwall, but this powerful insight transcends the local. What is being sensed here is not simply a consequence of the growth of literacy, that process was already well under way, what is at issue is a shift in everyday cosmology. Henry Quick, Zennor's 'People's Poet' caught the moment succinctly:

Our Cornish drolls are dead, each one;
The fairies from their haunts have gone;
There's scarce a witch in all the land,
The world has grown so learn'd and grand. [18]

What observers thought they saw happening was a decline in the 'simplicity' of the manners of the common people, indeed a keyword with several of them was 'peasantry.' 'The peasantry of the Duchy were, until recent years, a people apart' wrote J.S. Flynn in 1917, in regretting that:

> ...destructive criticism has succeeded in banishing many of the old and harmless beliefs, which in days long gone by, enlivened the peasant life of the county, and it is doubtful if, with a school in every village, they will ever get back again.

He also feared the effects of the arrival of universal schooling, which although inevitable, had come with a heavy price: the likelihood of the 'utter destruction of one of the quaintest and most fascinating dialects in England, and with its departure, the loss of humour, originality, and sweet old-world manners'. [19] It was a similar belief, which C. C. Rogers expressed in her sensitive essays. Writing in 1923 she anticipated an imminent end to the dialect and folkways of old Cornwall:

> Very soon, in ten years, fifteen years perhaps, these memories will be forgotten. The very words, those old expressive Cornish words, no longer will be heard, no longer understood. Surely it is well to gather up memories while we may... to keep alive the memory of... Cornish folk who lived their quiet lives in quiet places. [20]

Perhaps the 'quiet lives' were too quiet for little enough survives to tell us how far and in what forms the Cornish articulated feelings about many things, even about being Cornish, or for that matter English, and since we cannot hear their voices, we can do little other than assume that at least to some degree their writings, which survive, can show something of the way things were spoken. His biographer has perhaps sanitized Billy Bray the best known of the miner-preachers. His manuscript journal suggests perhaps less control of syntax and orthography, although an undeniable ability to express meaning is present:

Hee was good to me when i was a sarvant of the Devel so i shold been down in Hell now. But thanks bee to god I am out of hell in the way to heven, bles his holey name if aney one have reason to speak good of the Lord tis me for he have done great things for me. Bles the Lord for his goodness to the Childron of men. They think that there is none need for as much to do as to lepe and dance and make so much noise for the Lord is not deaf and he knaw harts, and you must know that Devil is not deaf neither and yet his sarventes make a great noise. [21]

Religious idioms and rhetoric are perhaps the easiest to find in the writings or recorded speech of the Cornish poor, but other discourses are also present in trace if not in full exposition. Henry Quick, the Zennor poet wrote in 1835:

Old England is my native plain
God did create and me sustain
Twas on fair Cornwall's northwest shore
On Zennor coast, December four,
Seventeen hundred ninety-two
Born was I in this world of woe. [22]

'Old' England is usually an affectionate usage of belonging, often tinged with nostalgia. But Quick moves on very quickly to locate, specifically, the Cornish site of his birth. Possibly 'fair' Cornwall outweighs 'old' England? Anonymous letters of protest can be considered to reveal something of popular usages. One pinned to a blacksmith's door at St Just in 1795 urging the inhabitants to arm themselves preparatory to a food riot, ended with the Cornish rallying cry: 'So one and all'... So one and all', while another posted at Stratton in 1801 called on the 'labouring men' to march 'one and all' in search of concealed corn, but it also urged that 'you show yourselves men and true born Englishmen not to be enslaved by any nation or power of men on earth'. This combination of the Cornish rallying call with the radical discourse of the 'Free-born Englishman' was not unique. [23] A handbill circulating in Hayle at the time of the Chartist rising of 1839 also invoked this discourse: 'Show yourselves not cowards or slaves but free Englishmen'. [24]

Few if any Cornish working-class radicals have left a longer record of their public speaking than the Truro Chartist Richard Spurr whose addresses at public meetings were regularly recorded in the local press. His targets were typical Chartist ones, like the New Poor Law, the urban police and the corn laws, and he was committed to the remedies sought in the National Petition for reform, but at times he injected elements of Cornish protest rhetoric into his orations. At a meeting called to petition for repeal of the corn laws, he interrupted to say that it was necessary to go further:

...the best way of getting these corn laws repealed is by enfranchising the people... he would say that Cornishmen should not want a working man to support their claims... the Cornish motto is one and all and let us all go together on this occasion. [25]

At the other end of things there was the élite discourse of Burkean conservatism, which was of course in itself older than Edmund Burke's celebrated counter-manifesto of 1790. William Borlase for example wrote to his Cornish neighbour Sir John St Aubyn in 1745, 'If I can see anything in our English History, 'tis that the poor nation is always the worse for alterations'. While Richard Polwhele's long poem of 1797 idealises 'The Old English Gentleman', in its title and nostalgic content, this vicar of Kenwyn and Kea could include a Cornish parvenu like Sir William Lemon within the discourse of traditional English paternalism:

In him we admire the old country gentleman, faithful to his king without servility, attached to the people without democracy. [26]

In a typically penetrating review of Cornish historiography Bernard Deacon has represented my work as 'prominent among' those who have developed a 'labour history' approach in which the emphasis is on the weakness of Chartism and early trade unionism. In particular he is concerned with my suggestion of a configuration of explanatory factors. His criticisms are well made, and responding to them in part explains the reappearance of the key article of 1992 in this collection. I, of course, accept my concern with the kind of consciousness that determined the take-up of the early labour movement, is a limiting one. [27]

But in fact the essay was first presented to a conference in Gronningen in 1990 of which the theme was the regional implementation of the labour movement. My argument was specifically concerned with early labour movements. I argued in the final section of my thesis that the configuration had clearly broken by the strikes of 1866, with shifts and changes taking place in its constituent elements. It is also fair to point out that it was contemporary opinion, which lauded this presumed characteristic of the Cornish miners. This opinion was surprisingly widely expressed both in the county and outside. It can be found in articles in periodicals and papers as diverse as the *Quarterly Review*, the *Penny Magazine* and the *Morning Chronicle*, as well as in specialist writings like the *Journal of the Statistical Society*. Economists of the highest calibre discussed it, John Stuart Mill returned to praise the tribute system several times, including in his major work the *Principles of Political Economy*, and a witness before a Select Committee recommended that employers generally adopted it. Neither were Methodists slow to take credit. It is the task of the historian to investigate why this was so.

So far as the consciousness revealed by food rioting is concerned. I have much to say about it in this volume, but it might be said at this point, that while Dr Deacon refers to it as the 'moral economy of labour', I don't think Thompson would have used that formulation. He was very cagey about extending a model derived from protests over food into other categories of crowd resistance. The contest over food prices was not between miners and those who managed and financed their industry. It was between the miners and those who were engaged in the production and distribution of corn. Recent work by Charlesworth suggesting a difference in pattern between food rioting in Cornwall and that in Devon in 1766, 1795 and 1801 can be linked to the background of labour clubs and combinations in the latter centred on Exeter, poses problems in that after the major industrial strikes and riots of 1725 to 1726 involving the Exeter woollen workers, there was a distinct lowering of the 'level and extent of conflict'. [28]

What is worth considering is the increasing sense that miners generally had of themselves as miners, separated from others by the fact and
nature of their underground labour. That outsiders were ready enough
to subscribe to this depiction of them, as 'a race apart', as mining became
overwhelmingly a deeper more distinctive occupation, is not difficult
to illustrate. However, an important work on the northern coal-mining
town of Whickham plays down this as a myth both in its own time and
as stereotyped by historians. I am not so sure. The sense of being a miner
can be a powerful one. Thirty-five years ago on my first visit to the North
East of England I was introduced to a retired pitman. He told me that his
grandfather had come from Cornwall. I held back from saying that it was
a near certainty that he had done so as a 'blackleg', for the old man was
a staunch trade unionist who still believed that government agents had
poisoned A. J. Cook the union leader! He then surprised me by reciting
from memory:

> *A dirge for the Cornish Miner,*
> *For Billy Bray the brave;*
> *He was not born to honour*
> *Such as the world would crave,*
> *But in the vale of labour*
> *His lot it was to tread*
> *Till Jesus called him higher,*
> *Where rests his weary head.*

He then declared proudly 'He was the best preacher ever, and he was
a miner!' I had myself made no mention of Bray, the name came straight
from his memory. The television was on, showing wrestling. One of the
contestants was a large Yorkshire man who fought under the name of
'Big Daddy'. The old pitman pointed to him and said with equal pride:
'And he is a miner too!' [29]

There is now in Cornwall much discussion over the appearance and
propagation of what has become known as the 'new Cornish historiography' in itself contained within and central to the 'new Cornish studies'. Like 'new Labour' this is a self-attribution, not a label imposed by

those external to its practice. The 'new Cornish historiography' has its centre, the Institute of Cornish Studies, its journal *Cornish Studies*, which has now reached thirteen annual issues since 1993, and a very accessible text in Philip Payton's impressive *Cornwall* published in 1996. What is new about NCS? In the first place it might simply be seen as the bringing into Cornish historical production those methods, approaches and subjects being taken up generally by historians. Examples might include discourse analysis (the so-called 'linguistic turn') as well as more adept and robust statistical methods. So far as subject inclusion is concerned, the attention now paid to women's history has become the most significant. [30] On the other hand there seems to have been little as yet in the way of parish register demography for the seventeenth and eighteenth centuries which can bring new knowledge, not only of changing rates of births, marriages and deaths, but also of rates of illegitimacy and bridal pregnancy and the patterning of mortality, for example the relative roles of fever and famine. So far as I know no one has published a full 'family reconstitution' for a Cornish parish, although the list of 26 parishes from which data thus obtained was used in the major synthesis published in 1983 included six from Devon. [31]

The new historiography stresses the value of an interdisciplinary approach, especially with the social sciences and related to this a willingness to engage with theory such as recent attempts to deploy the concept of 'proto-industrialisation' to a revised narrative of Cornwall's eighteenth and nineteenth century economic development. [32] If there is an over-arching purpose to all this it is clearly enough expressed in Payton's introduction to the first issue of Cornish Studies:

[There is] a common strand of Cornish distinctiveness, an emphasis on a Cornish 'difference' which finds its expression in everything from political behaviour to the natural environment. When all is said and done, it is this Cornish 'difference' that is at root the raison d'être *of Cornish Studies as an area of academic inquiry. It is a 'difference' that exists not in parochial isolation but as an integral part of that wider pattern of European cultural and territorial diversity.* [33]

The essays in this book are certainly directed towards explanation of the Cornish experience through a series of case studies. They are also of necessity case studies in the history of the polity of which Cornwall has been a part. For whatever Cornish feelings on the matter may have been, Westminster increasingly enacted statutes often backed by official inspection, which brought the state evermore into the lives of households and individuals. Writing on the eve of the Second Reform Act, J. M. Ludlow and Lloyd Jones, assessed the *Progress of the Working Class 1832-1867*. It took them more than a hundred pages to provide even an outline account of the work of the legislature. Chartism in part failed because after the mid-nineteenth century the 'state' in its enactments became something other than that which had been imagined by the radical artisans whose resistance amounted, according to Marx to a futile attempt to 'roll back the wheel of history'. [34]

Connections

My father, Leslie Rule died recently at the age of 91. In the sorting which such events bring about, we found a small archive of certificates and an exercise book labeled 'Family Connections'. In this, in his distinctive handwriting in 1986 he had entered what he remembered of the coming and goings of his family over the several preceding generations. None of us had known of this account, and reading it gave me a greater sense of connection with my Cornish past than I had previously felt.

I was born in 1944 at East End, Redruth, in the home of my grandparents. My grandfather Jack Meneer was a grocer: a trade which he followed for his working life, apart from four wartime years on the Western Front as a sergeant in the Royal Horse Artillery. He had had some career success as a manager for the Star Tea Company, but had failed in running his own shop, too generously allowing credit in the 1930s when Redruth was as depressed as any declining mining or manufacturing town. [35] His father was a guard with the Great Western Railway, which explains traces of a cockney accent, for he had spent several years of his childhood in London. Some of the GWR guards and footplate men took their families to live at the Paddington end of the line. As a young child,

I was puzzled by his middle name, which was 'Gladstone'. Not for some time did I realize that he had been named by his father after the 'Peoples' William', an expression of the long affair between the Cornish and the Liberal Party. [36]

His wife, my grandmother was simply baptised 'Annie' by the local Bible Christian Minister when she was a year old, in 1890 at a ceremony at her Camborne home. She was a miner's daughter as the certificate indicates, but it does not indicate that he was already dead. Henry Leah in fact had been killed in an underground explosion at South Crofty, several weeks before the birth of his daughter. He was 33 years old, born in the old mining town of St Just and had been married barely a year before the tragedy. A newspaper report of the coroner's verdict is headed 'Poor Henry Leah' and essentially blames the working miners for their careless disregard of the safety efforts being made by the legislature and the mine management. The story, which comes out of the coroner's inquest, was the old one of carelessness. The Inspector strongly condemned the loose way in which the dynamite was taken underground:

The law requires that it be packed in tins or canisters and not handled loosely like peas or beans. Legislation has done all that can be fairly expected from it; but if men will play with dangerous weapons; nothing can save them from disaster... while employers, inspectors and legislators are striving to reduce the accidents in mines, the men themselves whose lives are at stake ought to co-operate in the same good work. [37]

The judgment may be harsh. Carelessness by young miners had long been a noted factor in the debate over safety in the mines, but nothing of the little that is known of Henry Leah suggests him to have been other than a serious minded man. At 33 he was hardly inexperienced and his relatively late marriage also suggests a degree of prudence. But most remarkable is a brief report in the local press, published a week before the inquest. It seems that on the very evening before the exploding dynamite blew his head from his body, Leah who was 'a devout Wesleyan' was addressing a crowded meeting in a local mission hall. He exhorted his hearers, 'to always be ready to meet death, especially miners who like himself, were exposed to so many dangers'. [38] The family tradition as handed down by my grandmother and mother tells a rather different story. [39]

My other grandmother was also the daughter of a miner. The industry claimed his life too, but in circumstances that take rather longer to narrate.

Frederick John Simmons, my great grandfather, was born in the Helston area in 1867. He became a tin miner like his father, grandfather and brothers. He died in 1909 at the age of 42. Thirty years of working underground at home and abroad brought about this early end. He died four years before my father was born. So most of what is known of his life and ways has filtered to me via my father, from the memories of the widow, Grandma Bessie Simmons (see photograph at beginning of this chapter). She lived to be 81, dying in 1946. What my father knew of Fred-John, as he was known, was gathered from listening to her. She could not, even had she wanted to, have written anything down, for although she might have been able to read a little, she was unable to write. His mother, Fred-John's second child Agnes, could not have added much to my father's knowledge, for although she was 17 at his death, he had been mining abroad for most of her childhood. He was, like so many in the mining community, a Methodist. He was sufficiently committed to preach from time to time, but was certainly not an abstainer from beer. Some of his children remembered him as a strict father. But the youngest of them knew him only as a sick, indeed a dying man. His own father was primarily a miner, although several mentions of a cart and harness suggest he had also a collateral occupation. He perhaps married 'above himself' for his wife Ann Gilbert came from a well-to-do family. Unhappily, she died when Fred-John was still young, and his father's subsequent re-marriage brought into the household a stepmother with whom he did not develop a happy relationship. After one especially bad clash, his father punished him severely with a harness strap. This happened when he was about 14 years old and he consequently ran away from home, taking ship to South America, where he worked in the Brazilian mines for about seven years.

Still only 22 years of age on his return, he began to work again in the tin mines of the Redruth district living at South Turnpike. He would seem to have re-established some measure of Methodist involvement for it was on the annual Carnkie tea treat that he met Elizabeth Northey. They were married six weeks later on 3 August 1889 at the United Methodist Free Church in Redruth. The marriage certificate has two points of special interest. The two witnesses were both members of the Northey family although it was far more usual to have one from each side. Perhaps Fred-John was not yet fully reconciled with his family? More interesting is the evidence it provides on literacy, and how the ability to read and/or write could vary within families even as late as 1889. The bride herself made a mark, as did James Northey, her father, as a witness, but the second witness Elizabeth's younger sister Mary was able to sign. Using the four signatures needed on a certificate of marriage as a crude test of literacy, it seems that of marriages taking place among skilled workers from 1879 to 1894 about two-thirds involved four literate participants. While in one case in ten either the bride alone or the bride and a witness were unable to sign. In only one in 50 cases were four crosses made. For England and Wales, as a whole of brides marrying in 1889, about one in seven could not sign the register. For reasons that are not easy to find in 1884 Cornwall and Devon were the only counties in the southern half of England in which women were not marginally more literate than men. By 1904, Devon had joined the majority in this respect, while in Cornwall male literacy still lead, as it now also did in Dorset. [40]

While Elizabeth's situation was not rare, it did place her in a small and shrinking minority. Her father, James Northey, probably cared little about his illiteracy, the son of a miner he worked all his working life in the local mines. Born near St Day at Cregbrawse in 1838, he worked at Poldice among others and when these mines fell away, he found employment at Condurrow Mine in Troon, walking six miles to it and six back each day. James was reputed something of a 'rough', especially when in drink. A family tradition has it that he was on the spot and was among the first to rush to the factory fire in St Day in 1875 in which several young women perished.[41] He was not much of a Methodist and had clearly not been stimulated into literacy by a burning desire to read in the Bible.

Elizabeth's lack of literacy was above all the result of lack of schooling. No doubt she fell into the classic role of the eldest daughter. Although the marriage certificate describes her as a domestic servant, my firm impression is that for most of her 23 pre-marriage years, it was in her family's household that her labour was mostly deployed. She spoke often of the chore of cleaning the mine boots of her father and brothers. Little time was afforded for her education. She was already 13 by the time Mundella's Act of 1880 finally brought state compulsion. All that was 'purchased' for her was a short period at a dame school at a penny a week, and what she mostly remembered of that was doing the woman's washing. [42]

After their marriage Fred-John and Bessie, as she was generally known, lived in a cottage at Sparnick Redruth and two daughters, Maud and Agnes (my grandmother) were born in 1890 and 1892. There was to be a gap of eight years before a third child was born. Like so many others Fred-John had reacted to the progressive decline of mining in Cornwall, by emigrating. He joined a group of Redruth miners going to work in South Africa. Johannesburg was at that time so full of Cornishmen that it was described as a 'suburb of Cornwall'. [43] For a decade more as the mines at home shed labour, remittances from South Africa practically kept the Cornish economy afloat. Conditions of work were appalling. Fred-John remarked that there was little enough water to drink, and none available to lay the life-destroying dust thrown up by the rock drills. There is a photograph of the Redruth group including Fred-John Sixteen men, serious in expression; all but one hatted and most moustached, they look to be in early middle-age and fit enough for any occupation. Yet all were to die before they made old bones. Fred-John himself died at the age of 42. His father-in-law, the rough St Day miner James Northey outlived him, but then, unlike him, Northey had not gone to South Africa. Much of value was brought or sent back to Cornwall from these emigrant miners. But it seems that almost invariably working for any length of time in those mines brought on the dreaded phthisis. The miners' disease of

course shortened the life of many, who like Northey did all their mining in Cornwall, but investigations carried out in Redruth and elsewhere
during the first years of the twentieth century revealed the alarming extent to which working for any length of time in the South African mines
aggravated its incidence, its onset in the individual, and the severity and
speed with which it progressed. Even so it killed only after a decline of
several years. In Fred-John's case it took ten years. As Philip Payton has
described it those who returned from South Africa came home 'to endure
a rasping, lingering, but early death'. Fred-John came home in 1899 and
lived for just ten more years. Whether he was already experiencing the
first indications of phthisis is not clear. He was after all only then in his
early thirties. Possibly he was leaving as the crisis with the Boers was es-
calating. Most likely he had decided to leave believing that he had earned
enough to secure a comfortable life for his family. He seems to have returned with both a gold and a silver watch, or else to have purchased
them soon after, and enough to purchase both a house for the family and

Frederick John (Fred-John) Simmons (middle row, second left), South Africa.

two cottages for letting. The house was at Mount Carbis, along what later became Albany Road in Redruth. He began to work on his own account delivering first coal and then vegetables, also selling the latter from a small shop adjoining the house. To carry out these activities he had presumably purchased a horse and cart of some description.

Those who went to South Africa usually left their wives in Cornwall to head often, but not always, large families. So long as remitted earnings were regularly received, their experience was not necessarily one of even relative poverty. Accounts exist of conspicuous consumption, of extravagances of dress even being displayed in chapel on Sundays. Poverty was more likely to occur in the next stage of the mining-wives' life cycle. Consider Bessie's personal history. She was married at 23 and her marriage lasted 20 years for eight of which her husband was abroad. She had at least six pregnancies. She was widowed at 43, with two grown-up children and four below the age of ten. And she had outlived her husband by almost forty years. Clearly the increasing size of her family alongside the increasing debility of Fred-John, despite his desperately seeking such 'cures' as collecting and eating garden snails, made living increasingly difficult. However, his will drawn up very shortly before his death indicates no expectation that his dependents would be reduced to a less than comfortable life. The Widow Simmons was not such a conspicuous beneficiary as A.L. Rowse's Aunt Lelia whose miner husband had taken a pub on his return and purchased other property as well before he died of phthisis. This widow never went out without her several gold chains and other gold jewelry. [44] But Fred-John did leave an estate valued at £708. His will apart from leaving his gold and silver watches to his two sons, amounts to a clear strategy to deploy his assets in ensuring that his family was kept in reasonable comfort. As well as some cash and his savings, he owned the family house and three leasehold cottages besides. A trust was to administer the rent from these and anything deriving from the money and other non-property assets, to produce for his widow a weekly income of £1. If the fund became exhausted, then the cottages were to be sold and the money paid into the trust account to continue the weekly income. On his wife's death if the sale had not proved necessary, the properties were to be then sold and the proceeds divided among his children. It seems to me reading his will that it is a confident document. I imagine that Fred-John died with at least the comfort of believing that he had taken care of his family. At a time when skilled miners in Cornwall earned around £5 a month, and taking into account that Bessie had the family home rent free for life, he was entitled to die in peace.

For a few years the strategy of the will worked. But much sooner than anticipated the savings ran out. It was not only incipient phthisis that Fred-John had brought back from his Johannesburg sojourn. He also brought a bundle of share certificates having unwisely invested much of his savings in what proved to be a worthless gold mine. I remember these certificates turning up in a cupboard when my Grandmother died in 1955. So far as I know, they never made a contribution to the widow's support. As a consequence not only was the selling of the leasehold properties forced much sooner than expected, but the family house at Mount Carbis had also to go. Bessie's eldest child, Maud had married well to Thomas Rowse, a farmer at Treyew Mills on the outskirts of Truro. And they purchased one of the cottages into which the family moved. It was a distinct decline in comfort, lacking for example a water supply. The widow made the best of things and as the children grew into adulthood, things must have eased somewhat. After her family left, Bessie moved to live her last years with her second daughter Agnes and her family in Redruth's Rose Row. With so many women being widowed at such young ages that they typically outlived their miner husbands by thirty years or even longer, there was a need for a network of support especially from within the wider family. Bessie Simmons had a circle of other women with whom regular visits were exchanged on a much more frequent basis than simply keeping in touch. Of her own brothers, two had emigrated to America on a permanent basis, and a third had died from an industrial accident when only 17. Joseph Northey, the remaining brother stayed at home, but died aged 38, in 1903, seven years before his brother in law, Fred-John. His widow, known to my father as Aunt Jane, was a frequent visitor. As was her husband's widowed sister, Thursa who lived on a smallholding near Carharrack. She became a little strange after losing her only son in the First World War. Each Friday dressed as though she were penniless, she would walk the three miles to Redruth market carrying a large basket on each arm. After selling her butter and eggs, she would take the short cut home across Carn Marth, wearing a man's hat and whistling to keep her spirits up, for she had a mortal fear of being robbed as well as an obsession that she was due a substantial sum of money from her mother's family. Her one surviving child, Irene, had received a good schooling at the High School, and was to marry the keeper of a general store at Carharrack. Of Bessie's own sisters, Kate was the closest. She had been a domestic servant to the Rowse family and was presumably the link explaining how her niece Maud came to meet and marry Farmer Tom Rowse. Kate left service to marry Will Cock, a railway signalman. The Cocks saw a great deal of Bessie and Agnes and her family, becoming especially close to Agnes's three children. The youngest of Bessie's sisters, Mary, never married but worked as a housekeeper. She died in 1922, at 54 having been, it is said, alarmed into a stroke by her first ride in a motorcar, her nephew Tom's new Ford. On the other side of his family too, my father had his bevy of widowed aunts each of whom he saw quite often as he grew up. This may well have been a feature of Cornish working class society in the mining districts. I sometimes think of my father as enclosed inside a perimeter of great-aunts. A transient situation perhaps since it was produced by the impact of mining on the longevity of the underground workers, widening markedly an already existing differential in gender mortality. [46]

Mining was less evident, but not absent on the other side of my father's family. His great grandfather William Dunkin Rule was from a mining family, in fact by the time of William Dunkin's marriage to Mary Harris in 1859 his father James Rule had risen to the rank of mine agent. William himself however, became a carpenter, working on the Bickford Smith estate. Mary died in giving birth in 1861 to Richard (Dick) Rule, who was my father's grandfather. Dick was brought up by friends of his father. Although he worked as a boy streaming tin near Camborne, he later trained as a carpenter with his father. In 1883 he married Ann Thomas the daughter of James Thomas, the estate's head gardener. It is

Tom Rowse and his infamous Ford!

from this point in my exploration of my family's history that my thoughts were turned from mining to Methodism. James Thomas brought his children up in a strict Methodist tradition. Of his three sons, two became missionaries, and the third was likely to have become one had he not died at 16. Thomas, the eldest son, spent most of his adult life with lepers in unhealthy parts of Burma and after being twice widowed returned to Britain and lived with his sister. Edward Thomas did his missionary work in Africa, subsequently settling down as a Methodist minister at Port Elizabeth. He married the daughter of a well-to-do mine owner. She is buried on St Helena having died on a return voyage from a stay in Cornwall. In retirement in the 1920s Edward lived with his sister at Chyanhayle (Trevarno). He was a frequent visitor to his other sister and her husband Dick Rule. He continued to preach locally into old age. My father recalls that he once met him returning from Porthleven, and the aging minister it seems was thinking himself back in South Africa, as he remarked: 'I had an interesting time and met several Cornishmen'. The youngest son, James, was a fully committed Methodist and the writer of several hymns by the time he left for America at the age of 18. The ship went via Montreal to New York. But James became ill and died in Canada before the final leg.

Margaret was the eldest of four sisters. She worked at first as a nanny with the well-known Quaker Fox family at Falmouth and then as a maid in the Yorkshire house of some of their friends. [45] After her return she married Dick Rule and they set up home and business in Truro in 1884. They first lived in Edward Street, but later moved to a four-roomed terrace cottage in City Road on the corner with Calenick Street. They lived there until their deaths about fifty years later. A monument to their religious zeal was the founding of the City Road Mission, along with several other Truro families. The couple kept strictly to their Methodist beliefs and attitudes, but not in a joyless manner. Dick, for example loved singing, not only in the choir, but would lead singing on Saturday nights in Victoria Square. My father remembers seeing him thus engaged with two or three others of his associates including Johnnie Cockles, a former seaman, who was the father of the only black family in Truro.

Family Group. Richard and Margaret Rule and family.

Also among the family's friends was the prominent local Methodist, Joey Hunkin who shared much of Dick's open-hearted and publicly celebrated form of religion and worship. Hunkin's son converted to Anglicanism and became Bishop of Truro in 1930. Dick also shared the Cornish love of brass bands not being adverse to all secular music. He was a teetotaler and active in temperance organizations like the Band of Hope, as well as in the Truro Lodge of the Oddfellows. His wife's religious practice was less exuberant; after all, she had been a domestic servant to a household of Quakers. For Margaret Sundays were for Chapel and no other pursuits were allowed. My mother told me that on her approach even knitting and sewing had to be quickly hidden! At first Dick worked for a builder, but later went into business with his son, Hedley, occupying a workshop at the top of Calenick Street, then Truro's roughest street. The purpose indeed of the City Road Mission was to draw in the poorer sorts who were not attracted to Truro's more imposing St Mary's Chapel. Dick comes across to me as a sincere, honest and hard working man, whose religion was not worn at the expense of a sense of humour, and who was liked, respected and fondly remembered. His wife was more introvert, but remembered as a kindly person working hard to bring up her family of seven children, and who always had a welcome for visitors. She died in 1942 two years after her husband. Of the children the eldest Hedley eventually followed on in his father's carpenter's business, and Claude, my grandfather, became a bespoke tailor at Redruth and was, according to the headline on his funeral account, an 'ardent freemason'. Will worked hard to become an accountant and with his son, Howard ran a successful practice in Truro for many years. He, too, was an active freemason. Howard, the youngest of the sons, was by training a tailor, but he joined the army at the outbreak of war in 1914, aged 18 and served six years in India. He became a bandsman being talented on a number of instruments. He later became an ambulance man. Of the three daughters, Millicent married a foreman at his uncle's granite quarry at Mabe; Lillian married a regular soldier and moved to Torquay. Hilda remained unmarried and continued living in Truro until she died in 1983 at the age of 87. For those who remained in Truro, the City Road Mission continued to fill an important place, indeed. Hedley became its organist, in which role his nephew Derek followed him.

Looking back at Methodism through the lens of recent family history has given me much to think about. In my past writings my judgements on its effects upon Cornish lives have not been over kind. I would now place greater emphasis on its more positive attributes of concern, compassion and consolation. That does not mean I now think my earlier work was misdirected. It is rather a question of balance. The humanist can find neither comfort nor consolation in religion, but should not too easily overlook that others can. However much I might warm to the kindly Methodism of my great grandparents and their efforts around Truro's City Road Mission, I still find that what can be argued about earlier Methodism from its origins in the 1740s to the emergence of a more stable society from the 1850s, is that it was then emotionally more raw, theologically more stark, and behaviourally more repressive. Salome Hocking pointedly contrasted the freer attitude in chapel activities of her own childhood in the 1860s with the more serious and intolerant one of her parents generation. [48]

1. As well as the essays in this volume these include, 'Idle Hands? Controlling non-Work Time in England 1750-1815, *Il Tempo Libero Economia e Societa*, Secc. XIII-XVIII, ed., Simonetta Cavaciocchi, Prato, 1995, pp. 689-703 and 'Regional Variations in food consumption amongst agricultural labourers', in W. Minchinton, ed., *Agricultural Improvement: Medieval and Modern*, Exeter, 1981, pp. 112-137.
2.The Preface to Thompson's classic work has become an important historiographical essay in its own right and can be found in the front of all editions and reprintings.
3. For Thompson's influence see my entry, 'Edward Palmer Thompson, Historian, Writer and Political Activist' in the *New Oxford Dictionary of National Biography*.
4. Thanks to microform and digital recording many more of the national material relating to Cornwall can now be consulted there.
5. J. Rule, 'The British Fisherman 1840-1914', in *Bulletin of the Society for the Study of Labour History*, No. 27, 1973, pp. 53-65 and 'The Smacksmen of the North Sea: Labour Recruitment and Exploitation in British Deep-Sea Fishing, 1850-1890', in *International*

Review of Social History, xxi, Part 3, 1976, pp. 383-411.

6. J. Rule, 'Wrecking and Coastal Plunder', in D. Hay, P. Linebaugh and E. Thompson, eds., *Albion's Fatal Tree. Crime and Society in Eighteenth Century England*, 1975, pp. 167-189.

7. 'Social Crime in the Rural South in the Eighteenth and Nineteenth Centuries', in *Southern History*, 1, 1979, pp. 135-153, reproduced in J. Rule and R. Wells, *Crime, Protest and Popular Politics in Southern England* 1740-1850, 1997, pp. 237-254 and 'The Manifold Causes of Rural Crime: Sheep Stealing in England c. 1740-1840', ibid, pp. 237-254. Both articles contain Cornish material.

8. J. Rule, *The Experience of Labour in Eighteenth-Century Industry*, 1981; see for example, 'The Property of Skill in the Period of Manufacture', in P. Joyce, ed., *The Historical Meanings of Work*, 1987, pp. 99-118.

9. These points about smuggling and wrecking are made in my contribution to P. Payton, ed., *The Maritime History of Cornwall* (in preparation).

10. See R. Swift, 'Food Riots in mid-Victorian Exeter 1847-1867', in *Southern History*, II, 1980, pp. 101-127.

11. For an important mapping of food rioting see A. Charlesworth, ed., *An Atlas of Rural Protest in Britain 1548-1800*, 1983.

12. J. Flynn, *Cornwall Forty Years After*, 1917, p.140.

13. The attachments to the so-called 'Blue Books' are among the very best sources for the nineteenth century. See for example the superb report on Cornwall by Charles Barham appended to the Report of the Royal Commission on Child Employment, *British Parliamentary Papers*, 1842, xvi, and the Minutes of Evidence appended to the Report of the Royal Commission on the Condition of all Mines in Great Britain, *British Parliamentary Papers*, 1864, xxiv.

14. J. Buckingham, *Autobiography*, 1855, Vol. 1, p. 16.

15. A. Rowse, *A Cornish Childhood*, 1942, p. 13.

16. ibid, p. 14.

17. T. Hardy, *Tess of the d'Urbervilles*, Penguin, 1978, p. 61.

18. This verse is cited, but not dated in William Botrell, *Traditions and Hearth-side Tales of West Cornwall*, 1870, 1, p. 69. Quick died in 1857. The sense that that they were recording a dying tradition is strong both in Botrell and in Robert Hunt, see the introduction to his *Popular Romances of the West of England*, 1881.

19. J. Flynn, *Cornwall Forty Years After*, p. 100.

20. C. Rogers, *Echoes in Cornwall*, 1923, pp. 8-9.

21. MSS Journal of William Bray in the Methodist National Archive. Compare with the more polished attributions in the hugely selling *The King's Son. A Memoir of Billy Bray* written by F. Bourne, published in 1877, revised in 1890.

22. P. Pool, ed., *The Life and Progress of Henry Quick of Zennor*, Penzance, 1963, p. 11.

23. See Chapter 2 below.

24. Public Record Office, HO 40/41, From Reverend Hockin, Hayle, August 1839.

25. For Spurr see Chapter 8 below.

26. Cited in P. Pool, 'William Borlase', in *Journal of the Royal Institution of Cornwall*, 1966, pp. 122-123; cited in L. Namier, and J. Brooke, eds., *History of Parliament. The House of Commons*, 1964, Vol. III, p. 35.

27. B. Deacon, 'In Search of the Missing "Turn": The Spatial Dimension and Cornish Studies', in *Cornish Studies*, 8, 2000, pp. 219-221. For contemporary views on the 'system of mining in Cornwall' see Chapter 4.

28. For a discussion of the value of applying the concept to industrial disputes see J. Rule, 'Industrial Disputes, Wage Bargaining and the Moral Economy', A. Randall, and A. Charlesworth, eds., *Moral Economy and Popular Protest. Crowds, Conflict and Authority*, 2000, pp. 166-86; A. Charlesworth, 'The Spatial Diffusion of Riots: Popular Disturbances in England and Wales 1750-1850', in *Rural History*, 5, 1, 1994, pp. 2-12. It is however unclear that trade union activity continued in sufficient strength in the Exeter district after the strikes and industrial riots of 1725 to 1726. Food riots made their first appearance in 1756, see J. Rule, 'Labour Consciousness and Industrial Conflict in Eighteenth Century Exeter', in B. Stapleton, ed., *Conflict and Community in Southern England*, 1992, pp. 92-109.

29. D. Levine and K. Wrightson, *The Making of an Industrial Society, Whickham 1560-1765*, 1991, pp. 276-277. At the end of their book, Levine and Wrightson accept that: 'to be sure, they were something of a race apart, in the extraordinary environment they inhabited, the nature of their work, and the structure of their industry', p. 432. They further present the eighteenth century pitmen as having as well as having major strikes in 1731 and 1765, inhabited a culture, which generally demonstrated the 'unquiet nature of day-to-day industrial relations', p. 394. This 450 page study of 200 years in the history of a single parish on the Durham coalfield is a major achievement, and is perhaps the most valuable book on mining history to have appeared for some time. For later strikes on this coalfield see R. Colls, *The Pitmen of the Northern Coalfield: Work, Culture and Protest 1790-1850*, Chapter 16. Colls argues that: 'In 1820 the pitmen entered upon two decades of unprecedented coalfield expansion and conflict', p. 232, including the major disputes of 1810, 1831 to 1832 and 1844.

30. This is not of course to suggest that all those that are placed among those who practice and propagate the 'New Cornish History' are on the staff of the Institute of Cornish Studies. Mark Stoyle, for example, the most significant writer on Cornwall's seventeenth century history, has been a colleague of mine at Southampton and much of his work, now happily gathered into a book, first appeared in national journals including the *English Historical Review*, while leading members of the Institute have of course published in many places as well as *Cornish Studies*. See M. Stoyle, *West Britons: Cornish Identities and the Early Modern State*, 2002. What is the case is that pretty well all of us who currently write Cornish history have some measure of attachment or association. For a strong contribution to women's history see Sharron Schwartz, 'In Defence of Customary Rights: Labouring Women's Experience of Industrialization in Cornwall c. 1750-1870', in *Cornish Studies*, 7, 1999, pp. 8-31; and '"No Place for a Woman". Gender at Work in Cornwall's Metalliferous Mining Industry', in Cornish Studies, 8, 2000, pp. 69-96. This issue contains four other articles on women's history.

31. E. Wrigley, R. Davies, J. Oeppen and R. Schofield, *English Population History from Family Reconstitution 1580-1837*, 1997.

32. See B. Deacon, 'Proto-industrialization and Potatoes: A Revised Narrative for Nineteenth Century Cornwall', in *Cornish Studies*, 5, 1997, pp. 60-84. Deacon proposes

that the 1840s rather than the 1860s be considered, 'as a major structural turning point', p. 61. Roger Burt in a thoughtful and challenging article has argued for the inclusion of mining in the proto-industrialization model, see 'Proto-industrialization and "Stages of Growth" in the Metal Mining Industries', in *Journal of European Economic History 1*, XXVII, 1, 1998, pp. 85-104. I have no difficulty with the way either writer makes his case. If I prefer not to use the term, it is because since it was first used more than 30 years ago, its meaning has lost a great deal of precision and I was already treating it with a degree of caution in 1981, see J. Rule, The Experience of Labour in Eighteenth Century Industry, 1981 p. 53. For me the demographic dimensions were an essential element in the original model by F. Mendels. This is based on a cottage manufacture in which the cottage is a site of manufacturing production, not necessarily one of even limited food production. The existence of a dual economy, does not in itself define proto-industrialization. The family expands its labour by increasing in size. This is driven by the opportunity for earlier marriage, hence the rapid demographic growth as the old marriage pattern breaks down. In mining districts the population driver was more likely to be in-migration, as has been demonstrated for the Durham coalfield by Levine and Wrightson (see note 29 above) I prefer to continue to use, with care, the concept of 'Industrial Revolution', perhaps describing the period whose dynamic ended 1840 to 1850, as the 'First Industrial Revolution'. This was the revolution of coal, iron, metal and textiles and it was a regional phenomenon. Cornwall was one of these regions along with the North, the East and West Midlands, and beyond England, South Wales and Lowland Scotland.

33. P. Payton, *Introduction to Cornish Studies*, 1, 1993, pp. 2-3. For examples of the interdisciplinary nature of 'The New Cornish History' look especially at *Cornish Studies*, 10, 2002, with its impressive disciplinary range.

34. J. Ludlow and L. Jones, *The Progress of the Working Class 1832-1867*, 1867. I think the point is that if Cornishness needs sometimes to be defined against an English/ British state, then that is itself a definition, which needs periodic, if not constant adjustment.

35. In the 1930s mining employment all but ceased. It had fallen from 8700 in 1919 to 4500 in 1920, its post-war peak, which it would not again exceed. Holding up to 3269 in the 'good year' of 1928, it fell precipitously in the crisis of the early 1930s, never again to exceed 2000. J. Rowe, 'The declining years of Cornish tin mining', in J. Porter, ed., *Education and Labour in the South-West*, Exeter, 1975, p. 76.

36. The great railway companies presumably had an interest in having some of their footplate men and guards living near the terminal London stations. Single men could be housed in sleeping barracks, but experienced train drivers and others tended to be older and family men. Not every one born in Cornwall and having a London childhood came back. My grandfather's brother and two of his sisters stayed on and thereafter only came to Cornwall on visits.

37. *West Briton*, 30 May 1889.

38. ibid, 23 May 1889.

39. My grandmother until she was married worked as a trainee cook for the Holman family, whose head cook, was her mother. She insisted that the family had provided such secure employment for the widow, out of a sense of obligation, Leah having

been engaged in testing equipment for the great engineering works, which was situated very close to South Crofty.

40. Gillian Sutherland, 'Education', in F. Thompson, ed., *The Cambridge Social History of Britain 1750-1950, Vol. 3: Social Agencies and Institutions*, Cambridge, 1990, p. 124, Fig. 3.2. The other very rough figures are inferred from D. Vincent, *Literacy and Popular Culture: England 1750-1914*, Cambridge, 1989, p. 25, and Appendix B, p. 283, on the assumption that Cornish miners formed a similar group to Vincent's 'skilled labourers'. A count of Marriage Register signatures in Lanner indicates that adult non-signers had fallen to only one or two a year by the 1890s. See S. Schwartz and R. Parker, *Lanner: A Cornish Mining Parish*, 1998, Fig. 10.4, p. 218.

41. My father's notes refer to a fire at a 'plush' factory. A textile factory of this kind was at work in St Day between 1881 and 1895, see *The Mining Villages. An Exploration of the Gwennap Mining Area*, pp. 9-10. But I have never seen any reports of a fatal fire at the factory. There is probably a memory failure here, for instance confusion with the fire at the Unity Safety Fuse Company in 1875 that killed five women workers.

42. For school provision in the district before 1870 see *The Mining Villages*, pp. 26-28.

43. On the South African chapter in the Cornish miner's history see the excellent discussion in P. Payton, *The Cornish Overseas*, Fowey, 1999, pp. 343-371.

44. A. Rowse, *A Cornish Childhood*, 1962, p. 93.

45. My great grandmother Margaret is the subject of a perceptive biographical portrait by her granddaughter, Phyllis Jones née Margery Rule, in *Life I Could Not Know*, soon to be published.

46. In 1851 Cornwall had the highest proportion of widows to total population of women of any county and at 2:82 was second only to Northumberland in its ratio of female to male paupers.

47. A press cutting of my grandfather's funeral dwells heavily on his freemasonry. I assume it to be from the *West Briton*.

48. S. Hocking, *Some Old Cornish Folk*, 1903, reprint edited by Amy Hale, 2006, p. 175.

'The Tinners are Rising':
Food Rioting in Cornwall
1737-1847

The Cornish miners of the eighteenth and nineteenth centuries were notoriously prone to riot, demonstrating their grievances publicly, theatrically and forcefully. In England, generally the most frequent form of public disturbances were those riots provoked by rising food prices, which at times could rise so suddenly and steeply as to leave many of the lower orders unable to afford or even obtain corn, flour or bread for their families subsistence. In such situations hunger could be extreme. It was especially so in the wartime harvest crises of 1795 to 1796 and 1800 to 1801, and a leading historian of that period has not hesitated to label those years as ones of 'famine'. Cornwall was no exception, indeed it was among the foremost in food rioting. Its miners have been described by Edward Thompson as having an 'irascible consumer consciousness and a readiness to turn out in force'. [1]

The pioneering research of Rose and Rudé in the 1960s was able to form a basis for some understanding of these complex happenings. [2] The geographical structures that worked with historical process were beginning to be mapped, and with the multiplication of known incidents, it became possible to put forward a typology locating the various action forms encompassed by the simple term 'food riot'. There were no years of recorded food rioting between the earliest Cornish clear example in 1727 and the last in the county in 1847, except for 1740, in which the miners did not participate. In some of these years, such as 1766, and 1795 to 1796, it was a case of one among many, in others such as 1757, one amongst a few, while in 1831 the Cornish miners provide the only example. [3] Rioting was a recurrent phenomenon in the mining districts and while there were disturbances in reaction to presumed pressures other than rocketing food prices, food rioting was by far the most frequently occurring, and most widely supported form of protest. [4] In 1971 in an article of huge international influence, Edward Thompson brilliantly analyzed eighteenth century English food riots, as the fundamental phenomenon in what he famously called the 'moral economy of the English crowd'. [5] Moral economy was an over-arching concept that offered a way of interpreting an increasing number of research findings. It had become clear that the frequent outbreaks of food rioting in eighteenth and early nineteenth century England were very far from being the blind, unreasoning protests of the delinquent and empty-bellied poor against abuses, which in the true order of things, could not be removed. Thompson, in particular, showed that an examination of the food riot reveals the existence of customary practices in the marketing, milling, and baking of bread corn, amounting to a popular 'moral economy', at variance with the assumptions of the rulers, and in conflict with the supply and demand market model of the classical economists.

The conflict inherent in the food riot was between those who favoured, and had been increasingly operating a free inland trade in grain, and the poor who maintained that the corn trade should be regulated in the interests of supplying them with vital bread corn at a 'just' price. Rose had already identified four main types of food riot, ranging from simple outbreaks of looting, through riots to prevent the exporting of grain in times of scarcity, to direct action by rioters in imposing lower food prices on market sellers, and fourthly attempts to use mob pressure to force local magistrates to decree maximum prices. These four types can be found in Cornwall and a fifth is also identifiable. This was the invasion in force of the agricultural districts by miners in search of farmers withholding grain from the markets. Any hoarding farmers that were found were forced to sign agreements to bring their corn to the next market. This form was related to the attempts to prevent exportation of grain, in that it was often suspected that the hoarded grain was intended for export, but the fact that the site of conflict was the farm and not the port makes it more useful to consider this form as a distinct type.

Rose suggested that the English price-fixing riot originated in Oxfordshire in 1695. The choice of the 1690s as the period during which rioting of these types first achieved historical significance is based on sound reasons. Government policy towards the corn trade underwent a distinct change in 1660. Under the Tudors and early Stuarts, paternal bureaucracy had checked the activities of corn dealers and restricted exports when the interests of the consumer were believed threatened. After 1660, the producer was as favoured as the consumer. A law of 1665 removed practically all of the restrictions on the inland corn dealer, and also placed a duty on imported corn. Until the 1690s good harvests provided a counteracting influence. A series of good harvests ran with the exception of 1684 to 1692, after which they were not really good again for twenty-five years. For the first time in the 1690s the English people faced bad harvests in a situation in which local magistrates were no longer prepared or compelled to impose controls on the markets and dealers. In addition, there now existed a system of regulation designed to encourage exports, discourage imports and keep prices high. It is reasonable to accept Rose's arguments, and the more developed ones of Thompson, and date the growing prevalence of hunger and price-fixing riots to the closing decade of the seventeenth century and their subsequently more frequent and widespread occurrence to rising corn prices after mid-century.

Rose argued that the classic form of food riot, the seizure of corn in the market and its open re-selling there at an imposed 'just' price (taxation populaire) spreading from an Oxfordshire starting point in 1695, passed westward through Bristol in 1709, Somerset in 1753 and Exeter in 1756, to reach Cornwall in 1766. But by then food protests of other kinds had already been experienced from 1727 and possibly earlier. In fact the Cornish miners were stereotypical of the kind of community in which food protests most frequently occurred. Along with the Cornish miners in this regard, must be placed coalminers, keelmen, potters, weavers and other textile workers, glovers, and metal workers. In short it was from the settlements of miners and manufacturing workers that food rioters largely came. Barley rather than wheat, was the usual Cornish bread corn until well into the nineteenth century. Many may have preferred wheaten bread when they could afford it but there was no widespread prejudice against the eating of barley bread .The miners needed to be able to purchase barley either as grain or flour. Local supplies were generally bought as grain and then taken to the miller for grinding. There was little demand for baker's bread, partly because the miners' wives baked their own, and partly because of the local taste for flour baked in the forms of the traditional pasty, or hobban. Ideally the mining household needed to be supplied with barley at prices which bore a reasonable relationship to the level of their earnings, and in small quantities since they would hardly have the capital sufficient to lay in large amounts at one time. For this to happen, farmers should bring sufficient corn to the markets to meet the needs of the labouring poor, before any sales were made to factors seeking to purchase for resale at a profit. The corn could then be taken to the millers, who, for grinding, should charge the customary tolls but not seek undue profits. It was regarded as the producer's moral responsibility to see that the local markets did not lack supplies before sending any produce further afield. This model of a 'moral economy' broke down at several weak points. The enforcement of legal and cus-tomary restrictions on profiteering from the grain supply of the poor was at best haphazard, at worse non-existent. Moral condemnation was more often expressed than was positive action taken. In Cornwall there is little evidence to suggest that millers were very often regarded by the poor as exploiters. Few of the very many incidents of food rioting which took place were directed at them. Nevertheless, it was a Cornish member, Sir Francis Basset, who proposed changes in the law relating to millers' tolls, telling the House of Commons that they were often 'extremely oppres-sive to the poor', who were vulnerable to extortion and fraud from mill-ers in years of corn scarcity. [6]

The old bogeymen of the consumer - badgers, regraters, engrossers, and forestallers - undoubtedly operated in the county, but the limited survival of Quarter Sessions records makes it impossible to say whether such practices were often dealt with by eighteenth century magistrates. The weakest point in Cornwall was the preference of farmers for selling their corn in larger quantities to factors rather than undergo the chore and risks of selling piecemeal in the local markets. The seriousness from the point of view of the poor consumer was not just that middlemen enhanced prices, but that all too often corn disposed of to dealers never reached the local markets, but was transported to more profitable distant ones. Factors were especially active in the county in times of general bad harvest. London merchants appointed agents to buy up Cornish corn. A letter from a Falmouth factor to London merchants in 1757, mentioned three others besides himself as being so engaged and revealed that he had stored grain at Padstow and Helston ready for trans-shipment to London. Perhaps it was only in grimmer years that London merchants would seek as far as Cornwall for corn, but even if that pull was infrequently exerted it was at the very times when local supply was at its most precarious. Cornish farmers were naturally tempted to sell in large quantities to factors, and have the grain removed from their hands without the risk of it turning bad, or the prospect of a good harvest to come substantially lowering the price as the summer drew on. Thus, in years of short supply, a paradox would arise from an increase in both exports from, and imports to the county. The latter because of the efforts of the mineral lords and the mine adventurers to import supplies for their workers, and the former due to the increasing demand from London and elsewhere. Such was the situation in 1795 when extensive supplies had to be imported at a time when farmers were refusing to sell in small quantities to the poor. Exports from the county in such years go back at least to 1727, as the food riots of that year indicate. It is possible that the trade died down somewhat in mid-century to be revived in the final quarter.[7] The Corporation records of West Looe note in 1778 that for a long time there had been neither import nor export of grain from that place, but:

Now for some years past it hath become a great trade amongst them as corn factors, to buy very large quantities of corn among the country farmers and to lodge the same in their lofts and cellars in the borough and from hence to take the same on board ships or vessels. [8]

The crucial months were those of late spring and early summer when the reserves of the previous harvest were running out. Although fish formed an important part of the miner's diet the pilchard season did not begin in time to alleviate a spring food crisis. Some grain crisis years were also years of record pilchard catches, but these were taken in the autumn, too late to subsist the hungry poor. Potatoes were also an important dietary item, increasingly so as the eighteenth century moved in to the nineteenth, but it remains true that whilst potatoes and fish in a normal year might make the difference, between bare necessity and tolerable sufficiency they were by no means sufficient in bad years to remedy a serious failure in the grain harvest.

The winter of 1727 saw the first serious outbreak of food rioting by miners. It was especially prevalent in the Falmouth district, but also broke out further west around Penzance. Extremely violent threats were uttered. The townspeople of Falmouth were warned by the miners, that if insufficient corn were not offered for sale on the next market day, they would come in a body several thousand strong and attack the town from all sides. If resistance was offered and any of their number killed, then they would 'make the town run with blood'. Such threats were largely bombast, part of a war of nerves, but that they could be taken at all seriously by the townspeople indicates the fear of the miners which existed in the port towns at times of dearth. [9] Rioting in the spring of 1729 in the St Austell district brought about the issue of a Royal Proclamation naming twelve miners from four different parishes, and offering a treasury reward for their apprehension. Further west an interesting but isolated riot took place in St Ives. In 1737 a Falmouth corn factor named Pye engaged in buying activities sufficient to raise the local grain prices, and both Falmouth and neighbouring Penryn prepared to face 'invasion' by the tinners. Two attacks were made on Penryn where miners plundered several cellars where they heard 'the corn was taking in for exportation'.[10]

The middle years of the century saw rioting in 1748, 1756 to 1757, and 1766. Penryn was again the scene in 1748. The cellars of Benjamin Heame, described as a 'considerable merchant', were the main targets of the rioters. In 1756 the north coast port of Padstow experienced large scale food rioting, as in 1766 did Redruth, St Austell, and Truro. Apart from a possible single incident near Truro in 1767, food rioting next occurred in 1773 when rioting was widespread affecting the area around Truro, Wadebridge, Penryn and Padstow from which town a vivid and well observed account was sent:

> We had the devil and all of a riot at Padstow; some of the people have run to too great lengths in exporting of corn, it being a great corn country. Seven or eight hundred tinners went thither, who first offered the corn factors seventeen shillings for twenty-four gallons of wheat; but being told they should have none, they immediately broke open the cellar doors, and took away all in the place without money or price About sixteen or seventeen soldiers were called out to stop their progress, but the Cornishmen rushed forward and wrested the firelocks out of the soldiers hands: from thence they went to Wadebridge, where they found a great deal of corn cellared for exportation which they also took and carried away. We think 'tis but the beginning of a general insurrection, because as soon as the corn which they have taken away is expended, they will assemble in greater numbers armed, for 'tis an old saying, "The belly has no ears". [11]

There were expectations of rioting in 1789, but the next significant outbreaks came in the years of the Great War with France, in 1793, 1795, 1796, 1801 and 1812. To some extent these outbreaks were touched and coloured by the popular radicalism of those years, during which the severity of the food crises was exceptional and the incidence of food rioting broke previous geographical bounds. In 1793, incidents are recorded at Wadebridge, Looe, Falmouth, and the districts around Truro. In 1795 at Padstow, Penzance, Helston, Ruan, near Truro and Port Isaac on the north coast. In the following year Helston, Looe and Truro again experienced riot. 1801 was a bad year following another and disturbance must have seemed inevitable. Early in March, rioting already happening in Devon, reached Launceston, but did not begin in the western mining districts for a further month. Nationally 1812 saw some but less extensive disturbances, but in a year in which a local newspaper reported that large numbers were 'literally famishing', Truro, Redruth and, Padstow again experienced rioting. [12]

There were isolated outbreaks of food rioting in 1818, 1830 and 1831, but in none of these years was food rioting very widespread or serious.

By far the most serious outbreak since the years of the French Wars took place in 1847. In that year the disease caused failure of the potato crop and heavily aggravated the grain shortage. Corn prices which had been rising steadily week by week, suddenly shot up to famine level at the beginning of May 1847, at a time when a late spring was holding back the vegetable crop, and stormy weather hampering the fishing industry. Padstow, Wadebridge, Callington, Helston, Penzance, Redruth and St Austell experienced food rioting. Outbreaks in that year were on a scale and intensity not seen in the county for almost half a century. All the major types of food riot occurred in one place or another. Elsewhere food rioting was already largely a thing of the past. In Cornwall the riots of 1847 were the final fling of this traditional form of protest. [13]

Such, in outline, is the chronology and incidence of food rioting in Cornwall. The nature of the food riot now requires analysis. In Cornwall, as elsewhere, far from being the irrational and spontaneous response of a disorganized rabble, vainly resisting an invincible political economy, the food riot followed accepted patterns of action and was conducted with definite objectives in view. Although incidents of plunder and violence did occur, it is the rarity of such departures from good order and disciplined purpose that is striking. The evidence suggests that the food riots of the first half of the eighteenth century were more violent in their nature, and contained a larger element of simple looting than subsequent outbreaks. This is to be expected. The formalized tradition of the food riot in some of its almost ritual forms was not born at once (indeed it has been mentioned that the pure form of the price-fixing riot did not even reach Cornwall until 1766). After the mid-eighteenth century, violence and looting ceased to be characteristic of the majority of outbreaks. Prescribed action forms took over and protocols were developed and defined. It should be emphasized that the authorities if they were unfamiliar with the phenomenon of food rioting in its early years, and the descriptions which they rushed to the Secretary of State contain a far greater element of panic and fear than do later descriptions penned by a magistracy accustomed to food rioting. It is possible that the moderating influence of Wesleyan Methodism, which grew rapidly in the mining villages, may have helped to tone down the later outbreaks, but the most satisfactory explanation is that the sophistication of the form of protest employed grew with the experience of food rioting. It would, however, be wrong to assume that the early outbreaks bore little relationship to the poor's conception of a moral economy operating through a regulated grain trade. The miners who threatened Falmouth with savage retribution in 1727 stated that they intended to come only if at the next market, 'there did not come in a sufficient quantity of corn to supply their occasions'. The early riots were largely directed against the storing of grain for export hence a port was usually the scene, but it is striking how often a specific named merchant was the target of the rioters. John Pye was warned in 1757 in a letter that the tinners were incensed against 'you and your family'. Looting may have taken place but it was seldom indiscriminate. An account of the action against a Penryn merchant, Guide, in 1757 illustrates that the crowd were not necessarily of one mind even when it came to looting the stores of known corn merchants. The tinners had first gone to Guide's house and questioned him as to whether he had any corn in his cellars. He told them that he had only fifty bushels, and had no intention of storing more. He further offered to sell them the corn at cost price. Some of the miners wanted to agree to this, but others insisted they 'would have it for nothing'. The crowd forced Guide to open his cellar, but were still divided as to whether the corn should be seized or not. Just as before, a section of the crowd had wanted to pay for the corn and suggested that if the corn was no more than the fifty bushels Guide claimed was all that he had, then none of it should be touched. Moderate opinion lost out however and the corn was seized. Other eighteenth century occasions of apparently simple looting turn out to be not quite so simple. Corn looted at Padstow was taken only after the miners had offered to pay the corn factors seventeen shillings for the Cornish bushel for wheat which was intended for export, and had been told that they could have none. On another occasion in that year, 1773, corn seized by rioters was publicly offered by them at one shilling and sixpence a sack, clearly a symbolic protest price. [14]

By and large after the mid-eighteenth century the food riot followed more defined forms of action directed at the points where the idea of a regulated corn supply was clearly breaking down. Even on the occasional disorderly protest some notion of legitimacy usually underlay the protest. To the crowd, those farmers and factors who saw no reason to exclude the food supply of the poor from the governance of the laws of supply and demand were the offenders, not only against a strong sense of moral entitlement to food, but against the surviving elements of paternalist regulation. Against such offenders and exploiters action was popularly held to be both legitimate and justified. The language of the market had rapidly become the dominant economic discourse over the eighteenth century so that by its end it seemed only necessary to cite Dr Adam Smith to close any economic debate. The *West Briton* cautioned its readers in 1812:

The price of every commodity will naturally be regulated by the demand and supply, - grain will be cheap when it is in plenty and dear when it is scarce; and all attempts to alter this fixed and natural relation, whether they proceed from the rulers or the multitude, must inevitably produce and increase the very evils which they are intended to remedy. [15]

Such lectures in the basic principles of *laissez-faire* were frequently addressed to the poor, but they remained obstinate in their belief that there was a 'just' price for bread corn, and that that 'just' price could only prevail if a stop were put to the activities of grain-hoarding farmers, corn-jobbers, monopolists forestallers, regraters, exporters, and all others who had an interest in raising corn prices.

To support the claim that food riots were frequently well ordered and disciplined, it is worth quoting at length from the Annual Register of 1831, noting all the while that it was printed under the heading 'Riot':

...a party of 5,000 miners...passed through Helston in the greatest order, (having selected eight men to act as leaders) for the avowed purpose of preventing further shipments of grain near Mawgan they were accidentally met by Mr Grylls, who entreated them to return, but to this they would not consent. They said, "If you, Sir, and Mr Sylvester...will go with us, we will engage to do no

mischief". Finding that all entreaties to induce them to return were unavailing, Mr Grylls, Reverend Mr Black, and Mr Sylvester accompanied them to Geer, where about 100 Cornish Bushels of barley were deposited, which Mr Grylls promised should be sent to Helston market. They then proceeded to Treath, near Helford, where only a small quantity was found, and there also a promise was given that it should be brought to market. From Treath the party went to Gilling, and in the cellars belonging to Mr Roskruge found about 200 bushels of barley, 50 bushels of malt, and 50 of wheat. Three of the leaders entered the cellars and measuring the depth, length and breadth of each pile of grain, computed the quantity, and having obtained a promise…that all the barley should not be exported; and the wheat should be sent to market, they appeared satisfied and set out on their return home.

Before they broke up, Grylls addressed the miners, who agreed to return peacefully to their homes and gave him three cheers. Sylvester offered similar advice and also received three cheers. The report concludes:

Throughout the day the utmost regularity prevailed; all that the men required being that corn should be brought to market for which they alleged they could not afford to pay more than 12s per bushel.

A clear enough case of a large crowd in perfect order carrying out a planned action with discipline being preserved over a considerable mileage and length of time. [16]

On another occasion a hundred years previously a crowd of miners also invited a responsible person to accompany their demonstration to emphasize the legitimacy of their purpose. In 1729, tinners from St Austell visiting the port of Par took with them a parish constable named Rosevear. He, however, became so captured by the spirit of the occasion that when the tinners' request that stored corn be delivered to them was refused, he took the lead in breaking down the doors of a cellar. Being recognized, he was subsequently arrested, tried, and executed as a ringleader. His body was hung in chains on St Austell Downs as a warning to all miners who might be tempted to let their hunger and indignation over-rule their reason. [17]

Well-ordered conduct was evident on many other occasions. In 1801 miners entering Liskeard were met by the Mayor, who declared, 'his determination to act the part and duty of a magistrate'. To this the miners respectfully answered, 'So you ought'. The *West Briton* said of a party of young miners who entered Truro in 1812, that it could not have conceived that so many could quit their work under such circumstances and show less irritation and do so little mischief. [18]

Another outstanding example of strict self-discipline and confinement to purpose was reported in 1767. One of a party of miners seizing corn near Truro took advantage of the situation to slip a couple of silver spoons into his pocket. The leaders, according to the report of the incident, ordered that a search be conducted and when the culprit was discovered he was stripped and beaten by the rioters. [19] The broad question of violence needs to be set in context. It would seem, as a recent survey has pointed out, that English food rioters for all the apprehension their rhetoric might occasionally cause, killed no one. Such deaths as there were happened to the rioters. Rioters were shot in Cornwall in 1729 and in 1748 and two were hanged in 1729 and 1796. The most explicit and theatrical threat to the person came in the form of a riot used in Cornwall and in Devonshire when incursions were made into the countryside in search of grain-hoarding farmers. They carried with them a rope and a written contract. This bound the farmer to bring his corn to market to sell at an agreed price. Placing the rope around the necks of the reluctant ensured signing. This form of action was used in Cornwall in 1796, 1801 and 1812. It could well have been deployed on earlier occasions, when the reports state only that farmers were threatened without providing detail. The noose was symbolic and on only one occasion, in 1796, does it appear that any degree of implementation occurred. On that occasion two millers were actually hoisted, but quickly cut down before they had experienced any more than a slight choking. [20]

As John Bostedt has argued, particularly from Devonshire evidence, a protocol was being followed, a dramatic but serious game the rules of which were understood by both sides. [21] Many farmers seem to have

readily enough sent corn to market once the miners had forcefully demonstrated their need. Others withholding grain with enhanced profit in
mind must have accepted a visit from the miners as a risk, just as they
also took the risk of withholding too long and getting caught by falling prices, should expectation of a forthcoming good harvest take hold.
The contracts were not of course valid in law. And proclamations to that
effect were rapidly issued by the magistrates and prominently carried
in the local press. But the press could also carry expressions of disapproval of excess farmer profiteering from the distress of the poor. Once
the miners had forced attention onto their situation, the more 'griping'
of the farmers might expect strong pressure from their landlords, the
magistracy, and also find strong and directed criticism further echoed in
editorials. Public order may have been paramount, but this was compat-
ible with an extension of public and private relief.

In size Cornish crowds tended to be formidable, probably the largest assembled anywhere in England. Some accounts provide estimates
of the size of food rioting crowds, although more usually only adjectives
such as 'very large', 'numerous', or 'immense' are used. The following
are from the few accounts where estimates were given:

5000	Truro	1796
2000	Falmouth	1727
2000	Manccan	1831
7-800	Padstow	1773
500	Penryn	1775
400	Padstow	1795
300	Penzance	1831

Crowds at Penzance in 1795, and at St Austell and Redruth in 1757
were described as being 'several thousands' strong. It is small wonder
that in the absence of superior armed troops the townspeople could offer
little resistance to such large groups of rioters. As such large numbers indicate, the crowds were neither formed from single mines or from single
parishes. They cut across parish borders. At most times miners were very

conscious of parish identity, but in food rioting rivalries were set aside and the issue became one of miners against those seen as common oppressors. The Royal Proclamation of 1729 named eighteen rioters from four parishes. Affidavits against nine miners in 1773 show them to represent four parishes. Five rioters taken at Penryn in 1748 also represented four parishes. The rioters of 1831 came from at least five parishes, and the St Just miners before they marched to Penzance in 1795 sent circular letters to the miners of six different parishes inviting them to join them. In the only instance where the miners are identified by the mines at which they worked rather than by the parishes in which they lived, in 1831, six mines are listed. [22] Since large mines would employ men from several different parishes, it could well have been at the mine that communication between the parishes was established. Whatever the means of communication, a point of assembly was usually agreed upon, for example, Chacewater in 1757, Church Town, St Just in 1795 and Sithney Common in 1831. Within the parish, handbills were sometimes posted to advertise an intended demonstration. At St Just in 1795 the following notice was posted in a blacksmith's shop:

This is to give notice that all persons coming to this shop and all other shops in this parish to attend at Church Town Saturday 14 instant. All that have got firelocks are to bring them with them for there we do intend to muster and be independent ourselves and them that have not any firelocks to provide themselves with staffs 9 feet long fix spears in the end of the same and them that refuse to their peril be it. So one and all...So one and all.

A handwritten notice, very specific and to the point, was posted at Stratton in 1801:

To all the labouring men and tradesmen in the hundred of Stratton that are willing to save their wives and children from the dreadful condition of being starved to death by the unfeeling and griping farmer, My fellow sufferers and country men now is the time to exert yourselves and show yourselves men and true born Englishmen not to be enslaved by any nation or power of men on Earth; now is the time to come forward and take vengeance on your oppressors. Assemble all emeadiately (sic) and march in dreadful array to the habitations of the Griping Farmer, and compell them to sell their corn in the market, at a fair and reasonable price and if any refuse and will not comply with our just demands we must make them feel the punishment due to their oppression and extortion. Therefore you are desired to meet at Stratton next Monday by 2 of the clock in the afternoon and march one and all with determined hearts and hands to have redress or vengeance—Cato.

An old miner reminiscing in 1898, recollected seeing as a young boy notices which had been posted at Padstow calling upon fathers of starv-

Hardbill advertising a public demonstration, 1795
(Public Record Office, H.O.)

ing children, 'in the name of God and the King', to prevent vessels laden with corn from leaving that port, and to forcibly take their cargoes for their own use. [23]

Although a few attempts were made by local justices and the local Tory press to ascribe the riots to the agitating tactics of a disaffected few, they were unconvincing, if only because they were an attempt to attribute two particular and time-specific causes to a form of demonstration, which remained substantially unchanged for over a century. The food riots had the moral support of the community, and the active participation of a substantial part of it. Rewards offered for the detection of distributors and of posters handbills, and for the apprehending of ringleaders were rarely effective, a Penzance magistrate explained the difficulty in making arrests in 1795:

Almost every individual in the mining parts of the country where the riots happened, was more or less concerned in them, so that each man feels it his own cause.

He believed that rioters could only be taken at night, since at other times they found 'so safe and ready an asylum in the mines'. The men of the mining districts were expected to join in. A Penryn magistrate received information from his wife's maid whose father and brothers were miners, that though her relatives, 'are very adverse to the manner yet they shall be forced to join'. She added that they would run off as soon as they could. The reluctance of her family to take part is understandable in view of the fact that a magistrate knew their names. This can hardly be indicative of dissent from the intended action. [24] The food riot was the expression of the community as a whole, and the very real sense in which the miners constituted a community apart enabled their incursions to be regarded with real horror, even by the poorer tradesmen of the towns they visited, as well as by the farmers of the rural districts. James Silk Buckingham described a visit of the miners from the point of view of the inhabitants of a small non-mining village. A body of some three or four hundred of these men visited Flushing, and as they:

...were all dressed in the mud-stained frocks and trousers in which they worked underground, and armed with large clubs and sticks of various kinds and speaking an uncouth jargon, which none but themselves could understand they struck such terror where they went, and seemed like an irruption of barbarians Invading some more civilized country than their own.

It was claimed in 1737 that affidavits against only a few rioters could be obtained because 'the tinners have seldom occasion to go abroad from their parishes where they live, or places where they work, therefore are known to but a few'. [25] The miners collected in their villages and entered the market towns, or made incursions into the agricultural districts, or they went to the ports to prevent exportation. In each case they were taking the action outside of their own communities. The conflict was not simply one of poor against rich. The inhabitants of non-mining parishes and districts frequently used the term 'invasion' to describe the incursions of the miners. John Allen remembered from his Liskeard boyhood the shouts, 'The French are coming!' and 'The tinners are rising!' causing equal consternation among the townspeople. When the town of Looe received warning in 1793 that the miners intended to come in, the Sheriff of the county, who happened to be there, determined to resist and issued warrants for raising the *Posse Comitatus*:

...which brought there from the neighbouring parishes, a great number of men, most of the inhabitants of the town also came forward, and all was bustle and preparation expecting hourly the arrival of the Enemy. [26]

It is difficult to identify leaders of the rioters. That a man was taken and prosecuted need only imply that he was known to eyewitnesses and could be pointed out to the authorities. Those who attracted most notice, far from possessing the disciplined qualities of leadership, might well have been the hot-heads, sufficiently intoxicated by the excitement of the occasion to have taken the lead in plundering warehouses or assaulting opposers. The one rioter who was executed following the disturbances of 1796 was nicknamed 'Wildcat'. [27]

The impression gained from reading the examinations of witnesses of the Penryn riots of 1748 is one of surprise that the persons whom they identified should have become involved in such outrages. One saw a miner whom he knew driving a horse laden with corn. He asked the miner, 'How could you be so roguish as to take away Gentlemen's corn?' Another told a miner, whom he knew, that it was, 'a great shame for him to be there upon such an occasion'. Among those arrested at St Austell during the riots of 1847 was an old man to whom the magistrates spoke:

My good old man, what business can you have here, you show a very bad example, do go home, this is coming to a very serious matter. [28]

Two fishermen, John and William Richards, headed the Penzance riots of 1801 although the bulk of the crowd was miners. These two were described as 'notorious for their turbulent dispositions', but it is improbable that without their services no disturbance would have taken place. In that year of widespread rioting it is unlikely that the miners of that district would have stayed in their homes. They had rioted in 1793, 1795 and 1796 and were to do so again in 1812. Such a crisis year as 1801 would hardly have been missed. A certain violence of disposition may have lead such men to place themselves in the vanguard of the action, but it does not follow that they represented the aims and disposition of the main body of the rioters. It is, however, possible to identify a St Just miner, Henry Smith, as a leader in his district in 1847. He appears to have had a considerable popularity among his fellows, for when he was in dispute with the management of Boswidden Mine in 1853, the entire labour force struck work alleging that he was 'a marked man' both in consequence of his having played an active role in organizing a public meeting of miners to discuss strike action, and because:

…he acted a prominent part in the rise of the miners which took place some six years since, in consequence of the high price of flour'.

Smith's popularity clearly extended beyond the mine in which he worked, since a general strike of the St Just district was called in his support, which was especially impressive since Cornish miners were not at all accustomed to strike action. [29]

Some disturbances arose spontaneously. This would be more likely with price fixing in the markets in response to suddenly inflating prices, as at Launceston in 1801 and at Falmouth in the same year. But not all such disturbances can be viewed as spontaneous. A crowd at Penzance which tried to prevent the exportation of potatoes in 1818 had been was called together by a drum. [30] In general, given the involvement of more than one parish, the agreed assembly points, and the advance handbills and posters, it would seem that many food riots were organized and planned in advance. Indeed the miners, through threatening letters consciously used the threat of riots to achieve concessions.

So far the food riots have been considered as responses to an economic and social situation, and not as a politically motivated form of protest. It is true that the riots of the French War years were to some extent coloured by the popular Jacobinism of that time. Counter-revolutionary attitudes certainly coloured the reactions of the authorities, especially in 1795 and 1796. A more desperate spirit seems to have marked the actions of the rioters during those years. At Truro for instance, where a crowd openly assaulted the Worcestershire Militia, sent into the county to quell the disturbances, and where a miner from Redruth refused to depart after the reading of the Riot Act, saying, 'What use would it be to go home? He should have, 'as good or better living in prison', and that he would 'as soon be killed as starved. [31] The St Just handbill of 1795 invited miners to arm themselves with firearms and pikes for a visit to Penzance, but it was not displayed at the blacksmith's until after a party of miners had already visited the town unarmed and had been repulsed without difficulty by the Volunteers. In the same year a party of miners had told the magistrates at Helston that unless corn were procured for them on certain terms, they would come in and enforce such terms themselves. They would not 'come this time unarmed' as they had done the previous year, but would be 'prepared and properly armed, and that things should be more equal'. Nor were such threats the only signs of a different spirit abroad in those years. Rumours multiplied. According to one communication to the Home Office, the clerk of Kenwyn trying to have his horse shod in the mining village of St Agnes in March of 1795 could not find a blacksmith able to undertake the work for, 'they were busy at each forging pikes and making cutlasses'. Another communication tells the same story, but this time it is supposed to have happened to the Bailiff of Penryn. [32] In October of that year, the High Constable of Pydar was prevented from arresting four miners who had removed corn from a warehouse by a riotous crowd, and several shots were fired into the house into which he had fled for safety. In December, a Mrs Herring received a letter from the miners of Polgooth and other mines, which stated the cause of the miners' distress was 'such impious Monsters as you who have a plenty to spare and we perishing with hunger'. By the consent of 'many thousands of brave miners', and with the consent and advice of 'many respectable men of your parish', who knew that she possessed stored grain, she was being warned:

...if after this caution, you still persist to keep your corn, or from the same motive refuse to sell it at a moderate price, We are thareby (sic) determined to assemble and immediately to march till we come to your God or your Mows, whome (sic) you esteem as such and pull it down and likewise your house. [33]

Trouble continued into 1796. In April the following paper was circulated in the neighbourhood of Camborne:

Gentlemen of Camborne Church Town. This is to inform you, that unless you do stand to the agreement made concerning the butter and meat, that it shall be sold as we proposed (that is) meat of whatsoever kind shall not exceed 4d per pound, nor fresh butter 8d per pound, nor salt butter 6d per pound, nor salt pork 6d per pound, for if you do, we will take the liberty to call to see you again, for we have not given it up yet, for we will have it so - or we will burn the Town and you in the mits (sic) of it.

In the same month a crowd of grain-seeking miners roughly handled four servants of a Breage farmer. They were beaten with sticks and were dragged around by ropes placed around their necks. The farmer was not at home, but the miners still felt that they had a score to settle with him and a notice was nailed to his door:

This is to give notice that if the inhabitants of this house is not home tomor-row morning by ten o'clock in the forenoon they may expect to see it all broken open, and leveled to ground.

On the turnpike road about three miles from Truro, a corporal of the Worcestershire Militia was assaulted and beaten by a body of miners. All in all the propertied classes in the county must have wondered in 1795 to 1796 whether the greatest danger to their peace of mind threatened from the tinners or the French. [34]

All this was happening at the height of Jacobin phobia, when many of the gentry, whatever they thought at other times, could see the hand of Tom Paine behind even the most minor of disturbances. Sir Francis Basset, who possessed more influence in the western districts than any other single man, could even smell Jacobins from a distance of three hundred miles. Although living in London at the time, he wrote to the. Secretary of State, informing him that many of the miners 'seemed strongly tinged with Jacobinical principles'. Finding that his colleagues on the Cornish bench, closer to the scene of the riots than himself, were inclined to deal leniently with men who they had not realized had changed from hungry miners into seditious revolutionaries, Sir Francis hurried down to Corn-wall to rescue the situation. Securing fifty of the rioters, he conveyed them to Bodmin, where at the assize that followed one of the leaders was sentenced to death. All of the magistrates except Basset were in fa-vour of remitting the sentence. He was adamant claiming that his fellows were putting him in a very bad light, for in favouring leniency they were appearing to fix upon him the death of the condemned man. Despite this disagreeable situation he would not shrink from his duty and would not prevent 'an example being made which was highly necessary for the benefit of society'. Some years later Basset claimed with pride:

...the effect of this resolute conduct was soon visible throughout the coun-try, and the manners of the people were suddenly changed from rudeness and disrespect to proper obedience. [35]

Those who hold power are seldom uneasy without cause. Without

fire there may be no smoke, but that fire does not have to be a conflagra-
tion. There was just enough evidence of the circulation of Jacobin ideas
among the miners to intensify the unease, which the gentry would have
in any case felt in high food price years. William Jenkin, a Quaker mine
steward, not given to flights of fantasy, remarked of the miners around
Penzance in 1795:

> *I am told that in St Just, they went so far in imitation of our Gallic neigh-*
> *bours, as to plant the tree of liberty - I am sorry to hear several cant words*
> *amongst the tinners much in use amongst the French.* [36]

At Redruth in the same year, a miner, drinking at the 'Three Com-
passes', was blaspheming the evangelists, wishing perdition to all the
kings of the earth, and drinking the health of Tom Paine. On this occasion stern action from Sir Francis Basset was pre-empted by the intervention of Divine Providence. The unfortunate man was struck down
with lockjaw on the spot, at the very moment of his seditious toast. That
is how the *Gentlemen's Magazine* reported it; it might possibly have actually happened that way, but in any case even as an urban myth it is
strongly indicative of the tension and apprehension of the time. [37] Pro-
French Republican tinged sentiments continued to surface in 1801. A
printed broadsheet bearing two poems, 'The Complaints of the Poor of
Cornwall' and the 'Weeping Mother' was circulated. Its tone was quietist
rather than seditious. Although one verse was almost triumphalist in its
millenarianism:

> *My breth'ren do not mourn, Although you suffer here, We shall rejoice*
> *while others weep, When Christ in clouds appear.*

The farmers are again blamed for the food shortage:

> *You know the Lord did send*
> *The harvest dry and good,*
> *And thousands wept before the Lord*
> *That now is wanting food.*
> *My friends some pity take*

And lower the price of corn,
And do not let the poor be starv'd
Nor leave them for to mourn.

But the printed sentiment is transformed on a surviving example sent to the Home Office, for across the page in a strong hand has been written, 'Starving – Bonparte (sic) and Bread before oppression?

Other traces of radical political sentiment can also be found, but so too can evidence that they did not run very deeply or widely among the miners. A crowd of food rioting miners in Truro in 1796, who were desperate enough to offer fierce resistance to the soldiers present in the town, was approached by a small group of Jacobins. 'We declared that we were friends yet their jealousy or hatred ran to such a height that they threatened us with instant death'. [38]

Such revolutionary sentiment that there was manifested itself in talk of arms, and some other expressions being added to the protest language employed in some instances, rather than in any changes in the basic motivation and forms of action associated with the food riot. It is hard to believe that given their past record (or for that matter their future actions) that the miners would not have rioted in any event in the extreme food crises of 1795 to 1796 and 1800 to 1801.

The magistrates had to make a dual response to food riots. In the first place they were responsible for public order, and in the second place, it was from them and their class that any serious relief initiatives needed to come. At the earliest indication of a disposition to riot, they generally called a county meeting and issued a proclamation. Those issued in 1801, 1812, 1831 and 1847 are to a large degree interchangeable. A statement to the effect that the magistrates had already endeavored to lessen distress by raising money in the several parishes to provide flour for those most in need, is followed by a plain statement that the magistrates are firmly resolved to take further measures in this direction, but that nothing can be done to effectively remove the evil until it shall, 'please Providence to give a cheaper supply of food'. In the meantime the people were urged to bear their distress with patience, and the trust was expressed that the

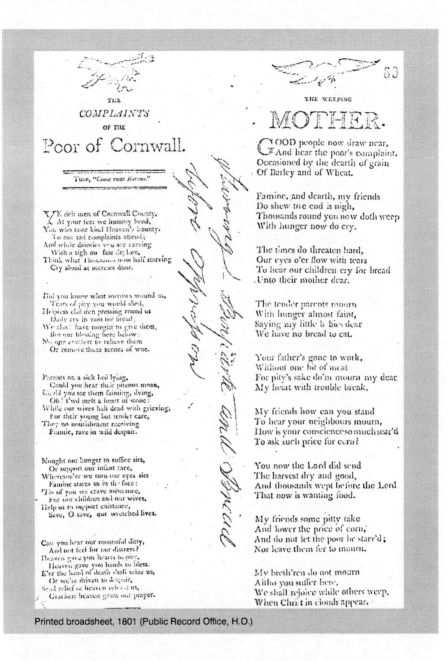

Printed broadsheet, 1801 (Public Record Office, H.O.)

Cornish miners 'would not allow their distress or their discontent or the persuasions of the ill-disposed to urge them on to acts of violence'. Such acts could do them no good, but would force the magistrates to use those powers that the law had given them to repress violence and punish its instigators. The poster of 1801 finishes with the uncompromising statement in extra-large print:

Resolved

That we will to the utmost of our power afford the fullest protection to property and the free supply of the markets.

A mixture of charity and repression was the usual reaction of authorities. Not perhaps charity always from the highest of motives, as a contributor to the *Gentlemen's Magazine* in 1795 pointed out:

Many plans are laid, and schemes proposed to keep our poor from perishing for want of bread; but alas, that is the lowest link in the chain of charity, except to ourselves - to prevent their rising and knocking us on the head. [39]

The food riot served to throw the distresses of the poor into sharp relief. Whether, compassion or fear was the ruling motive, it is clear that measures of relief were intensified after outbursts of rioting. Until their sufferings were forcibly expressed, many of the well-to-do lived in ignorance of the condition of the labouring miners and their families. When made aware, many of the gentry, took on a genuine, philanthropic role. At times in their efforts to procure corn or substitute foodstuffs, would-be relievers discovered for themselves the severity of the crisis, when only with the greatest difficulty could they find any food to procure, despite as the magistrates of the west of the county described it, in 1795, their, 'utmost endeavours'. A plea from St Hilary begged that the government might find means to send, 'pease or anything eatable less great numbers perish through absolute hunger'. In that year the vicar of Wendron who had had the foresight to secure a supply of barley for his poor parishioners at an early stage of the shortage, was offered an enhanced price for it by the inhabitants of a neighbouring parish. The vigilance of the authorities in taking action against traders, who exploited their customers by giving short weight or adulterating flour, was most evident in crisis years. The cases of this kind which are reported in such years, lead one to wonder just how extensive such practices were, when there was no food crisis to stir the magistracy into activity. It was not unknown for the poor to directly attempt to galvanise magistrates into taking some kind of action. In 1757 protesters appear to have wanted to push them into petitioning the king to prohibit maltsters from using any more scarce barley for brewing:

To Mr John Soal Esqr. at Penrice, St Austell, Cornwall, These Sir, Wee the poor of this niborhood (sic) desire you as you are chief at present that you will petishon His Majesties Grace to hinder the Malstors that the make no more Malt for this year, for Wee can live without Drink, but not without Bread, for Wee must-all starve if not Timely prevented. This wee implore you first with Tears. But if you lie sleeping and Wee starving by your side Wee will soon gather and burn your house, and destroys both You and Yours; For' if the Enemy be so near it is time to stirr - See Wee offer You life and death, Chuse which you please - Fortiskue, Grigar and Cariion shall share with you. [40]

The immediate concern of the magistrates was the restoration of order, using the local resources of the special constables and, during the French War years, the Volunteers where they proved sufficient, and hurriedly sending for the military when they did not. In normal times the strength of the military permanently stationed near the mining districts would be unequal to deal with any but the smallest and least determined of crowds. The small detachment normally kept at Pendennis Castle in Falmouth when summoned in 1727 to the assistance of the civil power was too weak to do other than stand by, while the rioters seized corn. The military were in any case always reluctant to involve themselves in civil matters unless especially authorized to do so by the War Office. The nearest large garrison on permanent duty was at Plymouth, two days march away. It was possible for a fast rider to get a request to the commander there within a day of an outbreak of rioting, but unless he had already been put on a general alert, the commanding officer was likely to await for War Office instructions before moving to the troubled district. The experience of 1773 illustrates this difficulty. The miners visited Penryn on the 8 February and the town officials wrote immediately to the Commanding Officer at Plymouth requesting assistance. He wrote to the War

Office on the 10 February informing them of the request, but saying that he had not complied with it as, 'he did not feel himself authorized to send a party upon the request of a deputy mayor and a deputy recorder'. Authorization from London was not sent until the 12 February, presumably reaching Plymouth on the 14 or 15 February. In any event troops did not arrive in the riot area until the 17 February, by which time, although isolated outbreaks caused the Secretary at War to authorize the sending of a further detachment on the 25 February, rioting had by then largely ceased. [41]

In 1796 the suppression of riots was assisted by the fact that the Worcestershire Militia, sent into the county during the disturbances of the previous year, remained there with standing orders to assist the civil authorities. In general, however, not only would the Government be reluctant to tie up troops in a restricted vicinity for a prolonged period of time once the immediate objective of restoring order had been achieved, but the civil authorities themselves often found the soldiers unwelcome guests once they again began to feel secure. The magistrates of Penryn in 1748 entreated a local peer to exert his influence and prevent any more troops from being sent there:

...as we have already more than we can reasonably accommodate and they make no question sufficient to protect us against any attempts the tinners will make on this place for the future'.

Troops had, after all to be provisioned at the very time when their presence was itself due to the fact that food prices were high. The troop, which marched from Falmouth to Redruth in 1812 to quell a riot, hardly had legitimate grounds for surprise when it could not find bread for itself on arrival. [42] Expense apart, relations between civil and military authorities were often strained, neither being fully inclined to take orders from the other, and the presence of troops in a town could in itself be, as at Truro in 1796, a provocation to violence on the part of the hungry local populace. In the French War years the local Volunteer companies were useful in holding a riot situation until regular troops could be obtained. It is perhaps more than coincidence that the Cornish towns that most zealously took up the patriotic call to arms were Penryn and Penzance, those most frequently visited by food rioters. Nobody was very keen to use the miners themselves to form armed companies of volunteers. It was not that they could not be relied upon to fight the French, their basic loyalty was not in doubt, but this was no guarantee of the use to which they might put their arms while awaiting a French invasion. In general the Volunteer companies could be relied upon to oppose effectively rioting miners, since their composition gave them little identity of interest with the miners. Formed from the tradesmen, lesser gentry, farmers and their servants, they were unlikely to take the side of rioting miners. The Penzance Volunteers were described in 1795 as, 'composed of shop-keeping Jews, butchers, and blacksmiths', and even the Volunteers of Illogan in the very heart of the mining district, turned out readily to quell disturbances at Redruth in 1801. [43] On one occasion, however, the loyalty of the Volunteers was not above question. The Tregony Company, called out in 1801 to deal with miners' incursions into the farming districts, did not, in the words of a magistrate, 'all deserve the thanks of Government'. One of their officers complained before setting out that the farmers' prices were too high, and later in the day suggested that farmers should sell at reduced prices. The whole company was said to have been 'mutinous and disorderly in the extreme'. [44]

In general the reactions of the magistracy to food rioting was far from both panic-stricken fear and from extreme severity in repression. After all, food rioting in Cornwall is basically explained by its effectiveness. In short, with disturbances so frequent, an adult miner whose life spanned the French Wars could have been involved in eight food riots. Magistrates in many cases sat on the bench, though as many a magistrate like Richard Polwhele, fervent anti-Jacobin that he was, could nevertheless describe those who saw the seeds of revolution in the riots of 1812 as showing, 'consternation without a cause'. Magistrates were familiar with such a recurrent form of protest. They expected riots to occur in expensive food years, and they were familiar with the forms that they customarily took. A Quarter Sessions chairman remarked that the disturbances of 1830 had arisen from a 'deep-rooted prejudice', which had existed as

long as he could remember. [45] Nothing so clearly underlines the excep-
tionality of Basset's action in insisting on the execution of a rioter in 1796,
as the lightness of the sentences passed on the ringleaders of 1801. Three
persons were imprisoned for three months, one for one month, two were
fined five shillings, and nine were fined one shilling. [46] The sympathy
of some magistrates with hungry miners was clearly displayed. In 1812
the Reverend John Collins arrived at a farm whose tenant was refusing
to supply wheat to a body of miners. He offered to pay himself for every bushel. When this was refused, he told the crowd to take what they
wanted. The farmer commenced a prosecution against Collins for felony.
The good vicar made a triumphal progress to the sessions receiving the
blessings and good wishes of the poor all the way, to be straightaway
acquitted by his brother justices. Polwhele, himself a magistrate, relates
this episode in a way which implies no disapproval of Collins' action. [47]

The frequency and longevity of food rioting was determined by the
fact that only through direct action could the eighteenth century poor express genuine grievances, and because it was in some senses an effective
form of protest. It could be so in two ways. Firstly, it precipitated relief
measures; and secondly, the immediate objectives of the rioters were often achieved. Grain was stopped from leaving ports, and hoarded grain
was brought out and sold in the markets. The general effect of food rioting in precipitating relief measures has been discussed above but on one
occasion the crowd set up its own relief programme. In 1831 a crowd of
two thousand miners visited Manaccan. Instead of departing upon being
assured that no more corn would be exported, they first, 'laid the village
under contribution for food, and the place was left perfectly destitute of
everything that could be ate or drunk'. [48] If the miners came into a town
or port without warning, and the inhabitants were unable to resist them,
then there was little to prevent them being successful. Jenkin wrote from
Redruth in 1801:

*I have had the disgusting sight of a riotous assemblage of tinners from
Gwennap who Broke into the Market and are now compelling the people to sell
potatoes, fish, butter, salt pork etc. at the prices they chose to fix - finding no body*

to stop them (for we have neither magistrates nor military here...)

Such success could not be hoped for on the next Market day, for by then the assistance of the military had been obtained:

The riots are finished for the present - Sir John St Aubyn and some other justices have attended here this week and a considerable force of Civil and Military power...has preserved (or rather restored) the peace.

In the same year prompt action against ringleaders was urged for fear that once the sense of urgency was past, courts would deal leniently with rioters, which would encourage such behaviour in the future, 'especially as the mobs have certainly in various incidents carried their point'. [49] The frequency of rioting suggests that its users had confidence in its usefulness. This confidence was not entirely misplaced. In general rioters were not treated with the full severity of the law, often succeeded in their short-term aims, and in precipitating measures of relief. If not all members of Cornish society would have appreciated such a functional justification of food rioting, the Home Office papers clearly reveal that those who screamed the loudest of outrage and revolution were the corporations of the market towns. The reports of the county magistrates were much less strident. There is little doubt that the troops sent into the county were protecting property rather than life or the Constitution, for only against the first was there any real threat.

Although food rioting was much their most frequently used form of protest, it is important to note that it was not the miners' only experience of crowd behavior. In the 1740s there were several outbursts of crowd hostility towards the Wesleys and their followers, but these were over by 1747, enabling John Wesley to write from St Ives:

Here is such a change within these two years as has hardly been seen in any other part of England. Wherever we went we used to carry our lives in our hands now there is not a dog to wag his tongue. [50]

There was a disturbance at Redruth in 1766, when around fifty tin miners protesting against the introduction to the County of Staffordshire earthenware, broke into the market and smashed all that they found there. They then proceeded to Falmouth intending to repeat their demonstration. Being unable to force their way into a building where pottery was stored, they were on the point of setting fire to it, when they were pacified by a group of town aldermen, who expressed sympathy and promised to do their best to discourage the use of pottery, and ordered a quantity of pewter dishes as an indication of their support. [51]

There were other uses than pottery to which a devious mind could put Cornwall's white china clay. A food-related disturbance took place at Truro in 1814 when a miller who used it to adulterate his flour was burned in effigy. A similar protest involving a crowd of 200 miners took place at Wendron in 1837 against a supplier of bread of a deplorable quality under his contract with the Helston Union. [52]

Industrial riots were rare among the Cornish miners. There is a record of miners from the Redruth area who entered into a dispute with the mine owners over a change in the method of calculating their wages. They, 'rose in large bodies, drove off or pressed into their number such as they found at their work, pulled up the ladders and then marched in a body to Truro.' There they succeeded in securing a promise that the change would not be introduced. [53]

Another rare instance of a disturbance resulting from an industrial grievance took place in 1831 at Fowey Consols, where the miners were attempting to form a combination to avoid tributers underbidding each other at the monthly settings. The refusal of two tributers to join, led to a riot for their part in which after reading of the Riot Act, seven miners were taken into custody and while they were being conveyed to Bodmin gaol an unsuccessful but violent attempt was made to release them, with the skirmishing taking upon hour-and-a-half. The following day a determined crowd of miners began to march on Bodmin to attempt once again the rescue of their comrades. The High Sheriff and other magistrates rushed to the town and swore in about forty special constables as well as calling out the Royal Cornwall Militia to surround the gaol. About six o'clock in the evening a crowd, perhaps surprisingly described as consisting mostly of women and children, entered the town and sent a deputation to the Sheriff. He remained firm, and eventually after some rather protracted negotiations, the crowd departed. [54]

During the 1780s competition with newly discovered and easily mined copper ore from Anglesey brought unemployment and falling earnings to the mining districts. As a result, desperate attempts were made by Cornish lords and adventurers to avoid mine closures. [55] Local resentment was directed against the great engineering firm of Boulton and Watt, whose steam engines first introduced in 1777 had quickly become essential to keep the deepening mines free of water. The firm was unwilling to lessen the burden of the premiums through which the engines were paid. On several occasions when word of closures circulated, large crowds of miners assembled. A crowd of 400 miners visited Truro in 1787. [56] In April 1788 the miners at North Downs reacted against its projected closure and so alarmed Boulton and Watt's agent, that he moved his family out of the district. Only the presence of soldiers prevented deeper disorder. In the following year the miners threatened that if another mine closed, they would, 'take down the greatest house in Truro'. [57] In that year 1789, John Wesley witnessed the arrival in Truro of, 'numberless tinners', who 'being nearly starved, were come to beg or demand an increase of their wages, without which they could not live'.[58] Although there was much muttering about the high cost of food, this incursion was hardly a food riot. It was directed at Truro because that was where the decisions that determined copper prices and output and through them the levels of employment, were taken. By the 1790s the easily worked out but comparatively poor ores of Anglesey were becoming worked out and the over-production crisis in Cornish copper mining ended. There was, however, yet to be an episode of crowd action directed at a local representative of Boulton and Watt in 1796. The problem on this occasion was their use of patent rights to obtain an injunction against the important Poldice mine completing the installation of a major steam engine designed by the Cornish engineer Bull which was needed to keep the promising deep levels of the mine free of water. With the injunction in place, the mine stopped its pumps causing ferment among the miners. A large body marched to Redruth. They forced William Murdock, who was then Boulton and Watt's agent in Cornwall, to accompany them back to the mine where, believing that he had copied the plans of the Bull engine and sent them to his employers, made him publicly promise never to come near the mine again. [59]

It is not being suggested that the industrial riots of the 1780s or the other riots not easily classified as food riots can be encompassed within an appropriate definition of the 'moral economy'. However, they do say something about the context in which food rioting took place. In particular they further indicate the familiarity of the miners with direct crowd action, and the comparative ease with which large bodies of them could be assembled. Arguments over the value of Edward Thompson's 'moral economy' will continue. In depth local evaluations will not necessarily indicate solutions to many of them. It does not, for example, seem that forms of evidence will surface which will conclusively settle the debate over the role of women both in instigating and participating in food riots. [60] They were responsible for the first two market place incidents in 1800 at Launceston and Falmouth, but are not singled out for mention, after the disturbances became more widespread and serious in the mining districts. The only incident in 1818 occurred when women took action over potato prices at Penzance. It seems probable that women were more evident in the market place, than on the enforcing 'long marches' typically undertaken by miners to ports or in to the country. In 1831 an estimated 2000 miners visited farms in the Helston area. A lengthy report of the day's activities makes no mention of any other than miners in the crowd. However, on the following day, some wagons loaded with corn through Breage were stopped and unloaded by a crowd described as 'principally female'. When it was learned that the corn was owned by a miller named Stevens and was actually on its way for sale at Penzance market, it was carefully stored to be restored intact to Miller Stevens, who presented the women with two bottles of brandy for taking such good care of his corn. [61]

It is the conclusion of this examination of food rioting in a Cornish occupational community in which it was recurrent, possibly to an extent and consistency beyond that of any other, that as a concept of explanation and interpretation, Thompson's 'moral economy' is indeed powerful. It is true that 'moral economy' was not a contemporary usage, but neither for that matter was 'market economy'. Thompson recognized this. He wrote to me in 1988 in answer to my query as to where he got the term 'moral economy' from and had he ever found it in an eighteenth century source? [62] In fact he first used the term in his classic of 1963 *The Making of the English Working Class.* It is used there without the emphasis of inverted commas as a label for the reactions of the poor to the encroachments of the market:

It [the food riot] was legitimized by the assumptions of an older moral economy, which taught the immorality of any unfair method of forcing up the price of provisions by profiteering upon the necessities of the people… the final years of the eighteenth century saw a last desperate effort by the people to reimpose the older moral economy as against the economy of the free market.

Importantly, he linked popular legitimation to 'the old paternalist moral economy'. Indeed, at times he seemed to use 'moral' and 'paternalist' interchangeably. [63]

It is possible that Thompson overstated the retention in the popular mentalité of specific elements such as the Book of Orders or the Assize of Bread. The moral economy is found in a wider vocabulary both spoken and, sometimes written. It is to be found too in a repertoire of actions and in a particularization of targets and objectives. When the rioters attempted to force a resetting of food prices, they described those they were seeking to impose as, 'fair and reasonable' and as moderate and their demands as 'just'. They warned of the consequences if any of the 'agreements' they made were not, 'stood to'. They described their targets as, 'griping farmers', or as an, 'avaricious woman', or, 'impious monsters'. They appealed to the justices to act as the enforcers of paternalist regulation. Thus, a letter circulating in 1796 was addressed to the 'Gentlemen of Camborne Church Town' while in 1757 the addressees of a demand that action be taken to restrict the activities of maltsters in buying up barley, 'We can live without drink, but not without bread' were four named magistrates in the St Austell region. Often in anonymous letters these meanings were wrapped in rhetoric of violence, sometimes extreme and set against the, 'starving poor' might as well, some of them asserted, be, 'hanged as starved'. But this is part of the language of the threatening poor, and grandiose as threats were to pull down houses or burn them while their inhabitants slept, none was carried out, even though arson was the weapon most readily available to the protesting or revengeful impoverished. [64]

1. E. Thompson, 'The Moral Economy of the English Crowd in the Eighteenth Century', in *Past and Present* No. 50 (February 1971), p. 99. The huge body of literature responding to this article was reviewed by Thompson in 'The Moral Economy Reviewed', *Customs in Common*, 1991, pp. 259-351. Of particular importance are R. Wells, *Wretched Faces: Famine in Wartime England 1790-1803*, Gloucester, 1988; R. Wells, 'The Revolt in the South West' in J. Rule and R. Wells, *Crime, Protest and Popular Politics in Southern England 1740-1850*, 1997, pp. 17-51; A. Charlesworth and A. Randall, 'Morals, Markets and the English Crowd in 1766', in *Past and Present*, No. 114, (19), pp. 200-213.
2. G. Rudé, *The Crowd in History*, 1964; R. Rose, 'Eighteenth-Century Price Riots and Public Policy in England', in *International Review of Social History*, VI, 1961, p. 27.
3. R. Rose, 'Eighteenth Century Price Riots and Public Policy in England', pp. 279-281.
4. G. Rudé, *The Crowd in History*, p. 37.
5. See Thompson, 'Moral Economy'; J. Whetter, 'Cornish Trade in the Seventeenth Century', in *Journal of Royal Institute of Cornwall*, IV, Part 4, 1964, p. 588; D. Rowe, *Revolution Cornwall in the Age of the Industrial Revolution*, Liverpool, 1953, p. 223; *Annals of Agriculture*, XXIV, 1793, pp. 217, 225-226; H.O. 42/61, J. Williams and Francis St. Aubyn to Duke of Portland, 14 April 1801; C. Redding, *An Illustrated Itinerary of Cornwall*, 1842, p. 142.
6. *Journals of House of Commons*, I, 1795, pp. 212-215.
7. Public Record Office, S. Dom, Pye to Rolfey and Weed, Falmouth 15 September 1737; See letter from Sir William Lemon, 27 March, 1795; HO 42/34.
8. N. Pounds, 'The Historical Geography of Cornwall', Ph.D Thesis, London, 1941, p. 555.
9. S. Dom, 36/4 Part 1, Mayor of Falmouth to Duke of Newcastle, 16 November and 18 December 1727; S. Dom, 56/5 t1, Newcastle to Secretary at War, 11 January 1727; W. Borlase, *Historical Sketch of the Tin Trade in Cornwall*, Plymouth, 1874, p. 54; Cornwall Record Office, Truro Borough Order Book, MSS, p. 156; S. Dom, 56/6, enclosure

in Mayor of Falmouth to Newcastle, 15 May 1728.

10. BM, Add. MSS, 52, 587 f. 557, Justices of the County to Newcastle, (n.d.); S. Dom, 56/10, Proclamation for Suppressing Riots etc; Calendar of Treasury Books and Papers 1729, p. 559; F. Hitchens and S. Drew, *History of Cornwall*, Helston, 1824, II, pp. 71-72; St Ives Borough MSS, transcribed by C. Noall, *Old Cornwall*, V, pp. 418-421; S. Dom, 36/42, W. Hicks to J. Pye, Truro, 18 Sep 1737; ibid, Mayor of Falmouth to Newcastle, 18 September 1737; ibid, Pye to Rolfey and Wood, 19 September 1737; BM, Add MSS 56690, f. 565; *Guide to Newcastle*, Penryn, 22 September 1737; S. Dom, 56/t & 8 42, Prideaux to Newcastle, 20 September 1737; *Gentlemen's Magazine*, VIII, October 1737, p. 656.

11. ibid, XVIII, October 1748, p. 474; S. Dom, 56/108, from Penryn, n.d., 1748; ibid, 56/80, Magistrates of Penryn to Lord Boscawen, 15 October 1748; 56/108, Mayor of Penryn to Bedford, 5 November 1748; H. Douch, *Cornish Inns*, Truro, 1966, p. 46; J. Hammond, A Cornish Parish, 1897, p. 555; A. Hamilton Jenkin, *The Cornish Miner*, 1927, pp. 151-2; WO, 40/17, J. Luke to Barrington, Tregony, 8 February 1773; *Gentlemen's Magazine*, April 1757, p. 185; *Annual Register*, IX, 1766, pp. 157-8; ibid, X, 1767, pp. 8; 4; Calendar of Home Office Papers of the Reign of George III, 1773-5, No. 30; S. Dom, 41/26, JPs to Secretary at War, 9 February 1773; Magistrates of Penryn to Commanding Officer, Plymouth, 9 February 1775, above to Secretary at War, 8 February 1773, Major Dunkin to Barrington, 27 February 1773, from principal inhabitants of Helston, 10 February 1773, Earl of Rocheford to Barrington, 25 February 1773; WO 40/17, Luke to Barrington, Tregony, 8 February 1773.

12. G. Unwin, 'Letters and Remarks etc with a view to open an ExtensiveTrade', *The Article of Tin*, 1790, pp. 2-3; HO, 50/581, Mayor of Penryn to Secretary at War, 3 August 1789; *The Times*, 6 February 1793; R. Polwhele, *Reminiscences*, 1856, I, p. 91; *Annual Register*, 1793, p. 21; HO, 42/25, Tippet to Secretary of State, Falmouth, 10 May 1795; Wendron Parish Register, CRO, Truro; HO, 43/6, p. 140, Portland to Mayor of Falmouth, 6 and 14 January 1795; HO, 42/54, Tremenheere to Secretary of State, 11 March 1795, from Mayor of Penzance, 25 March 1795, Grylls to Secretary of State, Helston, 15 March 1795, from Penryn, 20 March 1795, Penwarne to Sec of State, Penryn, 29 March 1795, from Sir William Molesworth (enclosure in letter from Sir William Lemon), 27 March 1795, from Carne, Falmouth, 19 April 1795; Jenkin MSB to G. Hunt, 25 March 1795; HO, 43/6, Portland to Price, p. 209, to Sir Francis Basset, 6 April 1795, to above 10 July 1795; HO, 45/7, to J. Foote, 10 November 1795; MSS Journal of Christopher Wallis, 3 October 1795, 6 April1796; *Burrow's Worcestershire Journal*, 21 April 1796, (reference supplied by Dr Malcolm Thomas); HO, 42/58, to Mt. Edgecumbe, 11 April 1796; from Major St John, Truro, 10 April 1796, from John Vivian, Truro, 26 April 1796, from J. Stackbouse, Pendarves, 28 April 1796; HO, 45/7, to Sheriff of Cornwall, 2 May 1796; T. Bond, *Topographical and Historical Sketches of the Boroughs of East and West Looe*, 1825, p. 86; W. Lovett, *Life and Struggles*, 1920, p. 15; *Cornwall Gazette*, 4 March, 11 April, 18 April, 2 May 1801; Jenkin MSS to S. Grose, 10 April 1801; *Sherborne Mercury*, 27 April 1801; HO, 42/122, 'Magistrates inform on the present state of the county', 9 April 1812; *West Briton*, 27 March, 10 April 1812; A. Hamilton Jenkin, *News from Cornwall*, 1951, p. 165.

13. *West Briton*, 18 Sep 1818; G. Rude, 'English Rural and Urban Disturbances 1830-

1', in *Past and Present*, No. 57, July 1967, p. 90; *West Briton*, 4 September 1830, 4 May, 1 May 1847; *Cornwall Gazette*, 27 November 1830, 26 February, 5 and 12 March 1831, 22 January 1847; *Cornubian*, 18 February l831; J. Rowe, op cit, p.l65; A. Rowe, ' The Food Riots of the Forties in Cornwall', in *Report of Royal Cornwall Polytechnic Society,* 1942, pp. 56-66; H.O. 41/18, Disturbance Entry Book, to Sir W. Trelawney, 1 June 1847. Food riots on a local scale lingered a little longer in South Devon with incidents in 1858 and 1867, in which year traces of the old tradition were to be found in Oxfordshire, R. Swift, 'Food Riots in mid-Victorian Exeter 1847-1867', in *Southern History*, 2, 1980, pp. 101-128, and R. Storch, 'Popular Festivity and Consumer Protest in the South West and Oxfordshire', in *Albion*, 14, pp. 3-4, 1982.

14. S. Dom, 36/42, Mayor of Truro to J. Pye, 18 September 1737; Newcastle MSS, BM, Add MSS 36690, f. 365, examination of Samuel Rouse; Calendar of Home Office Papers of the Reign of George III, 1753-1755; Document 30; S. Dom, 41/36, Justices of the Peace to Secretary at War, 7 February 1773.

15. *West Briton*, 10 April 1812.

16. *Annual Register*, 1831, Chronicle, pp. 38-39.

17. Hitchens and Drew, *History of Cornwall*, II, p 71-72; Thomas Tonkin, footnote to the 1811 edition of Carew's *Survey of Cornwall*, p. 66.

18. *Sherborne Mercury*, 15 April l801; *West Briton*, 11 April 1812.

19. *Annual Register*, X, 1767, p. 84. There are no other references to any riot in 1767. I suspect that the incident was a myth. If so it still remains significant.

20. PRO, WO, 40/17, J. Luke to Barrington, 8 February 1773; *Cornwall Gazette*, 18 April l801; HO, 42/58, from Major St John, Truro, 10 April 1796.

21. See John Bohstedt, *Riots and Community Politics in England and Wales 1790-1810*, Harvard University Press, 1983.

22. S. Dom, 36/10, Part 1, 'A Proclamation for Suppressing Riots 1729'; 36/108, Witness examinations from Penryn 1848; BM, Add MSS 36690, f. 365, Guide to Newcastle, 22 September 1737; HO, 42/34, from Captain Tremenheere, Penzance, 11 March 1795; *Cornubian*, 25 February 1831.

23. HO, 42/34, from Tremenheere, 14 March 1795 (enclosure); HO, 42/61, enclosure, hand written notice, posted 1801; *Cornish Magazine*, II, 1898, p. 113.

24. HO, 42/39, from Justices of Kerrler, Helston, 7 May 1796; HO, 42/34, from Penryn, 20 March 1795.

25. J. Buckingham, *Autobiography*, 1855, p.16; BM, Add MSS 36690, f. 365, *Guide to Newcastle, Penryn*, 22 September 1737.

26. J. Allen, *History of the Borough of Liskeard*, 1858, p. 360, f. Bond, op cit, pp. 84-85.

27. PRO, Assize 21/18, Summer Assize, Bodmin, 25 July 1796.

28. S. Dom, 36/108, Examinations of Witnesses from Penryn, 1748; A. Rowe, 'Food Riots of the 1840s', p. 65.

29. *Cornwall Gazette*, 9 May 1801; *West Briton*, 15 April 1855.

30. ibid, 18 September 1818.

31. HO, 42/38, Examinations and Proceedings against the Rioters taken into custody at Truro, 7 April 1796.

32. HO, 42/34, from Grylls, Helston, 31 March 1795; from Penryn, 20 March 1795; For the second version of the incident see Wells, *Wretched Faces*, p. 134.

33. *London Gazette*, 9 January, 30 April 1796.

34. ibid, 16 April, 3 May, 23 April 1796.

35. HO, 42/38, Basset to Portland, 20 April 1796; J. Farrington, Diary, (ed.), J. Grieg, 1926, VI, p. 134.

36. Jenkin MSS, to G. Hunt, 23 March 1795.

37. C. Gilbert, *Historical Survey of Cornwall*, 1817, I, p. 98.

38. HO, 42/61, Broadsheet Enclosure in Mt. Edgcumbe to Portland, 16 January 39. Minute Books of the London Corresponding Society, BM, Add MSS 27815, pp. 41-42, from Truro, pp. 39-43.

39. HO, 42/61, Printed Resolutions from Magistrates in poster form, *Gentlemen's Magazine*, IXV, Part 2, 1795, p. 824.

40. *Sherborne Mercury*, 9 February 1801; *West Briton*, 10 April 1812; PO, A27, A54, Penzance, 2 July 1795, Enclosure in letter from Basset, 2. July 1795; Parish Register of Wendron, CRO, Truro; *London Gazette*, 29 January 1757.

41. S. Dom, 56/4, Part 1, Mayor etc. of Falmouth to Newcastle, 16 November 1727; HO, 41/26, Prescott to Barrington, Plymouth, 10 February, Barrington to Rochford, 23 February, Rochford to Barrington, 25 February, Dunkin to Barrington, 27 February 1773.

42. HO, 45/6, to Sir Francis Bassett, 2 May 1795; S. Dom, 56/80, Magistrates of Penryn to Lord Boscawen, 15 October 1748; *West Briton*, 10 April 1812.

43. J. Western, 'The Recruitment of the Land Forces in Great Britain 1795-9', Ph.D thesis, Edinburgh, 1955, p. 202; *Sherborne Mercury*, 28 May 1798, 27 April 1801.

44. HO, 42/61, Mt. Edgcumbe to Portland, St Austell, 18 April 1801.

45. R. Polwhele, *Traditions and Recollections*, 1826, II, p. 582; *Cornwall Gazette*, 8 January 1831.

46. CRO, Quarter Sessions, 1801.

47. R. Polwhele, *Reminiscences*, 1836, p. 7.

48. *Cornubian*, 25 February 1831.

49. Jenkin MSS to S. Gross, 10 April 1801, to A. Hunt, 18 April 1801; HO, 42/61, W. Elford to Hatton, Falmouth, 19 April 1801.

50. John Wesley, Works, XII, p. 152, Wesley to Blackwell, St Ives, 18 July 1747.

51. A. Rees, 'Cornwall's Place in Ceramic History', *Report of Royal Cornwall Polytechnic Society*, 1935, p. 61.

52. *West Briton*, 10 November 1814; *Cornwall Gazette*, 17 September 1837.

53. Jenkin MSS, William Jenkin to George Hunt, Redruth, 11 August 1794.

54. *Cornwall Gazette*, 26 February 1831.

55. The economics of the contest between Cornish and Anglesey copper ore has often been examined by business historians, since after the setting up of the Cornish Metal Company to sell the copper output of the main mines, it entered into a price and quota agreement with Thomas Williams, the Anglesey mine owner, which is an early example of a metal cartel. A fine description of this background is provided in J. Rowe, *Cornwall in the Age of the Industrial Revolution*, pp. 68-113.

56. The main source for this section was the Boulton and Watt MSS, in Bir-

mingham City Library, Box 20. Letters from Boulton to Watt from Cornwall, 3, 5, 8, 11 October 1787.

57. Thomas Wilson to Boulton and Watt, 14, 18, 19, 21 April, 3, 4, 17, 24, 31 May, 2, August, 17 September 1788.

58. John Wesley, *Journal*, 18 August 1789.

59. Rowe, op cit, p. 106; Jenkin MSS, Jenkin to Richard Philips 30 July, 1795.

60. J. Bohstedt, 'Gender, Household and Community Politics. Women in English Riots 1790-1810', in *Past and Present*, No. 120, 1988, pp. 88-102, and E. Thompson, 'Moral Economy Reviewed', pp. 305-336.

61. *Cornwall Gazette*, 26 February 1831.

62. Edward Thompson to the author, Worcester, 24 November 1988.

63. E. Thompson, *The Making of the English Working Class*, 1963, pp. 63-66.

64. See C. Tilly, 'Conscientious Repertoires in Great Britain 1758-1834', in *Social Science*, Vol. 17, 1993, pp. 252-280.

3 A Risky Business: *Death, Injury and Religion in Cornish Mining c. 1780-1870*

Introduction

Around the tin and copper mines of Cornwall there had developed by the middle decades of the nineteenth century what was probably the largest long-settled metal mining community in the world. It is probably also the best documented in written sources of all kinds. The national population census provides basic demographic data from 1801, which was augmented from 1841 by additional statistics, including data on migration and on the distribution of occupations by age and gender. Several local weekly newspapers were in existence by the 1830s and the interest they showed in the morbidity and mortality of the working miners was shared by a number of local doctors who published detailed investigations at the parish level. There were several major Parliamentary inquires between 1825 and 1864 which assembled hundreds of pages of testimony to working and living conditions in the mining community from a large and varied population of local witnesses. These written sources provide the main evidence for this essay. They have been supplemented by others including manuscript letters and autobiographical and other authored printed works, especially those deriving from Methodism, the role of which religious denomination is a central concern of this essay. Aspects of the material culture of the mining community are frequently discussed in detail in the Parliamentary inquiries, but little archaeological research has been done on the area's later history. Visible reminders are hardly rare, from engine houses at the now disused mines to village chapels, now often converted to other uses, but a boom in industrial archaeology in the 1960s and 1970s concentrated almost exclusively on technical and engineering aspects of the mining industry and only marginally to social conditions.

Several contributions to this volume stress the importance of women as a presence even in mushrooming 'frontier' mining communities. In the long-settled mining districts of Cornwall, women outnumbered men; a consequence of the high death rate among miners. Young women worked at the mines, but only as surface labour breaking and sorting ores. In the Cornish mines there was no use of female labour underground. Occupational data sorted by gender and by age in the census tables of the mid-nineteenth century indicate that women usually ceased mine work on marriage. [1] They married young and were frequently pregnant at marriage. In the mining township of Camborne, calculation from the parish registers for the last quarter of the eighteenth century reveals that 45% of traceable first baptisms took place within eight-and-a-half months' of marriage. [2] Although the central purpose of this essay is to examine the high mortality and injury risks which daily faced the underground male workforce, it is clear that women too must be its subject. Young marriage and large families aggravated the material impact of the death or disablement of 'breadwinners'. If the folk religion, which it is argued below Methodism had become, provided for the miners a quietistic acceptance, it as importantly provided for the bereaved a culture of consolation.

Cornish Mining: Background

Cornish tin production has a very long history dating from pre-Roman times. The industry was protected and privileged by the Crown through the middle ages, although only from the sixteenth century did mining replace streaming as the predominant technology. [3] First arousing interest towards the end of the sixteenth century, copper came to exceed tin in importance, during the county's boom years from 1740 to 1860. It was only produced from deep mining. The two metals together already employed around 10,000 people by 1800. The underground labour force was male, but copper in particular also employed numbers of surface workers breaking and sorting ores and these were mostly young women and children. In 1851 total employment was 36,287. Decline set in by 1861 and was rapid after 1880. Large numbers emigrated famously taking their mining skills around the world. [4]

In Cornwall, by the mid-nineteenth century, settled mining communities had existed through several generations, although stereotyping miners as 'a race apart' has been overdone. [5] These communities had particular structural characteristics such as a very high male death rate and they also had distinctive cultural ones; among them the chapel culture deriving from a strong attachment to Methodism.

In the extensive literature on the middle decades of the nineteenth century words like 'risk', 'chance', 'speculation' or even 'lottery', appear frequently. Shares in Cornish mines, proven ones, promising ones and prospective ones, attracted great interest. Cornish mining involved a multiplicity of shareholders, who along with those historically who chanced their capital on the high seas, were known as 'adventurers'.

Mining booms do not occur simply because there is a shortage of other investment opportunities. The element of excitement is usually present, for metal mining is an industry that must at the same time produce and prospect. South Caradon commenced in 1835. Its original issue of one pound shares attracted little interest, but within a year they had reached £2,000. But such returns were not usual. Even adventuring in an established mine with a previous good history was not safe. All business ventures have a history, but in mining it is essentially a natural one. Higher lodes might prove profitable, but lower ones disappointing. Alternatively the best paying levels might prove to be deep down. Rewarding as they might ultimately become, staying in through the financial calls of a long, hard and deep sinking might prove too expensive for some. West Caradon, an enterprise stimulated by the success of South Caradon, found good ore in its higher levels in the 1850s and early 1860s and its shares peaked at £90, but by 1868 they were down to £6. Cook's Kitchen, near Redruth, was one of the largest single enterprises in the country already employing 1000 people by the 1790s. In its early years it had raised ore to an incredible two million pounds, but from 1810 did not manage to pay a dividend for 51 years. [6]

In 1837 copper mines employed 27,028 persons across 160 mines. However less than 12% worked in mines employing less than 100 persons; more than 60% in mines employing more than 250, and 31% in the five largest concerns which each employed more than 1000. Cornish mining had by then been a highly capitalised industry for more than a century. But corporate mining forms still retain some prospector aspects. They do not make, but discover and remove. [7]

Risks of Mining

An unusual feature of the mine economy of Cornwall was the sharing of prospecting risk by capital and labour. The miners who raised the ore were paid under the tribute system. Tributers formed small groups, perhaps only two men with a boy, to undertake measured portions of the mine, known as 'pitches', for an agreed share of the price which the ore they raised fetched when sold. Contracts usually ran for two months and was expressed in terms of a rate in the pound, ranging from a shilling or less (5p) to as much as fifteen shillings. This variation was due to the fact that pitches contained ores of different quality and in different amounts. Tributers had to judge the rate at which good wages could be made from a particular pitch on offer. If the ore was large in quantity or high in quality, this could be done at a lower rate in the pound. The prospective and speculative elements are evident. The selling price of the copper or tin was subject to fluctuation in a market beyond the miner's influence. Luck played a part in whether lodes turned out better or worse than they had promised. The skill and judgement of the tributer was critical, for the pitches were not allocated by lot, nor distributed by management. They were bid for at a form of auction, being taken by the tributers offering to work at the lowest rate. The system was acclaimed by those nurtured in the axioms of nineteenth century political economy. It promised a high degree of task application because the miners were paid by results and it associated labour with capital in the risks of enterprise. It naturally regulated the price of labour by supply and demand, for when work was scarce competition was fierce, and miners in effect bid down their own wages. Certainly, contemporaries noted that involving a miner in periodic competition with his comrades was hardly propitious for collective action, and contributed to the weak development of trade unionism in the mines. [8] The skilled miner was not offered constant wages but the chance of a windfall and the risk of poverty. However experienced the miners, the unexpected could happen in one direction or the other:

   ...within the last six or seven days two poor men were working in a part of the mine where the lode was very hard and poor, They suddenly cut into a bunch

of rich copper ore, very soft and consequently easy to break. The poor fellows hav-
ing by their contract 12s (60p) out of the pound...Their time expires at the end
of the month and if the lode continues so good... I expect they will get £100 each
for themselves for two weeks labour, and that same piece of ground will be taken
next month for less than one shilling in the pound. [9]

Such good fortune might happen only once or twice in a working life, but it helps explain the attachment of the miners to a system, which often denied them a living wage, and sometimes left them with nothing. The adventurers did not mind the occasional paying out of large sums, for when this happened they served to 'animate all the others who increase their exertion in the hopes of similar discovery'.[10] They also encouraged competition at the next bidding and helped to bring neglected parts of the mine into operation. In 1805 after a spectacular gain, a pitch was taken for only 5d (2p) in the pound, when the manager's own estimation was that at least a shilling (5p) was needed to make adequate earnings, but, 'there was no stopping them in the survey so eager were they to have that pitch'.[11] The tribute system meant that from time-to-time some miners and their families would suffer deprivation. Such reversals of fortune could in a religious community find themselves attributed to a greater power. When a Methodist miner had a good run in 1853, he knew who to thank: 'The Lord has greatly prospered me at the mine lately', while for another it was, 'Providence', which had blessed his labours.[12] When times were otherwise, hunger for the mining family linked a matter of risk to one of health. But working underground had more direct effects on miners' health than those consequent on poverty. Official figures reveal Cornish mining to have been the most unhealthy of employments. Mortality was more than two-and-a-half times that of coalminers and half as much again as that of seamen. Just as revealing is a comparison between miners and non-mining males in Cornwall itself. From a sample of six mining parishes from 1849 to 1853, if the latter are indexed at 100 then the respective age cohort figures for miners are as given in the table overleaf.

Index of Deaths in Age Cohorts: Non-miners = 100			
Age	No of deaths	Age	No of deaths
15-25	125	45-55	227
25-35	101	55-65	263
35-45	143	65-75	189

From this data two especially significant things emerge. In the age range 25-35, miners' mortality began to increasingly exceed that of non-miners, especially after that of 45. The death rate for miners in middle age was more than double that for non-miners. The heavier mortality between 15 and 25 is largely explained by the risks of mining, i.e. by the accident rate, which also crippled or blinded even larger numbers. Deaths and sickness in middle age are for the most part differently explained. Older miners were killed or maimed often enough, but there was a general consensus that their greater caution, patience and experience, made them less vulnerable. What explains their heavier mortality is not risk, but inevitably the impact of years of working in oxygen-deficient underground levels, breathing dust, the exhaustion of hard work in wet and hot places, and in particular the long ladder climbs back to the surface at the end of each shift. When miners answered the questioning of a Parliamentary inquiry in 1864, by stating, 'You cannot expect miners to live as long as other men', and when another said of the old miners, 'They dwindle down, they waste away in time', they were stating the simple facts of life and death as they knew and experienced them. The conclusion of the report was, in its official way, as clear:

At a comparatively early age the miners almost invariably exhibit in their features and persons the unmistakeable signs of debilitated constitutions. Their faces are sallow, they have an anxious expression of countenance, and their bodies are thin. At the border of middle-age, or soon after their health begins to fail, the maturity and confirmed strength of that time of life seems to be denied to them. [13]

The Poor Law relieving officer for the mining parish of Gwennap reported in 1847 that of 240 families receiving payments, 200 were miners' families. Of the fathers, 15 had been killed outright in the mines; 40 blinded or otherwise maimed to the point of being unable to earn a living; 63 had died after lingering for various periods after serious injury, and 15 others who had between them 80 children, were too ill from progressing lung disease to continue working. A local doctor estimated that in that parish one miner in five would be killed at work. [14]

Mining Disasters and Disease

Large-scale disasters were less common than in coalmines. Metal mines did not suffer the dreaded 'firedamp' produced by the explosive gases naturally occurring in the coal itself. There were exceptions like the flooding of West Wheal Rose in 1846, which drowned more than 40 men, but the toll was generally the aggregation of accidents to individuals, or at times a few men working together. These resulted from premature explosions of gunpowder, plunging falls from ladders, or faulty platforms, rock falls, or from incidents involving the lifting or pumping machinery.[15] Deaths from accidents accounted for 25% of miners dying between the ages of 20 and 30 in the four central mining poor law districts between 1837 and 1847, but for only 6% of deaths of non-miners. [16]

Newspaper reports suggest a link between the accident rate in the mines and youthful inexperience or carelessness. For example in a single issue of the weekly *West Briton* in 1853 reports are included of three inquests on young miners. One was killed when he went to the underground smith's to have his pick sharpened, and a spark ignited two sticks of gunpowder he was keeping dry beneath his shirt. Another fell to his death when climbing over the shaft casing to save time, while the third was killed when he put his head over the shaft just as the engine bob was coming up. Some died very young. William Lawry was just thirteen when he was blasted to death in 1848. He had been working with an older brother preparing a hole for blasting and had a can of gunpowder under one arm and a lighted candle in the other; the lid of the can fell off when he bent to pick up a cartridge. Henry Turner was only seventeen when he fell to his death from a ladder when a spark fell on his hand from a lighted length of rope he was carrying.[17] It was not always a matter of youth. Familiarity can breed contempt. As a mine agent remarked in 1801:

> *Men always in the habit of working [with gunpowder] seem to lose in a great measure a sense of their danger - so that many lives are lost, more than, I believe would have been had due care always been taken.* [18]

Ingrained work practices contributed too. A mine captain told the Accident Enquiry of 1835 how difficult it had been to persuade miners to reduce the chance of striking a spark by substituting copper needles for the iron ones they customarily used to tamp in explosive charges. The copper needles were offered at the same price as the iron ones, but it was only when the mine ruled that for those who were involved in accidents using the latter, no payment from the accident fund would be made, that they were more widely adopted. [19]

Of the greater toll taken by lung disease, (phthisis), much could have been prevented. A major investigation in 1864 while accepting that conditions had improved with assisted ventilation over the last thirty years still found only 17 of 142 samples contained the normal proportion of oxygen, while 87 were condemned as extremely bad. A mine captain in 1835 had defined an ill-ventilated place as one in which a candle would not burn. In fact candles could burn where the air was already harmful. Nor was the test always applied. The miners were paid according to the value of the ore they raised, and the best ore did not necessarily coincide with the best air. Miners working on good ore at the level-end were not inclined to give it up:

> *I have worked on tribute where I had the candle perhaps eight feet behind me, as it would not burn where I was working, and we were doing very well, and you do not think about the injury then.* [20]

The annual average death rate of Cornish miners per thousand miners between 1849 and 1853 exceeded that of northern coalminers in every age cohort, but was most noticeable in the age ranges 45-55 and 55-65 years. In the former group the Cornish rate was 33.51 per thousand, while that of northern coalminers was 16.81. In the second group Cornish miners suffered a mortality rate of 63.17 per thousand against a northern one of 24.43. Not surprisingly the proportion of widows to total female population in Cornwall in 1851 was higher than in any other county. [21]

The Mining Community and Methodism

How far can these unhappy statistics be linked to forms of behaviour and attitudes among the mining community other than through reference to careless habits or some generalised concept of fatalism? Popular religion may be one link. Statistics of membership and attendance reveal Cornwall to have been the most Methodist county in England and within it membership and influence were strongly concentrated in the mining communities. A report written in 1842 concluded that in them adherents of Methodism were, 'so numerous, that its qualities become prominent features of the whole body, when it is compared with other communities'. [22] Wesleyan Methodism in West Cornwall did not follow the national tendency of becoming a respectable 'middle-class' Victorian church, losing proletarian adherents to more democratic and revivalist splinter sects. In the religious census of 1851, the parent Wesleyan body in Cornwall had an attendance index equal to 20.5% of the county's population out of a figure of 32% for all Methodist denominations. Analysis of baptism lists reveals no marked occupational pattern sharply distinguishing the parent body from those that historians generally have considered more proletarian off-shoots, such as the Primitive Methodists. While it is true that middle-class Cornish Methodists were more likely to be Wesleyan, it is just as true that Wesleyan miners massively outnumbered those from other divisions. The recurrent revivalism found among the Cornish miners was a feature, which happened across Methodism, not the function of any particular segment. [23]

Jabez Bunting, the conservative head of the Wesleyan movement in the early Victorian era, reputedly described the Cornish as 'the mob of Methodism'. It was noisy, enthusiastic revivalism not political radicalism, which he had in mind. The independence of the Methodist communities of West Cornwall had long been notorious. John Wesley noted in 1788 that some at Redruth were, 'were apt to despise and very willing to govern the preachers'. It was a continuing characteristic. A minister remarked in 1908:

In the town...the minister represents the Connexion and takes over the chapel as his own...In the village the chapel belongs to the people...and the people take over the minister as a newcomer attached to them. [24]

If Cornish Methodism was controlled by local laymen, preachers and class leaders, to an extent unparalleled elsewhere, this is partly explained by the county's geographical and cultural remoteness, and partly by the special affinity of many aspects of Methodism to a traditional culture. The relative poverty of the members had the effect of limiting the number of official itinerant ministers who could be supported. In 1830 for example, Redruth had a ratio of members per minister of 658 and St Agnes of 929 against a national circuit average of 333. Whatever the pretensions of the London-based governing Conference, we can, following W. R. Ward, [25] represent Cornish Methodism as indigenised to the extent that it was a true *Volkskirche*. [26] Revivals were intense periods of mass conversions when large numbers were added to the Methodist societies. Phenomenologically they were mass displays of the conversion characteristics of sighs, groans, weepings and fits and, hopefully, the eventual joy of salvation.

In Cornwall widespread revivals have been noted for 1764, 1782, 1798, 1814, 1824, 1831-1833, 1841-1842, 1848-1849 and a period between 1862 and 1865. Up to 1814, the so-called 'Great Revival', they were separated by roughly sixteen years, thereafter they became somewhat more frequent. The usual features of Cornish revivals were remarkably consistent over time. Scenes of mass hysteria were common. Two descriptions from the revival of 1831-1832 illustrate this:

The loud and piercing cries of the broken hearted penitents drowned the voice of prayer, and all that could be done at this stage of the meeting was to stand still and see the salvation of God. At length the penitents were conducted and upheld, each of them by two persons, into one part of the chapel. And now when their cries and groans were concentrated, one of the most affecting scenes

*appeared before the people. Their humble wailings pierced the skies. Sometimes
a burst of praise from the pardoned penitents mingled with the loud cries of the
broken hearted; and this greatly encouraged those that were in distress.*

*The chapel was crowded almost to suffocation. The steam ran down the
walls; the gallery stairs were flooded with it; and had not all the windows been
opened, every light would have gone out. The people were yet determined to
enter into this kingdom; yet everyone suppressed his feelings as long as he
could. When any have cried out, it has been the involuntary burst of a soul
overwhelmed with a sense of guilt and a sense of danger. The seats in many
places were literally covered with tears. This night the preacher concluded the
first service about eight o'clock; but scarcely any left the chapel. From that hour
until nearly eleven the people were crying out for mercy in every part of the
chapel, both in the gallery and below. Nearly fifty found peace that night; and
more than double that number returned home weary and heavy-laden. Many of
these continued in prayer all night; and not a few during the night found peace
in their own houses.* [27]

It was not only in the chapels that miners were overcome:

*...in the bowels of the earth...the spirit strives with them. They come up
from their work and explain to...the captain..."we cannot work, we must cry for
mercy!"* [28]

In the 'Great Revival' of 1814, many were said to have believed it was
preparatory to the end of the world: [29]

*It continued for a few weeks, when the great noise subsided, but the fire
still existed. The same extraordinary agitation extended to divers neighbouring
parishes...But the great current seemed to run westward. It was not so very
rapid or noisy about Truro and its vicinity, as it was in the parish of Gwennap.
At Illogan and Camborne it was more violent. But at Hayle Copper works and
the adjoining villages (taking in Wheal Alfred mine) the agitation was extremely
so at the latter mine are about 800 labourers at the surface (male and female)
chiefly young people, where the torrent bore down everything that stood in its
way. Were I to attempt to describe it I could not find words sufficient to draw
in colours strong enough. All labour for some days was suspended, and the un-*

derground labourers (equally as numerous as those at the surface) seemed to be struck with the same power - but being more advanced in years. I think they appeared to have a greater mastery over their passions than the others had. [30]

Explaining Cornish revivalism in terms of 'frontier' mentalities derived from the 'burned-over district' experiences of North America does not seem applicable. For although elsewhere new up-heaved industrial and mining communities characterised by social dislocation may well have been susceptible to emotional and enthusiastic forms of religion, the mining villages of West Cornwall were by the nineteenth century long-standing industrial communities, characterised by established traditions and with marked cultural and social cohesion.

So far as the coalminers of North Eastern England are concerned, Colls has suggested that some outbreaks of revivalism can be linked to the psychological impact of colliery disasters. [31] However, in Cornwall, major disasters were rare while revivals were regular. I have argued elsewhere that Cornish revivalism was an internally driven phenomenon deriving from social imperatives within the local religious community itself. [32] The evidence is overwhelming that youth was the most likely point in the life cycle for an individual to experience conversion. The periodicity of revivalism meant that a major one would occur during this period of everyone's life. A revival could therefore function as a means of joining young people to the church, and to a lesser extent of re-joining older ones. This does not necessarily imply that revivals were deliberately staged with this end in view, but that they would perform this role whether or not deliberately. Once a revival had broken out, the neighbouring societies were naturally put into a state of expectation that they would soon experience it for themselves, or else a state of anxiety that they would not. Either way the necessary emotional state was attained. A miner later recalled of the revival of 1856:

...hearing of revivals around us, and feeling the want of one for ourselves and the people, we agreed three weeks ago, to have special services. [33]

Revival effects were in part produced by a style of preaching which could amount to mental terrorism. 'Stouthearted' men from the mines come to the prayer meetings and with tears, 'streaming over their faces and in great agony they fall down on their knees and wrestle till they have found mercy'. [34]

Contemporaries made no bones over this. Methodism's official historian wrote that the awakened sinner 'trembling in agony' beneath God's frown, could hardly be expected to control his emotions. During the 1814 revival some were said to have been, 'convinced that they are sinful, perishing, helpless creatures', and 'driven to the throne of mercy by terror'.[35]

If widespread revivals were exciting and spaced events, some of their features were nevertheless a not uncommon feature of worship in Cornish mining communities. A minister recalled:

In their meetings shouting and ecstasies were rather the rule than the exception...they let themselves go; they shouted, they wept, they groaned, they not seldom laughed aloud with a laugh of intense excitement. [36]

Discussion

Religious excitement was endemic and periodically epidemic in the mining communities, but can it be linked to the dangers of the mine and the constant need for consolation? The special need for the miners to be prepared for death is a recurrent theme of many forms of contemporary Methodist literature. Acceptance of their lot brought the miners much approval, from those who did not have to share it:

Nothing can indeed be more admirable than the cheerful confidence with, which, in trust of a future life, the miner contemplates that termination, often an early one, of his labours.

There was a political dimension to this attitude:

No rankling ill-will to those whom Providence had placed in easier circumstances arose in their minds. No hatred to their employers, or rebellious thoughts against the government of the country, for a moment found a place in their hearts. They laboured, they sorrowed, they suffered, but they patiently endured.

Botallack mine at St. Just.

More pertinent to our theme, perhaps, is another article in the same evangelical periodical, which drew lessons from the death of 40 miners in the flooding of East Wheal Rose in 1846:

We have mentioned the terror and dismay of those who were not pre-pared to die. But there were other and very different scenes which we rejoice to chronicle...[among the victims] were not a few, belonging to various Christian denominations, who had realised the power of godliness, and some of whom had been useful labourers in the cause of Christ. Although taken by surprise, they were not unprepared. Two...met in one of the levels, and conversed a moment on their awful situation. As they bid each other farewell, one of them exclaimed: "I hope to meet you soon in heaven". "Glory be to God!" was the reply...One [of those who died] was heard to exclaim as the waters rose about him, and just before he was drowned, "All is well! All is well!" [37]

The article concluded that among the 1260 men employed at the mine were, 'many of a very wicked and abandoned character; and by many persons on the spot, the visitation is looked upon in the light of a judgement'. Certainly there is an appeal to the whole community and especially to all similarly employed: 'Be ye also ready; for in such an hour as ye think not, The Son of man cometh'.

Working miners and their families did not generally read such homilies in middle-class periodicals, they did, however, receive them in another form, in verse from one of the broadsheets which were commonly produced after mine accidents. These follow a typical narrative and didactic form. The scene is set and the incident and its aftermath are described in great detail. The victims are named, and the painful consequences for their families described:

> *Young Peter Eddy's head was gone,*
> *Upon the skip he lay*
> *The sollar struck him as they passed*
> *And took his head away.*

> *Yet further down were others found,*
> *Thomas and Richard Wall*
> *Father and son -an awful sight*
> *Lay in that dreadful hole.*

> *Thomas Nankervis lay to death*
> *An awful sight to view*
> *And Michael Nicolas by his side,*
> *Both bruised and mangled too.*
> *Each one was injur'd fearfully,*
> *Bruis'd broken, smashed and dead;*
> *A sickening spectacle! for some*
> *Had lost part of the head.*
> *Near twenty children now are left*
> *Without a father's care;*

Three widows for their husbands mourn
In sorrow and despair.

The widow's mother too is left,
Her only son is gone;
His earnings did her wants provide,
Nought else to live upon.

Typically the closing verses carry the message:

An accident, or sudden death,
Above or under ground
May call thee, reader, but how blest
If waiting thou art found.

Then mourn not, weeping friends, for those
That suddenly are gone;
In Heaven they from their labours rest
Before the great white throne.

Prepare! prepare! to follow them,
While yet it's called today!
Lest unprepar'd, grim Death should come
And summon you away.

This particular broadsheet followed a tragedy at Botallack Mine in 1863, but the form is general. Another describing an accident through a cave-in in 1859, concludes:

May miners one and all prepare
Lest by some accident,
They may be hurried from this life,
With no time to repent.

Another, after seven lives were lost in 1858, concludes:

Great God, in mercy stay thine hand,
May this a warning be,
May sinners need no other call,
To bring them unto thee.
May they but think of those who lie,
Deep in Porkellis mine,
So many fathoms down below
Cut off just in their prime. [38]

To call such narratives of suffering a 'celebration of death' is perhaps unhelpful, but the mining communities certainly celebrated funerals:

Then borne unto the silent tomb,
What thousands gather'd there,
To mingle with the relatives,
Sorrow's lingering tear.

That such numbers attended funerals is well supported from other evidence. A correspondent to the *Mining Journal* described one of a miner killed in a rock fall in the late 1850s. A 'black mass' of 'several thousands' of people processed several miles to the church. It was headed by the Methodist minister, who gave out the verses of a hymn, the singing of which was then accomplished by the chapel choirs of the district, about 80 persons in number, after them came the representatives of the mine, the captains and agents. Then came the coffin, borne in the traditional underarm way by relays of bearers. Behind the body followed the widow with, 'a long string of relations', and behind them thousands of miners. At the church, matters were handed over to the clergyman, while the service was conducted, the crowd waited bare-headed until the moment of burial, before dispersing, many it must be said, to the neighbouring pubs. Cornish mining funerals have been described many times by historians of their communities - abroad as well as at home. [39] As well as the more sombre heavy hymns of the Wesleys, there seem to have been some peculiarly local songs. The best known of which was known as the 'burying tune':

"Gunpowder, Cap'n! There ain't a man had more
experience widdun."

"This place edden fit for a man to go into, Cap'n. Come in
and have a look at un."

Cornish humour - as illustrated in the cartoons of Oswald Pryor.

"Sing from the chamber to the grave",
I hear the dying miner say;
"A sound of melody I crave
Upon my burial day".

"Sing sweetly whilst you travel on
And keep the funeral slow;
The angels sing where I am gone
And you should sing below".

Attending funerals was part of life in the mining villages. Unrelated people and those who were not especially close to the deceased presumably went for a variety of reasons, among which were socialising and entertainment. When the dead was the victim of a mine accident, then there was a special sense of the need for the community to show its respect and its sympathy.

There is a humorous saying in Cornwall: 'If you don't go to other folk's funerals, then they won't come to yours'. Perhaps this links to another way in which oral traditions accommodate death and injury. Not all mining families were Methodists, and not all Methodists were too 'serious' to joke. There is a parallel tradition of black humour; it travelled with emigrating miners. At copper mines in South Australia, worked by expatriate Cornish from c. 1840 to the 1920s. One, Oswald Pryor, became known locally as a cartoonist. Many of his drawings illustrate this traditional humour. [40]

Conclusion

Things did not improve for the smaller numbers still working in Cornish mines at the end of the nineteenth and the beginning of the twentieth century. The introduction of powered rock drills abridged labour, but only at the expense of more dust. Around 1900 rock-drillers worked only around eight years before contacting phthisis. As Gillian Burke has remarked, 'To work a rock drill in Cornwall was to face almost certain death'. [41]

Over its long history, Cornish mining certainly created wealth, but it as certainly destroyed health. Exploitation is never an easy concept to define. Although their earnings were subject to fluctuation, Cornish miners were at most times among the relatively well-paid sections of the British working class, but, the death and injury rates among men and the consequences these also had for women and children, including desperate poverty, surely amount to a form of exploitation. Methodism helped the community to come to terms with this situation, although alongside consolation, it should be noted that its diversion of suffering from a cause of resentment and protest into a vehicle for personal redemption contributed to the reputation of Cornish miners by the mid-nineteenth century for industrial and political passivity.

1. Occupational data is discussed in J. Rule, 'The Labouring Miner in Cornwall c. 1740-1870', Ph.D thesis, University of Warwick, 1971 pp. 8-16.
2. J. Rule, *The Labouring Classes in Early Industrial England c. 1750-1850*, 1986, p. 197.
3. See A. Hamilton Jenkin, *The Cornish Miner*, 1962, pp. 38-9 and G. Lewis, *The Stannaries: A Study of the Medieval Tin Miners of Cornwall and Devon*, (reprint 1965).
4. J. Rowe, *The Hard-Rock Men: Cornish Immigrants and the North American Mining Frontier*, Liverpool, 1874, and especially P. Payton, *The Cornish Overseas*, Fowey, 1999.
5. D. Levine and K. Wrightson, *The Making of an Industrial Society. Whickham 1500-1750*, Oxford, 1991, pp. 275-278.
6. For these and other examples see J. Watson, *Cornish Mining Notes*, 1861, reprinted Truro 1961).
7. Sir Charles Lemon, 'The Statistics of the Copper Mines of Cornwall', *Journal of the Statistical Society of London*, I, 1838, pp. 65-84; D. Hardestyj, *The Archaeology of Mines and Miners. A View from the Silver State, Society for Historical Archaeology*, USA, special publication No. 6, 1988) p. 102.
8. For a summary argument see below Chapter 10.
9. Jenkin MSS, William Jenkin, 24 Nov 1804, Courtney Library, Truro.
10. R. Burt, *Cornish Mining: Essays on the Organization of Cornish Mines and the Cornish Mining Economy*, Newton Abbot, 1969, p. 25.
11. Jenkin Mss, from William Jenkin, 25 February 1805.
12. W. Tyack, *The Miner of Perranzabuloe*, 1866, pp. 54-55; M. Edwards, *John Wesley and the Eighteenth Century*, 1955, p. 38.
13. *British Parliamentary Papers*, 1864, VIII, pp. 6, 18.
14. R. Burt, The British Lead Mining Industry, Redruth, 1984, p. 186.
15. *BPP*, 1864, p. 186.
16. ibid.

17. *West Briton*, 1 April 1853, 18 Feb 1848, 2 March 1855.

18. Jenkin MSS, from William Jenkin, 27 Feb 1801.

19. *BPP*, 1835, V, 'Accidents in Mines', pp. 13-14.

20. *BPP*, 1864, XXIVI, p. 35; *BPP*, 1835, p. 12.

21. R. Burt, *The British Lead Mining Industry*, 1984, p. 184.

22. *BPP*, 1842, XVI, 'Child Employment', p.760.

23. T. Shaw, *History of Cornish Methodism*, 1967, pp. 81-82.

24. ibid, p. 78; R. Currie, *Methodism Divided*, 1968, pp. 30-31.

25. W. Ward, 'The Religion of the People and the Problem of Control', in *Studies in Church History*, 8, 1972, pp. 237-257, pp. 505-506.

26. D. Luker, 'Revivalism in Theory and Practice. The Case of Cornish Methodism', in *Journal of Ecclesiastical History*, 37, (4), 1986, p. 605-610.

27. R. Treffry, *Memoir of Mr John Edwards Tresize*, 1837, pp. 84-5, 91.

28. Methodist Archives, Fletcher-Tooth Letters, 30 March 1831.

29. Anon, *An Account of the Remarkable Revival of the Work of God in Cornwall*, Dublin, 1814, pp. 56; G. Smith, *History of Methodism*, Vol. III, 1888, p. 551.

30. A. Hamilton Jenkin, *News from Cornwall*, Bath, 1951, p. 179.

31. R. Colls, *The Pitmen of the Northern Coalfield. Work, Culture and Protest 1790-1850*, Manchester, 1987, p. 163.

32. See above Chapter 6.

33. W. Tyack, *Miner of Perranzabuloe*, p. 81.

34. Fletcher-Tooth Letters, 30 March 1831.

35. G. Smith, *History of Methodism*, pp. 604, 607; Anon, *An Account of the Remarkable Revival*, p. 12.

36. J. Rigg, *Wesleyan Methodist Reminiscences Sixty Years Ago*, 1904, pp. 67-68.

37. *BPP*, 1842, p. 760; *Cornish Banner*, 1846, pp. 22, 55-56; Broadsheets are from the collections in the Cornwall County Record Office and the County Museum in Truro.

38. C. Noall and P. Payton, *Cornish Mine Disasters*, 1989, pp. 186-187.

39. R. Burt, *Cornwall and its Miners*, Truro, 1974, pp. 12-14

40. Oswald Pryor, *Cornish Pasty: A Selection of Cartoons*, Adelaide, 1976. The cartoons reproduced here appear by kind permission of his family.

41. G. Burke, 'Disease, Labour Migration and Technological Change: The Case of the Cornish Miners', in P. Weindling, (ed), *The Social History of Occupational Health*, 1985, pp. 78-88.

4 The Perfect Wage System?
Tributing in the Cornish Mines

No group of nineteenth century workers received more praise for their conduct, order and intelligence than did the Cornish miners. This regard was in marked contrast to the reputation of the eighteenth century tinners for riot and disorder. In 1850, the writer, Wilkie Collins, found them to be a cheerful, contented race with the views of the working men so remarkably moderate and sensible that he had not met elsewhere with so few grumblers. Samuel Laing thought the Cornish section of the 1842 report on child labour in the mines, by many degrees, 'the brightest picture we have ever met of the condition of any considerable proportion of the labouring class in England at the present day.' To a writer in the *Quarterly Review* in 1857, they were one the most orderly and civilised societies in the world. [1] To a surprising degree the credit for this was to be given to the methods of wage payment used in the mines, especially to the much publicised 'tribute' system. [2]

In their pioneering history of trade unionism, first published in 1894, the Webbs commented that trade unionism among the tin and copper miners was absolutely unknown. [3] While they offered no explanation for this, for an earlier generation of observers it had been explained by the apparent effect of the tribute system in reducing industrial conflict to insignificant dimensions. An early nineteenth century propagator of tributing, John Taylor, an experienced mine manager, who introduced the system into metal mines elsewhere in Britain, was quite certain of its benefits:

The rate of wages...regulates itself by the circumstances that ought to control it - the demand for labour. No one has heard of disagreements between the Cornish miners and their employers, no combinations or unions on the one side or the other exist; nor have turn-outs or strikes been contemplated or attempted. [4]

Taylor's accounts were a main source for others' recommendation of the system. Charles Babbage was impressed enough by them to urge a more general extension of the principles of the tribute system to manufacturing as well as to mining, while John Stuart Mill was similarly approving. He wrote of the Cornish miners in 1845, that for, intelligence, independence, and good conduct, as well as prosperous circumstances, no labouring population in the island is understood to be comparable. Later in his classic *The Principles of Political Economy*, he described the tribute system as being responsible for lifting the condition of the Cornish miner far above that of the generality of the labouring class. A writer in 1834 thought it the perfect system to reconcile the conflicting interests of masters and men, letting normally difficult relationships adjust themselves in such a manner as to make strikes unknown among the Cornish miners. Giving evidence to a key select committee on trade union activities in 1834, a Birmingham steam engine manufacturer, who had experience of the county, advised that the tribute system, 'so perfectly prevented strikes that its extension would remove the necessity for any laws against combinations'. [5]

What was distinctive about the Cornish system? It paid by results, but hourly wages were generally rare in mining. In many industries piecework was used as a productivity incentive, but where underground labour was involved, the difficulty of supervising small gangs scattered over extensive workings made payment by results necessary, not as much to raise productivity but simply to stop output from falling below the norm. [6] In the Cornish mines underground work was divided into two categories: tribute work and tutwork. The former was used to pay the miners who excavated the actual ore; the latter the men who did the preparatory work of sinking shafts and driving levels. Tributers were paid a proportion of the value of the ore, which they produced. tutworkers were paid by the measure of the ground they excavated. There was little interest in the latter, but the peculiarities of tributing were the subject of numerous writings. What distinguished the tribute system from other methods of payment by results was that remuneration was not related simply to quantity, but also directly to quality: the wage eventually received by the miner was a proportion of the price the ore raised by him realized when sold by the mine. Observers were excited by what they persisted in seeing as a joint venture in speculation by capital and labour. John Stuart Mill headed his section on the Cornish mines: 'Examples of the Association of Labourers with Capitalists'. [7]

Tributers undertook to work measured portions of the mine, known as 'pitches', for so much in the pound of the price that the ore they raised fetched when sold. Rates varied from a shilling or less to as much as fifteen shillings in the pound, depending on the estimated prospects of the pitch in terms of both quantity and quality of ore. If it promised to produce a large amount of high quality ore, then the tributers would undertake it for a lower rate than if it did not promise to be very productive. The wage that the tributer received depended, therefore, not only on the amount and quality of ore that he produced, but also on the current market price for tin or copper.

A further distinctive feature of the tribute system was the manner in which agreements were made with the miners. Pitches were contracted for periods of one month or two months. They were put up to the men at a form of auction known as the survey or setting. Prior to the auction, the pitches were inspected by the mine captains (managers) who were to put up the pitches, and by the men. Each side formed its own estimate of the value of various pitches, and the rates at which it would be possible to make good wages from working them. The captain put up the pitches in turn, describing their location and the number of men required. The miners, in groups known as pares, bid against each other, the group offering to work it for the lowest rate securing the pitch on offer; the contract becoming then known as the 'bargain'. It has been suggested by a modern historian that, by forcing the miner to compete with his fellows at periodic settings of work for pitches offered to the lowest bidder, the system helped frustrate the growth of trade unionism in the mines and deprived the miner of the combined voice with which he could have demanded change. [8] L. L. Price, in a lengthy description first published in 1888, referred to the divergent interests of the men on setting day; and it is true that a situation in which labourers bid against each other to lower the price of their own labour was hardly a propitious one for the development of collective action. The miners' preference for the system and their willingness to sacrifice a certain steady income, for the freedom and chance of great profit, can be difficult to understand. An unwise attachment it may have been, but that does not mean that it was made unwillingly. [9] A writer in 1849, who wondered that such a speculative system should be preferred at all by the miners, found that tributers would be on the verge of starvation before they would undertake tutwork, driving levels and sinking shafts in the dead ground- he was a tributer and tributers look with as great a contempt upon the tutman as upon the surface labourers. [10]

Status considerations certainly played a part. Tributers felt themselves to be the proper miners. But the fundamental attraction was the possibility of great gain. The chance was offered of a sudden and substantial windfall. Although accurate estimation of the potential of a pitch was brought to a fine art by the captains and by the tributers, there were always times, given the geological uncertainties of hard-rock mining, when the mineral content might prove to be in excess of expectations. The following case, reported in 1804, will serve as an example:

...within the last six or seven days two poor men [were] working in a part of the mine where the lode was very hard and poor, they sudainly [sic] cut into a bunch of rich copper or, very soft and consequently easy to break. The poor fellows having by their contract 12s. out of the pound for their labour of all the ores they can break...Their time expires at the end of the month, and if the lode continues so good as it is now in sight, I expect, they will get a hundred pounds each for themselves for two weeks' labour, and that same piece of ground will be taken next month for less than one shilling in the pound. [11]

The possibility of earnings of this size goes a long way toward explaining the working miners' attachment to a system that often denied them a worthwhile wage, and sometimes allowed them less than a living one. The mineral content of the pitch could as well deteriorate as improve; false promise binding a man to a pitch which offered him little chance of good earnings The occasional worker's bonanza did not affect the shareholders adversely, for, as John Taylor has pointed out, they were likely to be rare enough. When they did occur they would animate all the others who increase their exertion in hopes of some similar discovery; they encourage competition, and frequently bring neglected parts of the mine into effective and profitable working. The discovery of a good lode could indeed have just this effect of intensifying competition and so lowering wages. [12] In 1805, following a good discovery, a pitch was taken as 5d. in the pound. The captain's estimate had been a shilling but, 'there was no stopping them in the survey so eager were they to have that pitch'. [13]

Professor Roger Burt has suggested that few miners could afford such speculation, and that most were the losers by it. [14] This was certainly the opinion of James Sims, whose account of the system was written in 1849:

It may be urged that the present system gives every man a chance of having work; - granted; but it does not give to everyone the means of purchasing the necessaries of life. [15]

The local poet John Harris, himself for many years a tributer, summed up the less attractive side of the system in his poem 'The Unsuccessful Miner':

A month had nearly ended,
And he severe had wrought
Day after day in darkness,
And it was all for nought.
The mineral vein had faded
And now all hope was fled
Tomorrow should be pay day
His children have no bread. [16]

The average earnings of tributers were higher than those of tutwork-ers (in 1843, £3 11s. 7d. compared with £3 1s. 11d.), but the earnings of the latter were much more consistent, although they depended to a certain extent on the hardness of the ground. [17] A witness in 1864 thought that 'nine times out often' their wages would be between £3 and £3 3s. per month. [18]

A monthly advance known as 'subsist' was made to the tributers on the security of their expected wages, in order that they might survive in the long intervals between the payments of their irregular earnings.[19] It has been suggested that this practice gave the mine a financial hold over the men and lessened their ability to change their place of employ-ment. In fact the evidence suggests that, although there was considerable movement between mines at some times and in some districts, generally speaking there were advantages to be gained from becoming established at a mine. Established tributers were usually given preferential treatment by the captains, a tendency which led to the practice known as 'taking farthing pitches', that is working at a nominal tribute rate in order to get a footing in a mine with the option of renewing the pitch bargain on more favourable terms at the next setting. [20]

L. L. Price, in 1888, wrote of a district and industry, which seems to have escaped the disturbing influences of the industrial revolution. [21] It was not, however, the divergent interests of the miners at the setting which seemed to him the most important contribution of the tribute system to promoting this state of affairs. He asked why there were no strikes, and why the relations between the miners and the mine owners seemed to adjust themselves so successfully. The real reason he suggest-ed was that the workman is in a sense his own employer. He stressed the point that the comparative absence of strife is due, not to the elimination of the capitalist, but to the practical disappearance of the employer. [22] Men who saw themselves as independent contractors, bargaining with the shareholders through the medium of captains (who were sometimes alternatively called the 'agents') might well have been slow to exhibit the collective solidarity of a wage earning working class. Since earnings were determined by individual bargaining and estimating skill, and by the fluctuating price of tin or copper, there was no need for any direct confrontation with the labourers in enforcing wage reductions in times of recession. Competition among the men would naturally achieve this end.

The practical disappearance of the employer was not just the result of the adoption of the tribute system; it derived as well from the financial organization of the industry, which was based on the so-called cost-book system. To spread risk, mining enterprises were undertaken not by single owner-entrepreneurs but by a group of adventurers, who provided the working capital when called upon in proportion to their share holding. Day-to-day management was in the hands of the captains, men promoted from the ranks of the skilled miners. So far as Cornish mining was concerned, the representative capitalist was a financial investor, not a working entrepreneur. This was emphasised in a major Parliamentary report of 1842:

The mine adventurers, the real employers, are not brought into contact in anyway as masters with the working miners; so that the agents, men taken for the most part from their own ranks, are the only superiors with whom they have to do. [23]

The absence of a boss class in direct daily contact with the mineworkers might well be expected to have slowed the development of an articulate class-consciousness. An experienced mine inspector, who remarked in 1855 that one excellence of the tribute system was that it prevented strikes sensed that it did not provide the complete answer:

...it may be questioned whether this is not rather due to other causes than the excellence of the system of tribute and tutwork...the system of the colliers in the north also shows excellence of plan and method, but still the colliers are as often ready to strike as if they were most unfairly dealt with. [24]

Trade unionism should not perhaps be expected to have been weak almost to the point of non-existence in a particular industry because of a single feature of its organization. Its weakness was more likely to have been the product of a variety of factors, which together formed an environment unpropitious for its early flourishing. Charles Barham thought that the tributer's hope of material and social betterment was an important factor: the hope that through fortunate contracting he might find himself, on a parity as to station, with the wealthier individuals near him, who have for the most part, at no remote period, occupied the lowest steps of the ladder on which he himself stands. [25] H. S. Tremenheere agreed:

They see around them numerous examples of individuals from their own ranks in every stage of progress towards independence and well-being; many possessing cottages and land, many placed in honourable and responsible situations in the mines, many who have risen to still higher points of social elevation. [26]

In the absence of a class comparable to the mill owner of the Northern industrial revolution, power and influence in the mining districts was wielded not so much by the adventurers, as by the lords, the landowners under whose lands the mineral lodes ran. Men like Sir Francis Basset, Sir John St Aubyn and Sir Charles Lemon were tied to the working miners by all the strings of patronage and deference. This was a relationship more subtle and complex than the cash nexus, in which charity and ceremony were important components.

Being paid under the tribute system, and not seeing a class of employers visibly opposed to their interests, the miners continued to see the profiteering middleman or grain-hoarding farmer as the enemy in hard times. They continued to express their discontent in the form of food rioting down to 1847. In addition in the Cornish mines, sickness and accident relief were paid from a mine club which was controlled solely by the mine, but to which miner's contributions were compulsory. The miners lacked the experience of the independent mutual funds, which played a clear role in the development of artisan trade unions. A letter from some miners in 1853 claimed that in many instances the dependence inherent in the prevailing system made it worse than parochial aid. [27]

A factor more difficult to evaluate is the influence of Wesleyan Methodism perhaps the strongest single cultural influence in the county. In

Cornwall, the Methodists provided positive opposition to political and industrial radicalism openly opposing it; and competitive opposition by monopolizing local working class talents and energies. A writer in 1865 remarked:

> *We have few turbulent demagogues in Cornwall. A miner who has any rhetorical powers and strong lungs prefers the pulpit to the platform.* [28]

Another writing in 1857 found it surprising that such a hot-blooded people should be comparatively indifferent to political agitation:

> *Leagues and unions, and Chartist gatherings have had small attraction for them, nor has any merely political cause found numerous and sanguine adherents in Cornwall.* [29]

Much of the explanation, the writer thought, lay in the county's geographical position, which almost cut it off from 'the contagion of foreign zeal'. This isolation helps to explain the ignorance of the miners' struggle in the North of England, which both the Chartist missionaries in 1839 and the delegates of the Miners Association in 1844 found in Cornwall. It also helps to explain why the Cornish miners could be used as 'blacklegs' in several coalfield disputes. The tribute system may have been of considerable importance in explaining the weakness of Cornish trade unionism but, with so many other factors playing a part, it can hardly be said that any significant lessening of the frequency of industrial conflict would have necessarily followed its introduction into other regions.

Contemporary writers and subsequent historians have tended to overstress the antiquity of the tribute system, seeing it as an inheritance from the 'free mining' of the middle ages. [30] To a degree it was, importantly so in the sense of the 'independence' that the tributer was widely acknowledged to have, but there is a danger of overlooking the way in which from the mid-eighteenth century the tribute system further developed to meet the needs of an increasingly capitalised and yet highly speculative enterprise. The continued use of 'tinner' as synonymous with 'miner' through the eighteenth century, and into the nineteenth, obscured the fact that the period of the industrial revolution was associated with a largely new product - copper. In 1787 an enumeration of copper mines gave 7196 adult male and 2684 women and child employees. Tin mining at that time probably employed around 2000. By 1851, despite considerable expansion and recovery in tin mining, within a total labour force, male and female, child and adult, of 36,284, adult male copper miners at 15,608 still outnumbered tin miners by 3000. [31] The copper boom brought new capital into mining and, though only to an extent, operated without some of the traditional constraints of the older industry. It was not brought within the jurisdiction of the Stannary Courts, which had administered tin mining since the middle ages, until 1836.

Those writers like Babbage and Mill who, as we have seen, praised the tribute system for producing exceptionally good industrial relations had never observed the system closely at first hand. Their accounts were based on a number of well-known descriptions. In fact there was not a complete absence of combination and conflict and in the industry; and in its day-to-day operation, the system, was far from perfect from the point of view of labour management. [32] R. M. Ballantyne, who did closely observe the industry before writing his novel *Deep Down* in 1869, provided a very full account of a setting at Botallack mine:

The men assembled in a cluster round the window…while Mr Cornish read of as follows:

"John Thomas's pitch at back of the hundred and five. By two men. To extend from the end of the tram hole four fathom west and from back of level five fathom above.

John Thomas… at once offered 'ten shillings' but the captain also knew the ground and the labour that would be required and his estimate was eight shillings a fact which was announced by Mr. Cornish simply uttering the words: 'At eight shillings'.

'Put her down, s' pose', said John Thomas after a moment's consideration… The pitch was therefore set to John Thomas.

'Jim Hockings pitch at back of the hundred and ten'.

'Won't have nothing to do with her', said Jim Hocking resolving to try his chance in a more promising part of the mine.

'Will anyone offer for this pitch?' inquired Mr Cornish.

Eight and six shillings were immediately named by men who thought the pitch looked more promising than Jim did.

'Anyone offer more for this pitch?' asked the manager taking up a pebble and casting it into the air. While that pebble was in flight, anyone might offer for the pitch, but the instant it touched the ground the bargain was held to be concluded". [33]

It will be noticed that John Thomas and Jim Hocking were given the opportunity to agree terms for continuing at their pitches for a further period and that when the former accepted the captain's estimate matters were concluded. When the latter declined, then the pitch was auctioned. In theory in the former case a lower bid could have been offered and accepted. None was offered, nor did the management expect one to be. At most times there was a strong convention not to bid against the old pare. At times when work was scarce, or in new areas, it broke down. The miners of the St Just region had a meeting in 1853 respecting some bad customs among themselves to re-establish the convention after a period of disregard. The captain at Boswidden Mine resolved to crush this combination, and his action in setting reserve prices precipitated one of the very few strikes in Cornish mining history. [34]

In general so confident were tributers of being allowed first refusal on reasonable terms that at times, as we have noted above, it was known for pitches to be worked for nothing:

To my surprise two of them were taken for nothing. The reason given was the expectation of being employed the following months and the hope of a better price next survey day. [35]

Through the late eighteenth century and the nineteenth, several of the practices described below, viewed as fraud or ore stealing by the management and by the courts depended upon the assumption that tribute bargains were commonly renewable. Pryce in 1778 complained of the bribing of captains with drink or presents by 'takers upon tribute' whom they then allowed, 'to mix and manage the ores in such manner as will most conduce to their own advantage'. [36] Twenty years later a mine steward wrote of one mine: 'there was never a mine worse managed, nor was the process of Kitting ever carried to such a height.' [37]

'Kitting' was the local name for fraudulent mixing of ores and complaints about it were made throughout the period. In 1832 a clause was inserted into an Act (2 & 3 Victoria, cap. 58), for the prosecution and punishment of frauds in mines by idle and dishonest workmen removing or concealing ore for the purpose of obtaining more wages than are 'of right due to them'. The clause, specific to Cornwall, defined this fraud as a felony and prescribed punishment as for simple larceny. Ore concealing was the simplest form, and all the ethnographic evidence points to it as widespread and considered fair game if it could be got away with. If a tributer working at a low rate broke towards the end of a 'bargain' into good ore, he would have only a very limited time in which to raise it before his rate would be considerably reduced at the next setting. Accordingly, such ore was sometimes concealed or disguised in the hope that the captain's impression of the pitch's potential would not be revised and the pitch set again at a high rate. The concealed ore could then be presented along with the ore raised during the second period.

Another form rested upon cooperation between two pares working on different tribute rates. They would mix their ores underground. If one had agreed thirteen shillings and the other five shillings, ores from the second would be presented by the former taker as having been raised from his pitch. Taking place underground, such practices were difficult to guard against. The Act of 1839 does not seem to have brought any increase in cases before the courts. When detected, 'kitting' miners were usually dealt with by dismissal and the attachment of a stigma, which made it difficult for them to find work in other mines in the district. As a mine steward wrote in 1809:

Altho' we might fail in bringing these men to a legal conviction, yet I hope the Agents in every copper mine in the County will faithfully unite in repelling those men from obtaining employment under them either as tributers or otherwise. [38]

Four tributers at East Pool were sentenced to six months at Quarter Sessions in 1835, having been convicted 'of a conspiracy to defraud the Adventurers of certain sums of money but details are not reported'. In a case before the Stannaries Court in 1847 a tribute pare, father and son, sued Wheal Bud nick for recovery of wages of £11 7s. 3d. due as tribute for working in a pitch set at ten shillings in the pound. It was claimed they had forfeited their earnings by breach of an article of the mine regulations directed against fraudulent and irregular working. The captain in this case did not dispute the quality but the quantity of ore presented by the tributers. He had observed them to work only irregularly; too irregularly to have raised that amount in the time. He claimed they had presented ore raised by another tributer. Three miners were called as witnesses and, despite their evidence that the pare had done 'a pretty good month's work for two men', that they had been seen regularly at work and that they had worked in 'a miner like manner', the jury did not find the case proved. At no point was it suggested that the men stole the ore. [39]

But this was the accusation made by a captain against two poor men in 1836. They were suing the mine for recovery of £39 2s. due to them as tribute on copper ore which had been set at eleven shillings in the pound. This case has much interest. The tributers had been working with only modest expectations when they broke into a good bunch. The captain went down to their pitch and accused them of taking ore from beyond its denned limits. He turned them forcibly off the mine and refused them pay, alleging that they had forfeited their ore to the use of the adventurers. The tributers established their case by producing witnesses to their having actually broken the ore within their pitch; and also by satisfying the court that in the course of mining, lodes are found varying in colour, size and quality. What won their case was their lawyer's convincing of the jury that the captain, having set a pitch at a rate which made it much more profitable to the men than had been anticipated, sought to cover himself from employer dissatisfaction by turning off the men with a false accusation. In reporting the case, the local newspaper sympathized with the tributers, but changed its position somewhat the following week, claiming to have been made aware of evidence in support of the captain which would have caused the jury to find otherwise had it not been concealed from motives of compassion. [40]

Cases of ore stealing only sometimes involved taking ore from beyond the bounds of a pitch, as in 1842 when two tributers were discovered by the captain, 'concealing themselves in a part of the mine which was not set to anyone'. At other times it meant stealing from a pitch set to another tributer. In such a case the offending tributer could be charged with stealing ore, 'the property of the adventurers and the men working at tribute'. A case from 1847 can serve as an example. Two tributers were charged with stealing ore from a fellow tributer at United Hills Mine. The accused had taken a pitch at twelve shillings, the victim at eleven shillings, but had broken into better ore and was expected to take a next setting at eight or nine shillings. Experienced miners from United Hills testified that among the ore presented by the accused was some that was clearly from the good bunch into which the other tributer had broken. They were found guilty and sentenced to six months. It should be noticed that in this, as in other cases where the charge was stealing from a fellow miner as well as from the adventurers, there seems to have been no reluctance to testify. [41]

Shortly before its sale to the smelters, raised ore was piled on the surface, a separate pile for each pitch. Sometimes when a really good lode had been discovered, the owners would not let it tribute but agree its working for direct wages by miners who were then described as working on 'owners' account'. Accordingly, as well as piles raised by the tribute 'pares', there could be others which had been raised by directly waged miners. There was an obvious temptation for tributers to surreptitiously add good ore from one of these piles to their own: 'Oh that we should have been so foolish!' lamented one of two tributers convicted of this offence in 1835. They had been seen by several witnesses 'feloniously mixing certain ores… the property of the Adventurers with a view to fraud'. But it was piles belonging to other tributers which had been depleted by a tributer in 1833. The footprints left by him were easily traced, thanks to his having a wooden leg! His victim had recognized ore from his pitch in the pile of the one-legged miner and knew, 'the prisoners had worked where no such ore could have been raised'. He had summoned the Captain who confirmed that the ore in question was peculiar to one of the mine's shafts. If further evidence was needed, it came from a female surface worker employed sorting and breaking ores. She testified that the accused and his accomplice had presented her with some of the richer ore. Faced with such overwhelming evidence, the two men confessed and revealed where more caches of ore had been concealed. Being the only one-legged tributer at the mine, was probably conclusive enough, but the case again suggests that when the ore of fellow miners was stolen, witnesses were ready enough to appear. [42]

So far as punishment was concerned ore stealing was dealt with differently from other forms of stealing from mines. It usually involved dismissal from employment and sentences of three to six months, some times with a small fine. Yet when a miner stole a piece of iron valued at 6d, from Dolcoath Mine in 1778, he was sentenced:

> To be confined to hard labour in the Bride well for a month and that he be then conveyed to Dolcoath mine and be there stripped naked from the middle upwards and whipped till his body be bloody. [43]

Sentences including the element of public floggings continued to be passed on those who stole property other than ore through the early nineteenth century. For example on two men for stealing a brass sieve in 1831 and two in 1835 for the theft of eleven candles. On the other hand, no increase in severity of the sentencing for ore stealing seems to have followed the passing of the specific Act in 1839, inviting them to be punished in the same manner as in the case of Simple Larceny. Cases in the 1840s do not suggest any change in practice, but presumably the clause was intended to resolve some confusion. Two tributers in 1835 who took ore from piles and added it to their own are reported as charged with feloniously mixing certain ores, 'the property of the Adventurers' with a view to fraud presenting it as their own for wages to which they were not entitled. Yet two years before two others had been charged with stealing copper ore, the property of the adventurers and the men working at tribute. They had done exactly the same thing. Both cases were heard at the Assize. [44]

Of more than a dozen descriptions of the tribute system published nationally in the early nineteenth century, while all commended it as offering freedom from industrial conflict and from trade unionism, only one chose to mention some of the imperfect practices indulged in by some of these model workers. Yet, as we have seen, frauds and certain forms of stealing were inherent in the system. The *Quarterly Review* in 1827 did describe practices, [45] which have otherwise to be gleaned from few and scattered local sources. How big was the iceberg of which a handful of court cases a year represented the tip? It is impossible to know. What is certain is that the derivative and bare accounts presented by nineteenth century writers, even by those of the distinction of Mill or Babbage were idealized economic models. They were not humanized descriptions of the social dimensions of a wage system whose peculiarities were of great importance in the lives of the thousands who made up a distinctive occupational community.

1. W. Collins, *Rambles beyond Railway*, 1852, p. 78; R. Laing, *National Distress: its Causes and Remedies*, 1844, p. 41; *Quarterly Review*, 102, 1857, pp. 331-332.
2. For a detailed description of the systems of wage payment in the Cornish mines see my unpublished thesis, 'The Labouring Miner in Cornwall 1740-1870', University of Warwick, 1971, pp. 34-72.
3. S. and B. Webb, *History of Trade Unionism*, London, 1911, p. 421.
4. Taylor's article is among several reprinted in R. Burt, (ed.), *Cornish Mining: Essays on the Organization of the Cornish Mines and the Mining Economy*, Newton Abbott, 1969, pp. 38-39. The original publication was in *Transactions of the Geological Society*, 12, 1814, pp. 309-327.
5. ibid, p. 48; J. Mill, *Principles of Political Economy*, (1845 edition), W. Ashley (ed.), 1917, p. 765; *The Claims of Labour*, 1845, in Toronto edition of *Collected Works*, 1967, p. 383; *Penny Magazine*, 27, December, 1834, p. 500; *British Parliamentary Publications*, Select Committee, House of Commons, 1824, V, 51, 'Artisans and Machinery', pp. 323-324.
6. E. Hobsbawm, 'Customs, Wages and Workload in Nineteenth Century Industry',

in *Labouring Men*, London, 1965, p. 353.

7. J. Mill, *Principles of Political Economy*, p. 765.

8. R. Burt, *Cornish Mining*, p. 10.

9. L. Price, "West Barbary" or Notes on the System of Work and Wages in the Cornish Mines', 1891, reprinted in *Cornish Mining*, p. 115. First printed in *Journal of the Statistical Society*, 50, 1888, pp. 494-566.

10. *Morning Chronicle*, 24 November 1849.

11. Jenkin Papers, W. Jenkin to R. Hunt, 24 November 1804, Courtney Library, Truro.

12. R. Burt, *Cornish Mining*, p. 25.

13. W. Jenkin to Dr Colewell, 25 February 1805.

14. R. Burt, *Cornish Mining*, p. 10.

15. J. Sims, 'On the Economy of Mining in Cornwall', in *The Mining Almanac for 1849*, reprinted in R. Burt, Cornish Mining, p. 10.

16. J. Harris, *Wayside Picture, Hymns and Poems*, 1874, p. 158.

17. J. Watson, *A Compendium of British Mining*, 1843, p. 6; *Morning Chronicle*, 24 November 1849.

18. *BPP*, 1864, XXIV, Part 1, Report of the Mine Commissioners; Minutes of Evidence, p. 564.

19. R. Burt, *Cornish Mining*, p. 11.

20. *Morning Chronicle*, 24 November 1849.

21. R. Burt, *Cornish Mining*, p. 122.

22. ibid, pp. 155-157.

23. *BPP*, Select Committee, House of Commons, 1842, XVI, The Employment of Children in Mines, p. 759.

24. J. Liefchild, *Cornwall, Its Mines and Miners*, 1855, pp. 147, 155.

25. *BPP*, 1842, XVI, p. 759.

26. *BPP*, 1841, XX, Report of the Committee of Council on Education, p. 94.

27. *West Briton*, 26 August 1853.

28. *Western Morning News*, 10 January 1865.

29. *Quarterly Review*, 1857, p. 312.

30. See for example E. Thompson, ' The Traditions of the Free Miner Coloured Responses into the Nineteenth Century', in the author's seminal work *The Making of the English Working Class*, 1968, p. 68.

31. Boulton and Watt Papers, Box 32, Birmingham City Library, 1851 figures from General Census.

32. I am aware of seven strikes between 1793 and 1859, but none were long-lasting and they were over local grievances at individual mines. The first long-running strike with an underlying union organization, the Miners' Mutual Benefit Association, took place in the newly developing mining districts of East Cornwall and West Devon in 1866. See *Cornwall Gazette*, 1, 8 and 29 March 1866.

33. R. Ballantyne, *Deep Down: A Tale of the Cornish Mines*, 1869, pp. 267, 271-271.

34. *BPP*, 1842, XVI, Report of the Committee on Child Employment; Minutes, p. 833. However, the witnesses remarked that convention was better kept in some districts than others; *West Briton*, 25 March, 15 April, 22 April 1853.

35. Jenkin Papers. 5 August 1816.
36. W. Pryce, *Mineralogia Cornubiensis*, 1778, pp. 175-177.
37. Jenkin Papers, 15 February 1791.
38. ibid, 16 September 1809.
39. *Cornwall Gazette*, 4 July 1835, 9 April 1847.
40. ibid, 8, 15 April 1836.
41. ibid, 18 March 1842, 9 April 1847.
42. ibid, 28 March 1835, 30 March 1833.
43. Quarter Sessions Minutes, CRO, 17 July 1788.
44. *Cornwall Gazette*, 8 January 1831, 30 March 1833, 28 March, 10 April 1835; *West Briton*, 11 April 1835.
45. *Quarterly Review*, 72, 1827, pp. 85-86.

A poem by John Harris the Cornish poet contains this verse:

> *A month was nearly ended,*
> *And he severe had wrought*
> *Day after day in darkness,*
> *And it was all for nought*
> *The mineral vein had faded*
> *And now all hope was fled,*
> *Tomorrow should be pay day*
> *His children have no bread.* [1]

Harris had worked many years as a miner and well knew the vicissitudes of the tribute system of wage payment used in the Cornish mines. Indeed the verse could be considered autobiographical. Harris had married in 1845 and recalled almost a year of privation as a tributer before a remarkable upturn in his fortune:

> *For the first ten months of my married life, fortune was against me so that my earnings amounted to no more than ten pence a day. Then the tide turned, providence blessed my labours, and I soon became the owner of two hundred pounds.* [2]

Harris had managed to live on around five shillings a week; managed because his poor run had happened before children enlarged the household. In 1840 the local newspaper carried a report from a mining district that a farmer had caught a tributer stealing swill from his pig trough to feed his family. Taking pity he loaned the miner money, which the man was able to repay with ease on the next pay day. The episode is instructive. A visitor to the district in 1788, by which time the system was already general, described it as, 'the merest lottery in the world'. Miners could earn as much as £20 a month, a week or even a day or as little as 20 farthings:

> *Thus we find the generality of these inhabitants wafted from time to time on the variable waves of prosperity and adversity.* [3]

Under the tribute system small groups of men undertook to

work a measured section of the mine known as a 'pitch'. They contracted for a rate in £1 of the value of the ore raised from it. According to the expectation from it, a pitch might be taken for as little as 5p or as much as 75p. It needed experienced judgement. If a tributer estimated more accurately than the mine agent, he might be getting a high tribute rate for larger quantities of better quality ore than the pitch had been judged by the agent to contain. If, on the other hand, he had overestimated the potential and accepted a low rate in £1, then he could hardly make wages. In extreme cases mineral lodes could disappear, due to rock faulting and a tributer find himself working for a month or even two months for nothing. Periodically after inspection by the miners and the mine management pitches were put up at a 'setting'; a form of dutch auction at which the tributers offering to work for the lowest rate secured the 'bargain'. A report in 1849 accepted the view that although miners earned typically 14s or 15s a week, they could not be considered as 'so well off as an agricultural labourer with constant work at 10 shillings'. [4]

That was in fact a pessimistic view. For the middle decades of the nineteenth century when the Cornish industry was at its peak, £3 a month was constantly cited as an average wage for a steady competent tributer. That is that taking the highs with the lows a miner earned perhaps 50% more than an agricultural labourer, and further had perhaps once or twice in an earning lifetime the good fortune to enjoy a considerable windfall. Harris's £200 in a matter of weeks was not a far-fetched hope, for as William Pryce the writer in 1778 of the first treatise on the industry put it: 'A tinner is never broke until his neck is broke'. [5]

The survival strategies of Cornish mining families were not, then, those driven by a need to manage in conditions of extreme and persistent poverty, nor of periods of deprivation resulting from seasonal employment patterns. This essay is not concerned either with periods of exceptional general distress, such as the grain crises of 1795-1796 and 1800-1801, or with the widespread distress associated with the potato famine of the late 1840s. [6] Nor is it concerned with the decline of Cornish mining after the 1860s. Its purpose is to examine the 'mixed economy of welfare' among families dependent on a particular industry that is with endemic situations, which could happen in any mining household in normal times, and with the means and methods through which available resources could be managed to best effect. [7]

In general terms some groups in the nineteenth century working class fared better, but many fared worse, however the management of the fluctuations of the tribute system needed from time to time a fall back to other sources of household income and onto considerable skills of domestic management. As well as this, for a miner to obtain the best outcome from the tribute system he needed to work that system in a particular way in which a satisfactory relationship with the mine management was paramount. Consider this evidence from a mine captain (manager) in 1864:

We have a first rate old man at North Roskear, a first rate old man, who has been working here for thirty years; the last two years he has always been speculating, and has done badly. I said to him the other day, "You are doing badly". "Yes" said he, "I never had such a long run before, but I will make it up again soon". I said, "You have not done badly on the whole, you have been here from a boy". He is worth £200 or £300 probably; he has one or two cottages, and keeps a cow and so on; we never let him go on less than £2 5s a month, though for a long time he has not earned any money. [8]

Several things stand out here (apart from the fact that someone who was probably in his later forties is described without any sense of misuse as an old man!) First, the importance of being a long serving and well regarded workman. Secondly, the fact that the mine was paying the man close to the average wage even though he was raising little copper ore. Thirdly, the probability of several 'starts' (windfalls) which had allowed the accumulation of savings and the acquisition of a cottage. Tributers who were established and trusted to work to good effect in winning copper or tin ores were usually paid an advance for subsistence, a payment known as 'subsist'. At the end of the pay period, usually a month in the mid-nineteenth century, any balancing amount was paid over, while if total earnings did not cover subsist and other deductions, then the debt was carried forward. Clearly this practice, for a considerable section of the workforce, went a long way towards ironing out the fluctuations in the system. It was however, not a right, but a favour and there was clearly a limit to the debt a mine would allow to build, and it could be used with discrimination as on one occasion in 1838 when it was refused to miners known to spend time in alehouses.[9]

It was important to get established in a well-run and generally prosperous mine:

It is seldom there is any indiscriminate bidding, or any great scamble at the settings. Men who have gained a footing in the mine have generally the preference over strangers.

The practice of sons first going underground with their fathers was a main route to 'natural' or hereditary establishment as it was in many other occupations, but there also developed a strategy by the 1840s of securing a footing known as taking 'farthing pitches'. This was the taking of tribute bargains at almost nominal rates with no expectation of making sound wages, and it depended on the convention that having proved themselves effective miners the pare would be offered the pitch again the following month, this time at a paying rate.[10] For those who were unable or unwilling to carry on after a poor run of tributing, there was an alternative employment strategy. They could seek work in the mine on 'tutwork'. Tutworkers worked in the 'dead ground', that is did not excavate the ore, but prepared the access by sinking shafts or driving levels.

They 'bargained' according to the hardness of the rock and on the time it took to drive a measured distance at a rate per fathom. There was fluctuations but wages were much more steady, so that in the mid-nineteenth century few mines found it necessary to pay subsist to tutworkers. The average earnings of tutworkers were lower, but not by very much. In 1841 for instance in the main mining Redruth district Tributers earned from £2 15s to £3 2s per month whilst tutworkmen from £2 12s to £3.00. In normal times it is clear that the preference of most miners was for tributing, its much greater risks notwithstanding. Significantly, though, there is evidence that miners' wives might have preferred the steadier income from tutwork.[11] In the first place it was a matter of status:

He was a tributer, and tributers look with as great contempt upon the tut-men, as the latter do upon the surface labourers.

A tributer according to one account in 1849 would have to be on the point of starvation before he undertook tutwork.[12] This statement is perhaps an exaggeration. Most miners had probably worked at both over their working lives. That was not surprising. The amount of work available of each kind varied. For example, during a period of optimism and high expectations the opening of new ventures and the extension of old ones would bring at first a large demand for tutworkers while even in a time normal activity, as suggested by an estimate made in 1838, that of 100 employees 50 would be underground miners and of these 30 would be tributers and 20 tutworkers. In the second place the tributer was strongly attracted to the possibility of a 'start'. Attached to this hope was what one witness described as the miner's 'grand desideratum' to own a cottage. When John Harris's luck changed after ten poor months he acquired a lease and built himself a home, just as his father had once done:

If they have managed to live without getting into debt, when they get this start, the first thing they do is to build a house.[13]

Estimated costs, expecting that a miner was usually his own builder, in the mid-nineteenth century were around £50. Given that a plot of land could usually be leased cheaply on a three-life tenancy from landown-ers in the mining districts, where the value of the land for commercial agriculture was low, then for many tributers aspiration to a cottage and plot can be regarded as central to their living strategies. For many it re-mained an ideal, but as such it probably had a powerful role to play in the preference for tributing over more steadily remunerated forms of mine labour.

Collateral Aids to Living

This raises the question of how important were non-mining sources of support for mining households? John Harris describes himself as growing up in the 1820s in a cottage built by his grandfather on a small farm of seven or eight acres, then being worked by his father:

He followed his daily avocation underground, and performed his farm work in the evenings and mornings and on holidays and leisureable opportunities. [14]

In fact the farm work was input by the family rather than by the father singularly. The double description 'tinner and husbandman' occurs often in parish registers of the early eighteenth century and probably describes a genuine dual occupation. It occurs rarely later and the miners who produced some at least of their family food from small plots thereafter are better considered as pursuing a supplementary activity. From the late eighteenth century it was common for local landowners to lease portions of downland and wastes to miners in plots of three to six acres. Sir Francis Bassett, the dominant owner in the important mining parish of Illogan, estimated in 1795 that over the previous few years 50 miners had built cottages on such plots on his lands, while the steward for a neighbouring estate in 1802 was even more of an enthusiast. Remarking on the temptation of the alehouse, which faced the miner in his spare time, he continued:

To guard against an evil of such extensive magnitude, I have often wished that the proprietors of wastelands would endeavour to direct and guide the industry of these people to such efforts as would soon lessen these evils [by leasing small plots]...When ever this has been tried...you may now see them busily employed in enclosing and cultivating their little fields.

He continued to describe how beginning with a crop of potatoes to break and clear the ground, over a few years the miners were able to grow a small amount of corn, using the ashes from the turf they used as fuel as manure. With hard work within six years the poor ground could be improved to the extent of allowing the pasturing of a cow and overall to make a very substantial contribution to the family food supply, as well as having become 'careful and thrifty', self-respecting and better fathers and husbands. [15]

The practice continued into the nineteenth century. A landowner telling an enquiry in 1842 that he and others leased such small plots in and near the mining villages, but that it was hardly possible for the increasing numbers of miners who lived in towns like Redruth or Camborne to all have access to such plots. In 1841 it was estimated that a quarter of all miners lived in such cottage allotments. Of the rest many, but not all, had gardens. Even more important was the practice which seems to have become widespread in the nineteenth century of potato allotments under which farmers allowed miners to take plots rent free under condition that they dressed the ground when cultivating their potatoes in readiness for the farmer to take a corn crop from it the following year. Charles Barham, in his authoritative account of 1842, did not use the term 'small farm' at all. He regarded the plots as 'collateral aids', that is as a distinctly secondary employment. Indeed by then attempts to combine significant farming activity with mining were no longer meeting with unqualified approval. Barham himself considered attempts to work more than a very few acres were rarely successful, while the manager of a large mine stated that he preferred employing men with small plots to those with large ones, since the latter could not be depended on to work as fully at the mine. Keeping in good standing with the major mines was, as has already been noted, an important condition for tributers. [16]

In parts of the county fishing offered 'collateral aid'. Around St Ives ten or so miners sometimes combined to share an inshore fishing boat. Perhaps one in ten of miner heads of household there were involved in such ventures. However, the object was to secure a supply of fish for family consumption rather than for sale. Pig keeping was an activity of practically any miner who had the small amount of space needed. [17]

Family Income

Once children began to grow they would contribute increasingly to family income. The report of 1842 gives a detailed example of the family earning structure of a miner:

Miner aged 47, wife 45, married 26 years, 12 children - 4 dead, 1 married. Highest wages have been 55s per month. Whole gettings of family are now:

Constance (21) earns 15s 0d
John (19) earns £2 0s 0d
Richard (17) earns £1 6s 0d
James (14) earns 16s 0d
Elizabeth (12) earns 2s 0d
Total with his own wages £7 10s 0d a mont.

Another miner earning £3 a month depended upon his children for an additional £1. [18]

On the basis of the detailed example it is possible to make adjustments to ages and earnings and some for marriage of older children and construct a possible history of the family's income over time.

Year	Number in family	Earnings per head (new pence)
1827	6	46
1832	8	38
1837	10	52.5
1842	9	83
1847	7	117

The effect of the family cycle is clear. Family per capita income at its lowest point was less than a third of its highest level.

Miner's wives, although many of them would have worked before marriage at the mines as surface workers, do not seem to have done so after marriage and bridal pregnancy was in any case common, [19] even usual. Pre-marriage employment was frequently blamed for a supposed lack of domestic skills, while the importance of a wife's management of the household was clearly recognised:

You will find two men, and one has got a clean, decent, wholesome industrious wife, and that man's children will be kept as clean and comfortable as possible. You will then see one of the same "pare" who has got a dirty careless wife, and that family will be in rags, and yet that man will make the same earnings. One man will be well off and the other always in misery. [20]

The heavy tones of Victorian domestic ideology are apparent here. But the importance of wives to household functioning is clear enough. Among other things they had to cope with the problem of the erratic re-munerations of the tribute system. Few sought their opinion of it. Further, in a region where salted fish and potatoes had become dietary staples, wives had to manage the storage and preservation of food as well as its purchase. The extent to which wives might have worked from home still needs research. One miner described his wife as having a fish hawking round, and further of his intention of leaving the mine to join her as soon as he could afford a donkey and cart. In the meantime she presumably was bearing the fish on her back in a cowl. [21] Cornwall as a county offered little opportunities in domestic textiles, although the spinning needs of the Devonshire serge manufacture had reached into eastern parts of the county during its eighteenth century boom period.

Death, Injury and Sickness

Miners' wives too frequently became their widows. Cornwall had the highest proportion of widows to its total female population of any county in 1851. Some of these had been made so from deaths in mine accidents and frequently in early life. But more were widowed later in middle age by the toll taken by the lung disease which overcame the miners typically in late middle age. Accidental death was a risk; a lingering decline from miners' phthisis almost inevitable for those who continued working in the mine. Around 1850 miners in the age range 45 to 55 had a death rate two-and-a-quarter times that of non-miners in the same sample of six parishes. Between the ages 55 and 65 it was more than two-and-a-half times. The contribution to widow-making is clear. In the mining parish of Gwennap in 1837 the average age of death in persons dying over 30 years of age was 46 for miners, 60 for non-mining males and 64 for wom-en. This was not something that the mining community could put out of mind. Death or injury from accident might be considered a risk, howbeit a high one. A survey made in the early years after civil registration began in 1837 indicated that as a percentage of male deaths above ten years of age in four populous mining parishes, accidents accounted for 14.1%

for miners compared with 5.4% for non-miners. Diseases of the chest accounted respectively for 61.1% and 36.1%. It was the latter that a working miner had in mind when he replied simply to an inquiry in 1864: 'You cannot expect miners to live as long as other men'. [22]

Given that miners consciously pursued an occupation with a shorter working life but higher total earnings, compared with available alternatives then becoming a miner in the first place could be considered a strategy for economic survival. [23] But was there any strategy which could minimise the effect on life and earnings of the onset of phthisis or other lung conditions brought on by working in dust-laden or oxygen deficient air? Since local medical opinion was generally agreed that the final crippling and killing stages came on quite suddenly, but after giving some preliminary indications, a life-employment strategy which suggests itself is to leave underground work at an appropriate stage, say around 40 and move to another employment. Mine doctors constantly advised this, but it would seem very few adopted it. A doctor retained by a large mine, Fowey Consols, which at the time employed more than 1600 persons of whom more than a thousand were adult males, explained his situation in 1841:

I have frequently felt it my duty to point out to a patient in the strongest terms, the necessity of his leaving off working underground, and what has been the reply? "I have a wife and a large family of young children to support, how can I keep them on nine or ten shillings a week when I can barely manage on twelve or thirteen shillings a week; I will try it on a little longer". That little longer renders the case soon hopeless. [24]

He added a further consideration, which was that so long as a miner worked at the mine he would be entitled to receive seven shillings a week from the 'sick club' when disabled for the rest of his life. In this important respect the decision of putting by something from each pay for a fund to cover some disability either permanent or short-term was not a strategy left up to the miner. From well back into the eighteenth century compulsory deductions were made at most mines for the retention of a doctor and for the sick club. But in what circumstances was relief from this fund allowed? From the evidence just cited it would seem that at Fowey Consols a weekly relief was payable in cases where disease had resulted in the inability to continue working underground, although it is also clear that that point would only be reached once the disease had become fatally advanced. It did nothing to allow a miner to quit in time, but worked the other way. In fact payment from the club in cases of disease rather than accidental injury does not seem to have been the norm. In many mines only 'hurt pay' was given for visible injuries. As a manager pointed out in 1864 sometimes men were taken on in whom the disease had already commenced its ravages unseen, and that to allow pay from the fund would take too much out of it at the expense of those who did suffer injury. But Fowey Consols was probably representative of other large mines, for example East Crofty, employing around 450 adult males. The manager there indicated a significant area of discretion allowed by the larger funds built up in sizeable enterprises. The rule was still visible hurt only, but it was often overlooked: 'We have many men home for years who have been fairly worn out in the mine, because miners do not live to be very old'. While another mine stated that it had always been liberal:

We apply it to pensioning off old men who are unable to work any longer on the mine, who have been there for many years and whose money is spent. We always make them some allowance...We treat an illness brought on by working in the mine as a visible hurt.

Here as in the matter of wages it seems that the best economic survival strategy for a miner was to become established in one of the larger enterprises. In 1838 ten copper mines employing more than 500 persons accounted for 43% of the total labour force, while this is a significant proportion, it still suggests that for the majority of the workforce relief when disease ended their working lives was obtainable only from the Poor Law, or from any private provision they might have been able to make. [25]

Did many make some provision of this nature? Here the necessary research has yet to be done, but there are some indications that it might have been more common than has been assumed. Gorsky's figures for Friendly Society membership in the early nineteenth century place Cornwall twelfth among England's forty-two counties. [26] The two mining parishes sampled by Eden in his classic inquiry of 1797 are suggestive of an early and significant role. In Gwennap he found three societies with 400 members and in Kenwyn four with 400. In both case, that is one in ten of the total population, suggesting that a high proportion of the adult male population did belong, although the nature of the benefits covered is not specified. [27] Illogan in 1803 had a Friendly Society to population ratio of 1:5. [28] Overall in 1831, Cornwall was in a small group of counties where total society membership was in excess of 10% of the population.[29] Nor were Friendly Societies the only means of making a measure of provision. Barham's report of 1842 suggested that of £28,2541 deposited in Cornish savings banks, two-thirds probably belonged to miners. [30]

When all this is taken into account, however, there is still little doubt that to a partial or total extent, sick or injured miners and their families were likely to fall into dependence on official poor relief. After a miner's death, whether lingering or sudden, that was even more likely to become the fate of widows and orphaned children. [31] The Union Workhouse at Redruth at Christmas 1843 contained 120 women, 150 children, but only 33 men. Redruth Union covered the most densely populated of the mining parishes, so the small number of men who were among its inmates is worth noting. [32] It seems clear that despite the Act of 1834 workhouse-based relief had not become the usual final destination of worn-out miners. The parish of Gwennap was part of that union and in one quarter of 1848 miners made up 200 of 240 families receiving relief. Of the fathers of these mining families, 15 had been killed in accidents; 40 had been injured or blinded; 65 had died and 15 others, who had between them 80 children were dying from miners' consumption. [33] It is important to note the structure of Poor Law relieved poverty in the mining districts. Overall levels of poor rate expenditure were low at times when there was no food or employment crisis. The overall figure for county expenditure in 1838 was 23p a head of the 1841 population. In the Redruth Union it was 17p and for the districts of Gwennap and St Day within it was 21p. The mining parish of St Just in Penwith had a rate of only 7p against an over-all figure for the Penzance Union of 17p. In the non-industrial Stratton Union, on the other hand, the per capita rate was 34p. There is certainly a suggestion here that the poor rate cost of relieving the poverty situations which arose in mining households in the middle years of the nineteenth century was less than that of relieving the structural problems of low rural wages and unemployment. [34]

However, an important qualification needs to be made. Cornwall may have been a low-spending county in overall terms, but in one re-spect it was well above the average for England and Wales. In 1851-1856 its ratio of female to male paupers at 2.82 was exceeded only by North-umberland at 3.09. Cornwall was almost matched by Durham at 2.79, South Wales at 2.8 and the West Riding at 2.75. There is a strong sugges-tion of a link between mining and proportionately high female to male pauper ratios. [35]

Miners dying or being crippled in accidents created in the immedi-ate term a larger problem of relief simply because they were much more likely to leave families including young children. We noted above the significance of the family cycle in determining household income gener-ally. Using the example family from 1842 (see p.124) it can be shown how significant it was for the impact of a loss of a mining fathers earnings. The miner was 47 and had he died in that year with five children between the ages of 12 and 21 at work, family per capita income would have fallen from 83p to 59.4p a significant fall, but one which would hardly have brought the family to destitution. Had however his death happened in 1832, ten years earlier, the fall would have been from 38p to 4p. A total family income of 29p less than 6s in old money. In short the references to the destitution of widows and children are real enough. Fifteen of the 40 miners who perished in the flooding disaster at East Wheal Rose Mine in 1846 were married and together left 60 children orphaned. Relief sub-scriptions were collected and they were often done so for individual cas-es, but while they met immediate expenses they provided for little more than short-term relief. [36]

The role of charity

Special subscriptions following particular episodes of distress were a re-active form of charity. What needs fuller consideration is the role of char-ity generally. It is said by historians of many groups of 'proud' workmen such as the Cornish miners that their pride and independence stood be-tween them and the willing receipt of charity. This may have been more true after the mid-nineteenth century than before. Victorian attitudes symbolised by the awesome authoritarianism exampled by organiza-tions like London's Charity Organization Society, perhaps represented a cultural shift on the part of the providers, which was reciprocated by a change in attitude from potential recipients. There is certainly evidence that the Cornish lower classes of the eighteenth and earlier nineteenth century, as elsewhere, could exhibit in certain circumstances expecta-tions from charity, which could even be expressed in a language of enti-tlement. In particular, charity expectations were part of the network of social relations which existed between the mining community and the mine and land-owning elite. This charity typically operated through the mediation of estate stewards. One wrote to his employer during the food crisis of 1847:

> *Wheal Prosper is not your property neither are you at present receiving any dues of consequence, but merely on Halvana...I do not think you can be expected to subscribe to anything more than the relief fund of the Parish which I consider they are in great want of.*

On another occasion he wrote that he had not forwarded his em-ployer's agreed donation because he had heard that some of the other landowners, 'had not come forward on the occasion'.[37]

The language here is one of calculation and instrumentality as well as sympathy and expectation. Solicitations came on behalf of individuals as well as for parish funds. In 1799 another steward had written to his employer:

> *There was a poor man unfortunately killed in Herland Mine...he has left a widow and several small children. The man bore a good character...a neighbour-*

ing gentleman and one of the Lords of the mine was so kind as to send the poor woman a guinea. I took the liberty of doing the like on your behalf. [38]

The man 'bore a good character'; clearly such a bearing and conduct was an important consideration for those who might one day need charity. When Lady Bassett's 'venerable' steward died in 1841, the local press praised his concern over fifty years for the miners of Illogan, especially his care in bringing 'deserving persons' to the notice of his employers. [39] William Jenkin brought a general need to the attention of his employer in 1799 reminding him of 'some little assistance to the poor families of Illogan' which he had given in the previous year, and advising him that, 'the poor creatures are enquiring whether anything of that sort is to be expected this year', while in 1845 another landowner was also reminded of the nature of the poor's expectations from him:

A subscription of two guineas has generally been given to the poor of Probus and the like at Grampound for purchasing coals…if it is your wish to give £5 had it not better be divided between them?…as the poor of Grampound in consequence of living in your houses and your paying a large part of the poor's rates consider they have similar claims on you to those of Probus. [40]

These are indicative examples. A full account of the working of charity is as wanting for Cornwall as it is for other counties. It is an important subject. At some point in their history many families had recourse to it. Its total impact may well have been hardly less than that of official poor relief.

Consolation

Concern with a community with such a distinct mortality profile, with death and bereavement at such high levels, raises questions not only over strategies for economic survival, but also for emotional survival: ways of dealing with death, injury and illness. So far as the mining villages of Cornwall were concerned consolation came overwhelmingly in a religious idiom. Contemporary descriptions and the evidence of the Religious Census of 1851 indicate that the religiosity of these communities was perhaps their most striking cultural characteristic. It took the form of Methodism, mostly in the form of the parent Wesleyan, and was extremely revivalist in its nature. I have written elsewhere in detail on the relationship of Methodism to the risks of mining life. [41] But what I have in mind is the kind of sentiment expressed in some of the verses in a broadsheet published in 1842 after an explosion killed eight miners:

Seven beside the youth are dead
His dear father too is fled
Crying with his latest breath,
Jesus is my strength in death.

O what solace thus to see
Christ had set his spirit free,
Born on angel wings away
To the realms of endless day.

Some have shouting crossed the flood,
They were washed in Jesus blood,
Now before the throne they shine,
Clothed with victory divine

Widow, dry the falling tear.
God will be thy husband here,
Orphan cease they accents wild,
God will be thy Father, child.

Now on him your griefs repose,
He will listen to your woes,
Feed you, guide you with his hand,
To that holy, happy land.

Or from another example after seven were killed in 1858:

Ah, no! they cannot come again;
No more their voice you'll hear;
But may we hope in heaven they rest,
And may we meet them there.

Widows and orphans now are left,
Their sad bereave to mourn
May David's God their father be,
And serve him in return

Funerals of mine victims were hugely attended:

Then borne unto the silent tomb,
What thousands gathered there,
To mingle with the relatives
Sorrow's lingering tear.

The *Mining Journal* described the funeral of one of mining's victims at the end of the 1850s as being attended by a 'black mass of several thousands' who processed several miles to the churchyard. [42]

Conclusion

There are links that can be made and conflicts that can be noted. Pursuit of short-term economic strategies may at times have contributed to the onset of disease. For example tributers knew well enough that the failure of a candle to burn as a level end indicated that the air was too deficient in oxygen to be safely breathed. But if their gettings were proving good, then they moved the candle further back from the end and carried on working. A mine doctor too considered it common to find a miner in whom the signs of disease were already apparent, struggling on in the hope of just one more lucky strike. One miner stayed working in an unhealthy mine because his children also worked there and he feared for their jobs if he left. [43] Religion too offered explanation and consolation in the face of the ups and downs of tributing. When a Methodist miner had a good run in 1853, he knew who to thank: 'the Lord has greatly prospered me at the mine lately', while for another it was 'Providence' which had blessed his labours. When things went badly an essay stereotyping the Cornish miner in 1846 suggested that even after months of dismal wages and extreme privation:

Their hope was in his truth; and often at night, after a long season of labour underground, when the miner returned to his family, and was sitting at his supper of salt fish and potatoes, would he comfort his wife in her trouble, by assuring her that God had said, "I will never leave thee; I will never forsake thee". [44]

John Harris wrote of his hatred of work in the mine: 'Yet I never complained, God had placed me there, and I knew it was right'. This essay began with a verse from this miner-poet. It can end with one from another of his poems:

> *A miner in his smoky cave,*
> *Amid his course employ*
> *In clouds of darkness visible*
> *Thus sweetly sang for joy*
> *His toil wet face and brow were pale*
> *And very ill he seemed*
> *When carolling those thrilling words*
> *Mankind are all redeemed.* [45]

1 J. Harris, *Wayside Pictures, Hymns and Poems,* 1874, pp. 158-159. This essay is concerned with the period of mining prosperity. It does not cover the effects of the later nineteenth century decline.

2 J. Harris, *My Autobiography,* 1882, p. 60.

3 *West Briton,* 15 May 1840; S. Shaw, *A Tour to the West of England in 1788,* 1789, p. 383.

4 *Morning Chronicle,* 24 Nov 1849. For a full discussion of the tribute system see above Chapter 4.

5 W. Pryce, *Mineralogia Cornubiensis,* 1778, p. 1755.

6 On the grain crises see R. Wells, *Wretched Faces. Famine in Wartime England 1793-1803,* Gloucester, 1988. For the potato crisis see B. Deacon, 'Proto-industrialization and potatoes: a revised narrative for nineteenth century Cornwall', *Cornish Studies,* (5), 1997, pp. 73-75 and P. Payton,' 'Reforming Thirties and Hungry Forties': the Genesis of Cornwall's Emigration Trade', *Cornish Studies,* 4, 1996, pp. 110-115.

7 For the 'mixed economy of welfare' see A. Kidd, *State, Society and the Poor in Nineteenth Century England*, 1999, Chapter 1.

8 *British Parliamentary Publications*, 1864, Report of the Royal Commissioners....
appointed to enquire into the condition of all mines in Britain. Epitome of Evidence, p.564.

9 *Cornwall Gazette*, 16 March 1838.

10 *Morning Chronicle*, 24 November 1849.

11 C. Pascoe, *Walks about St Hilary*, 1879.

12 *Morning Chronicle*, 24 Nov 1849.

13 J. Harris, *My Autobiography*, p.60; BPP, 1864, Minutes, p. 565.

14 J. Harris, *My Autobiography*, p. 5.

15 J. Rowe, *Cornwall in the Age of the Industrial Revolution*, Liverpool, 1953, p. 25; Jenkin MSS, Courtney Library, County Museum, Truro, Jenkin to J. Britten, 4 April 1802.

16 BPP, 1842, XVI, Report of Royal Commission on Child Employment, pp. 763-4; BPP, 1864, p. XXV; BPP, 1841, XX, Report of the Committee of Council on Education, p. 84. For potato allotments see Deacon, 'Protoindustrialization and potatoes', pp. 60-85.

17 *BBP*, 1842, pp. 754, 848.

18 *BPP*, 1842, p. 840.

19 On the scarcity of employment for women once through the ages at which child surface workers were usually employed see S. Schwartz, 'In defence of custom: Labouring women's experience of industrialization in Cornwall 1750-1870', in *Cornish Studies*, 7, 1999, pp. 8-31.

20 BPP, 1864, p. 45; BPP, 1842, pp. 834, 838.

21 *BBP*, 1842, p. 847. The buying strategy for fish, usually pilchards, but sometimes herrings, was to purchase in bulk from the autumn fisheries and salt a supply in large earthenware vessels known as bussas. If large shoals had not been coming inshore to the reach of the seine fisheries by the late autumn, local newspapers began to express concern over the winter food supply for the poor. As purchasers the mining families were quick to take advantage of any unexpectedly large catches, as gluts could bring fish down in the short term to almost give-away prices. When in 1893, a large shoal was taken at Perranporth late on a winter's evening, the town crier at the nearby town of Redruth was taking the news to the streets by dawn and the sale of the fish was underway by 8.00 a.m. *West Briton*, 13 November 1893. Carts from the mining parishes are reported to arrive at large landings in their hundreds. The importance of buying in fish is evident in the action of two sisters from Truro who pushed a wheelbarrow from Truro to Perranporth and back, an 18 mile round trip to return with 700 pilchards. *West Briton*, 7 September 1855.

22 For the sources of these statistics and an analysis of mortality and morbidity see J. Rule, ' "A Risky Business": Death, injury and religion in Cornish mining 1780 to 1870', in A. Bernard Knapp et al, *Social Approaches to an Industrial Past. The Archaeology and Anthropology of Mining*, 1998, pp. 45-76. See also above Chapter 3.

23 See R. Burt and S. Kippen, 'Rational Choice and a lifetime in metal mining: Employment Decisions by Nineteenth Century Cornish Miners, in *International Review*

of Social History, XLVI, 1, April 2001, pp. 45-76.

24 'Enquiry into the Health and General Condition of the Mining Population of Cornwall', *Report of the Royal Cornwall Polytechnic Society*, 1841, pp. 133-135.

25 See the discussion in A. Hamilton Jenkin, *The Cornish Miner*, 1962 edition pp. 265-267.

26 M. Gorsky, 'The Growth and Dstribution of English Friendly Societies in the Early Nineteenth Century', in *Economic History Review*, LI, 1998, pp. 493-495.

27 F. Eden, *The State of the Poor*, (abridged), A. Rogers, 1928, pp. 146-7.

28 Based on the 1801 Census and the friendly society returns in *BPP* 1803/4, XIII. See also M. Gorsky, 'English Friendly Societies in the early nineteenth century', p. 495.

29 A. Kidd, *State, Society and the Poor*, p. 112.

30 Cited in L. Price, *West Barbary or notes on the system of work and wages in the Cornish Mines*, 1891. Reprinted in R. Burt, (ed), *Cornish Mining*, Newton Abbot, 1969, p. 162.

31 For the concern of parish officials with the relief of widows once the Poor Law of 1834 came into operation see S. Schwartz, R. Parker and A. Lanner, *Cornish Mining Parish*, Tiverton, 1998, p. 29. Much needed further study of the Poor Law in Cornwall seems likely to suggest that officials shared the view usually associated with the industrial north that the workhouse was not an effective solution to local relief problems.

32 F. Mitchell, *Annals of an Ancient Cornish Town: Redruth*, Redruth, 1972, p. 122.

33 R. Blee, 'On the Comparative Longevity of Cornish Miners', *Report of the Royal Cornwall Polytechnic Society*, 1847, p.18.

34 Poor Law statistics tables in appendix to C. Redding, *Illustrated Itinerary of Cornwall*, 1842, pp. 247-253. The Cornish unions were set up in 1837.

35 See Tables in L. Lees, *The Solidarities of Strangers. The English Poor Laws and the People, 1700 to 1948*, 1998 p. 199.

36 'Accident at East Wheal Rose Mine', *Cornish Banner*, August 1846, p. 56.

37 Hawkins MSS, CRO, DDJ 1227, Letter book of Henry Trethewey, 7 and 12 June 1847.

38 Courtney Library, Jenkin MSS, Jenkin to A. M. Hunt, 27 February 1799.

39 *Cornwall Gazette*, 9 July 1841.

40 Jenkin to G. Hunt, 28 May 1798; Hawkins MSS, Trethewey to J. Hawkins, 2 March 1842.

41 See J. Rule, 'Explaining Revivalism: the Case of Cornish Methodism', see below Chapter 6; See also the introduction by P. Payton to C. Noall, *Cornish Mine Disasters*, Redruth, 1989, pp. 7-8.

42 Cited in R. Burt, (ed), *Cornwall's Mines and Miners*, Truro 1972, pp. 12-14. Broadsheets in the collections of the Courtney Library and the Cornwall CRO.

43 *BPP*, 1864, p. 35; *BPP*, 1842, p. 840.

44 See Chapter 3, p. *Cornish Banner*, July 1846, p. 24.

45 J. Gill, *John Harris the Cornish Poet*, n.d., p. 10; J. Harris, *My Autobiography*, p. 36.

Explaining Revivalism:
The Case of Cornish Methodism

In the period since Edward Thompson's extraordinary attack on Methodism, its historians have tended to emphasise the local. They have been especially concerned to demonstrate that the conservative or even reactionary policies of Methodism's national leadership could not easily be imposed on local chapel communities. David Hempton, for example, stresses that it was precisely over the issues of radicalism and revivalism that the divergence over national attitude and local practice was most evident. [1] Alan Gilbert has stressed the same ambiguity:

Conservative leaders seeking to impose a "no politics rule" on rank and file members often found themselves defied by the very independence of mind which had pre-disposed such people to Methodism in the first place.

He goes further to argue that it was grass-roots moderate radicalism rather than elite anti-radicalism which was the more important in assessing the political role of Methodism in the era of the industrial revolution:

...it was the radical element, the undercurrent of protest, the reformist sympathies and egalitarianism - the attitudes and concerns of the ordinary chapel folk - which determined the primary political significance of the movement. [2]

In part, re-assessment of the great question posed by Halévy and carried further by Thompson over the counter-revolutionary nature of Methodism, has correctly stressed the importance of distinguishing from the 1820s between the different divisions in to which the original body of Wesleyan Methodism split. In particular the local links, especially in leadership, between Primitive Methodism and early trade unionism have been demonstrated, for example by Robert Colls for the North-East coalfield, and James Epstein for parts of the industrial Midlands. [3] Yet one indication of the importance of local context is that this connection itself only works for some areas. In Cornwall, an area of great strength, it is hard to see very much in the way of difference in attitude between the Wesleyans and the major off-shoots like the Primitive Methodists or the Bible Christians. [4]

Thompson's most discussed assertion was a theory of 'oscillation' linking radicalism to revivalism through a pattern in which the latter took over, 'just at the point where political or temporal aspiration met with defeat'. Local testing of this particular rhythm has not generally offered much support for the thesis (although a study of the West Riding revival of 1792-1796 by John Baxter does leave the question open). [5] What seems to be emerging is a growing sense that in communities where Methodism was strongly entrenched, and these after all are the ones, that matter in terms of the thesis, revivalism was essentially the manifestation of a community dynamic, to which radical politics were largely irrelevant. This chapter will draw from a close study of the great era of Cornish revivalism from the late eighteenth century through the early nineteenth an explanation which certainly seems capable of transfer in the sense that it does not need the presence of particular externalities.

Statistics of membership and attendance indicate Cornwall as easily the most Methodist county in England. Since membership and influence was strongly concentrated in the western mining parts, it is not too difficult to defend the proposition that this district was even more Methodist than any part of Wales. The summing-up of Charles Barham, reporting for the Parliamentary enquiry into child labour in 1842 seems much to the point when he claimed that adherents of Methodism were 'so numerous, that its qualities become prominent features of the whole body, when it is compared with other communities'.

The Vicar of Redruth claimed in writing to Dr Pusey in 1851, that securing six 'poor mine girls' for an Anglican sisterhood was a major achievement in a parish 'with Methodism in every house'. [6] Further testimony to the same effect would be easy to provide. What West Cornwall does not reveal is any general sense of Wesleyan Methodism becoming a respectable 'middle class' church, losing its proletarian adherents to more democratic and revivalist inclined divisions. In 1851 the parent body had an attendance index equal to 20.5% of the county's population out of a total Methodist figure of 32%. Bible Christians with 6% came second, and the rest was shared between four other divisions including the Primitive Methodists. [7] Analysis of baptism lists reveals no marked occupational pattern. While it is true that middle class Cornish Methodists were more likely to be Wesleyan, it is just as true that Wesleyan miners massively outnumbered those from other divisions. Recurrent revivalism among the Cornish miners was accordingly a feature that happened across Methodism, not the function of any particular segment.

Jabez Bunting is reputed to have described the Cornish as, 'the mob of Methodism'. If he did, then it was noisy, enthusiastic revivalism not radicalism which he had in mind, for he did remark in 1843, 'In Cornwall there are great revivals, but the regular work there is little done'. [8] The independence of the Methodist communities of West Cornwall had long been notorious. John Wesley noted in 1788:

It has been observed for many years that some at Redruth were apt to despise and very willing to govern the preachers. [9]

It was a characteristic, which continued into the present century, a minister remarking in 1908:

In the town...the minister represents the Connexion and takes over the chapel as his own...In the village the chapel belongs to the people...and the people take over the minister as a newcomer attached to them.

When a minister remarked to a local leader in 1842 that the work of God was processing well, he replied, 'I hope that you do not think that you have done it'. Ten years earlier the same minister's wife wrote to a friend that when they came to St Agnes, 'the preachers who had preceded us had with their families suffered most keenly through the fault finding of the people'. [10] David Luker has suggested that Cornish Methodism was controlled by local laymen, preachers and class leaders, to an extent unparalleled elsewhere. He points to the county's geographical and cultural remoteness and to the special affinity of many aspects of Methodism to a traditional culture. The relative poverty of the members limited the number of official itinerants employed. In 1830 for example Redruth had a ratio of members per minister of 658 and St Agnes of 929 against a national circuit average of 333; suggesting a practical problem in maintaining full Conference control. [11] Following the argumentation of W. R. Ward, Luker presents Cornish Methodism as indigenised to the extent that it was a true *Volkskirche*. It is in this context that an explanation for recurrent revivalism should perhaps be sought.

Numerically revivals were periods of mass conversions when large numbers were added to the Methodist societies in a short period: as for example in 1831 when the Camborne and Redruth circuits added 1700 members over four months. [12] Phenomenologically they were manifested in mass displays of the conversion characteristics of sighs, groans, weepings and fits and, ultimately, joy uncontainable. Lasting typically for several hectic months, they were as often as not followed by a sharp decline in membership, although usually of smaller dimensions than the original increase. In Cornwall there were widespread revivals in 1764, 1782, 1798, 1814, 1824, 1831-1833, 1841-1842, 1847-1849 and a period between 1862 and 1865. Up to 1814 (the so-called 'Great Revival') they were separated by roughly sixteen years, thereafter they became somewhat more frequent. Closer analysis suggests a less clear-cut pattern. The dates represent sudden explosions of religious enthusiasm, but an upward trend in membership may have existed for several years before the revival broke out. The great revival of 1814 followed an upward trend in the two western circuits of Penzance and Helston: [13]

Year	Penzance	Helston
1808	1287	864
1809	1372	906
1810	1384	955
1811	1363	1080
1812	1612	1280
1813	2247	2000
1814	2500	3288

The total membership for west Cornwall before the revival of 1824 shows a similar pattern: [14]

Year	Membership
1820	8951
1821	8823
1822	9125
1823	9170
1824	11041

Annual membership returns can in any case flatten the revival phenomenon. In the first place they are annual figures and a major revival often had a period of a few months or even weeks of special intensity. In the second if a revival took place towards the end of a year, then the most rapid period of augmentation might be split between two membership years. Further, the timing could vary from circuit to circuit, and smaller revivals unconnected with the bigger ones might occur in individual areas in the intervening periods. Since revivals tended to spread by contagion, there might be a period of several months between the outbreak of a revival in one place, and the peak of intensity in another. A revival might therefore appear in different year's membership figures.

Nevertheless a pattern can be mooted. The widespread revivals occurred regularly, with decreasing intervals after 1814, but the longest period between two major outbreaks was the eighteen years from 1764 to 1782. The increasing frequency in the nineteenth century, probably reflects the fact that with membership more than keeping pace with demographic increase, there was a larger population of potential converts.

The usual features of Cornish revivals were frequently described. That of 1764 broke out while Thomas Rankin was the itinerant in the Redruth circuit and a brief retrospect of it is in his memoir:

The work of God more or less prospered in every society in the county. In two or three months, hundreds were added to the societies in the west, and many savingly brought to the knowledge of the Lord Jesus Christ; many backsliders were restored, and a most wonderful change took place in every parish where the gospel was preached. Most of the country villages were like Eden, and as the garden of the Lord. It was not uncommon for ten or twenty to find peace with God in one day, or at one sermon, or love feast. [15]

The revival of 1782 began in December 1781:

Many persons met at Gabriel Thomas's house in St Just church-town in order to sing and pray. In a little time several began to cry aloud, and would not be comforted; and some struggled in the agonies of death; one of whom fainted away. They continued in prayer until the preaching began at five in the morning, and six of the mourners found peace with God. Some were also deeply distressed for full salvation: but they were not yet set at liberty. On Tuesday December 25th, many met at three in the morning at Gabriel Thomas's. The power of the Lord fell upon them, so the six were as if in agony; two of whom were soon filled with peace. At seven they removed to the preaching house, where the same power was present. They continued in prayer until about nine. In that time four more found a sense of pardon. They met there again in the evening, and very soon began to cry for mercy. But two women who though they had been long in the society, were not convinced of sin, were much offended, saying, "It is all hypocrisy". In a short time, the cries of the mourners were turned into praise; at this they were still more offended. But in about two hours they were both cut to the heart, and cried out as loud as any. About one o'clock God put a new song in their mouths. About seven, the meeting broke up; but not before eleven more were enabled to declare that their sins were blotted out.

During all February, the work of God went on with power. Many were justified and some sanctifies. It was about this time that four score persons were justified in one week... [16]

Scenes of mass hysteria were common. Two descriptions from the revival of 1831-1832 illustrate this:

The loud and piercing cries of the broken hearted penitents drowned the voice of prayer, and all that could be done at this stage of the meeting was to stand still and see the salvation of God. At length the penitents were conducted and upheld, each of them by two persons, into one part of the chapel. And now when their cries and groans were concentrated, one of the most affecting scenes appeared before the people. Their humble wailings pierced the skies. Sometimes a burst of praise from the pardoned penitents mingled with the loud cries of the broken hearted; and this greatly encouraged those that were in distress. [17]

The chapel was crowded almost to suffocation. The steam ran down the walls; the gallery stairs were flooded with it; and had not all the windows been opened, every light would have gone out. The people were yet determined to enter into this kingdom; yet everyone suppressed his feelings as long as he could. When any have cried out, it has been the involuntary burst of a soul overwhelmed with a sense of guilt and a sense of danger. The seats in many places were literally covered with tears. This night the preacher concluded the first service about eight o'clock; but scarcely any left the chapel. From that hour until nearly eleven the people were crying out for mercy in every part of the chapel, both in the gallery and below. Nearly fifty found peace that night; and more than double that number returned home weary and heavy laden. Many of these continued in prayer all night; and not a few during the night found peace in their own houses. [18]

During this revival it was not only in the chapel that strong men were overcome:

It is also while they are at their work in the bowels of the earth...that the spirit strives with them. They come up from their work and explain to...the captain...we cannot work, we must cry for mercy! [19]

In the 'Great Revival' of 1814 not only the chapels and mines, but houses, barns and stables became scenes of frantic prayer. [20] So striking were the scenes during this most widespread of Cornish revivals, that many were said to have believed it was preparatory to the end of the world. [21] Its astonishing sweep through the central mining district is revealed in a remarkable contemporary description:

It began...in the parish of Gwennap, and then extended to Redruth, where... the Lord was pleased to pour out such a measure of his Holy Spirit upon the people, that the chapel doors were not shut till the Monday or Tuesday se-ennight after. During this time, it is said hundreds were converted to God and set at liberty, so that their change appeared as raise from death to life. For at their first conviction the people dropped down as dead, and became quite stiff, and after some time revived again, and the first words were, "Christ have mercy upon us, Lord have mercy upon us", and this repeated (in some cases) not only for hours, but for days, till the Lord on whom they called, sent salvation in an answer of peace to their souls. Such a sight as the chapel of Redruth afforded, and the other towns and parishes in succession was never witnessed here. Men crying with loud and bitter cries, till the anguish of their souls had opened every pore of the body, and produced a perspiration which fell from their face to the ground. From this you may form some idea of their distress, and the holy violence used in entering the strait gate. Almost all temporal business was at a stand, and the shops mostly shut up. When market day came there was scarce any buying or selling, for all were "labouring for the bread which endureth to eternal life". The cries for mercy were not confined to the chapel, but extended to the streets, [where] men and women were seen... supported on each side from the chapel to their houses, for they could neither stand nor walk and were not ashamed, to "cry for Him who is able to save".[22]

Two thousand were added to the societies in the Redruth circuit and a local mine steward, a Quaker, provided a rare detailed description from an outsider:

It continued for a few weeks, when the great noise subsided, but the fire still existed. The same extraordinary agitation extended to divers neighbouring parishes... But the great current seemed to run westward. It was not so very rapid or noisy about Truro and its vicinity, as it was in the parish of Gwennap. At Illogan and Camborne it was more violent. But at Hayle Copper works and the adjoining villages (taking in Wheal Alfred mine) the agitation was extremely so - at the latter mine are about 800 labourers at the surface (male and female) chiefly young people, where the torrent bore down everything that stood in its way. Were I to attempt to describe it I could not find words sufficient to draw in colours strong enough. All labour for some days was suspended, and the underground labourers (equally as numerous as those at the surface) seemed to be struck with the same power - but being more advanced in years. I think they appeared to have a greater mastery over their passions than the others had. [23]

Ten years later the glorious memory of 1814 was recalled in a private letter between two Methodists as Redruth once again became the centre of stirring events:

Its first beginnings were observed and felt at a prayer meeting held at Redruth Highway...To this favoured spot multitudes resorted...and were seized with powerful convictions. Many whole nights were spent in prayer and great numbers found peace with God...It is supposed that the place contains about 200 houses and it is reported by our friends that there is not more than five of these dwellings in which family worship is not now regularly observed. [24]

Not intended for publication, this account is noticeably less dramatic than those above taken from connexional magazines and pamphlets, but it still comes from a sympathetic insider. The middle class Quaker who provided the description of the 1814 revival quoted above can perhaps be described as a 'sympathetic outsider'. He concluded by writing that although people did not all see religion alike in all respects, 'yet who can but rejoice on seeing the apparent marks of outward reformation'. This approval of the end, with an implied distrust of the means was also characteristic of some within Methodism. The most obvious 'intellectual' produced from the Cornish Methodist community was Samuel Drew. Beginning life as a child labourer in the mines in the 1780s Drew improved himself to the extent that he wrote philosophy well enough to be offered the Chair of Moral Philosophy at the newly opened University College London. In old age when asked for his views on the revivalism of his native county, he gave a considered reply:

If the phrase revival of religion, be taken in its proper sense, as denoting the extension and increase of vital godliness, I should be no Christian were I to view it with indifference or aversion. If you couple it with noise and excited feeling (and without these many people would think the term inapplicable), I pause before I either approve or condemn. In point of reason, speculation, propriety, and decorum, my voice is decidedly against the manner; and if I thought it was the effect of human artifice operating upon weak intellects and strong passions, I would condemn it altogether. But when, without any ground for this suspicion, I

see the profligate reclaimed, the abandoned reformed, and the vicious undergoing
a moral renovation, I abandon all my fine-spun objections, and remain silent at a
spectacle so salutary in its effects, and so mysterious in its process. [25]

A more unusual, but hostile witness, who found nothing mysterious
about the process, was the Chartist missionary, Robert Lowery, whose
visit to St Ives in 1839 coincided with a revival:

A large chapel was full of people; there was an open space within the door
in front of the pews, where a number of people - neighbours who had slipped
out without hats or bonnets, as they would to see a passing sight - were looking
coolly on and passing their remarks. They had not caught the enthusiasm. But
all within the pews were in a state of delirium. Amidst the confusion of tongues
it was impossible to connect coherently the utterances. There were three persons
in the pulpit, one of whom was preaching, or rather uttering unconnected ex-
clamations. In the gallery some were singing 'rapturously', others were praying
aloud. Similar proceedings were taking place under the gallery, and in the body
of the chapel. I shall never forget the sight we observed in one of the large pews
close by us. A young woman was 'smitten' as they call it. She was uttering loud,
passionate, and convulsive exclamations of grief, and tearing her hair, which
hung dishevelled round her neck. Afterwards she sank on the ground, exhausted,
panting for breath and foaming at the mouth. There were two men beside her,
not at all excited themselves, who coolly watched her emotions, and excited her
as if they were merely applying galvanism. One of them particularly disgusted
us. There were no signs of honest fanaticism in his looks; on the contrary he was
cold and calculating…When her spent nature could no longer utter ravings, and
seemed to be recovering its reason, he would kneel down by her and exclaim close
to her ear, "Shout! Shout! Shout! there is no quietness until the devil is cast out,
and then you will find mercy".

Lowery offered an explanation for the breaking out of revivals:

The population possesses all the materials for such explosions being full of
warm religious feelings, which overrules knowledge. Their daily languages and
religious services they attend are replete with rapturous exclamations. Perhaps
the mother is out on some errand, and she has left the children to play with those

of a neighbour…Bye and bye in imitation of their elders, they begin singing a
hymn and uttering the expressions they have heard at chapel. In the midst of this
the mother returns. Her parental (sic) feelings are delighted, and she exclaims,
'Bless the Lord!' She joins the hymn, calls in her neighbours, who become simi-
larly affected, and the enthusiasm spreads from house to house, then the chapel
is sought, and the whole neighbourhood are infected. [26]

What is interesting about this offered explanation, is that Lowery had only been in Cornwall for a few days, he had come to St Ives after the revival had broken out, and on his own account, left the town without doing anything which could be considered local research. In short Lowery's observation was based on experience gained elsewhere. In fact he came from the Northumberland and Durham coalfield, a community for which Robert Colls has produced an interesting analysis of revivalism. He is rather sceptical about general explanations:

There are general theories about conversions and revivals which have been
tested and speculated upon in other works, but theories referring to say, the West
Riding of Yorkshire or the East Coast of the United States, will not necessarily
apply here. [27]

This may be a little guarded. The theory to be offered here as a partial explanation of revivalism does not depend on Cornish peculiarities, and is at least capable of testing in other communities. The accounts of the recurrent rivals of the Cornish mining districts thus far presented come from published and private Methodist sources, from the sympathetic, but qualified position of a local Quaker and from the hostile one of a Chartist agitator. There are also hostile reactions deriving from those who took a more conservative view of religion. These usually expressed extreme distaste for 'enthusiasm' and were often ready to accuse Methodist preachers of manipulating simple minds in their search for souls. Considerable descriptive evidence, then, from various sources survives, and from this and from the periodicity of the revivals a theory of explanation for recurrent revivalism can be suggested.

Outbreaks of revivalism in the eighteenth century do not coincide with the frequent visits of John Wesley. Even the widespread one of 1782-1783 broke out before he arrived in Cornwall in 1782. He wrote ahead of his visit, 'I must see them in the west of Cornwall, where there is a great revival of the work of God'. [28] Neither do revivals coincide with the food rioting years of extreme hunger and harvest failure. The revival of 1798, for example, comes between the two major food crises of 1796 to 1797 and 1800 to 1801. The marked proclivity towards food rioting of the Cornish miners continued down to 1847, but apart from that year itself, there is no year in which both a food riot and a revival took place. Even in 1847 the revival seems to have begun at least a month before the sudden upward movement in food prices which precipitated the riots. [29] So far as radical political agitation is concerned, Edward Thompson's famous theory of oscillation cannot be effectively tested in a county where radical politics never really took hold. [30]

Robert Colls has rightly discarded for the mining districts of Northumberland and Durham, explanations of the 'frontier', or 'burned over' district kind. Although new upheaved industrial and mining communities characterised by social dislocation have proved susceptible to emotional and enthusiastic forms of religion, the mining villages of Northumberland and Durham were traditional industrial communities, characterised by established traditions and with marked cultural and social cohesion. [31] The mining and fishing villages of west Cornwall were similarly established, not new industrial communities. Colls suggests that some outbreaks of revivalism can be linked to the psychological impact of colliery disasters, the best example being that of 1839 centred on South Shields after a disaster which killed fifty-one men. The three societies nearest to the mine doubled their membership. [32] However, this explanation will not transfer easily to the Cornish mining districts where the hardness of the rock and the absence of explosive gasses meant that despite the extraordinary toll taken by individual accidents, major disasters hardly ever occurred. [33]

*   *   *   *   *

The pattern of causation which will be suggested for Cornwall, does not in fact depend on the identification of external factors, for the argument is that revivalism was an internally driven phenomenon which although it could be sparked by any number of occurrences, was an expected and recurrent feature deriving from imperatives within the local religious community itself. The longest gap between major revivals was the eighteen year one between 1764 and 1782. However, the pattern I am suggesting would relate more to the established Methodist community of the early nineteenth century than to the emerging one of the eighteenth. In the former period, major revivals followed a cycle of approximately sixteen years. This parallels roughly the age cohort from the teens to the late twenties. The evidence is overwhelming that youth was the most likely period in the life cycle for an individual to experience conversion. The periodicity of revivalism meant that a major one would occur during this period in most people's lives. A revival could therefore function as a means of joining young people to the church. This does not necessarily imply that revivals were deliberately staged with this end in view, but that they would perform this role whether or not deliberately. As the conversion of young people in the community, in most cases the children of Methodist parents, came to be awaited, there was a reservoir of 'serious' or expecting to be converted penitents. The example of one or several of these 'proto-saved' experiencing first conviction and then conversion, could break the dam locally, that is within a particular society, and a flood of conversions ensue as the message spread by example through the circuit.

It has been said that the revivals of the 'burned-over' district of New York State in the 1830s and 1840s:

... did not customarily bring outsiders into the church so much as they promoted the hopeful onlookers to the sanctity of church membership. Most of the persons usually described by Baptist and Presbyterian clergymen as irreligious, immoral or profane went to church regularly and expected at some future time to experience conversion during a revival. [34]

If this has any relevance to explanations of Cornish revivalism, then the evidence needs to demonstrate several things. Firstly, that revival converts did come predominantly from this age group; secondly that a fair percentage came from Methodist families and thirdly that prior to a revival there was as feeling of the need for one on the part of older established members. The converts taken during the Great Revival of 1814 are described as young in a range of published and unpublished sources:

The subjects of this work are various: though perhaps the greatest number are young persons of both sexes, from about fourteen to twenty-eight years of age, and of the labouring classes in society. [35]

A large proportion of the new converts consisted of young people: [36]

At the latter mine are about 800 labourers, at the surface (male and female) chiefly young people, where the torrent bore down everything that stood in its way. [37]

Most of the converts at the revival of 1825 were also said to be young people, 'some even so, young as ten or twelve years of age'. [38]   At Truro in the revival of 1847 it was observed of the converts:

Generally speaking, they were young persons between fifteen and thirty years of age. Comparatively few older than thirty years were among the number…

and that:

…although some notoriously wicked and profligate persons have been awakened and renewed, by far the largest portion of the new converts consists of young persons, previously steady in their habits, regular members of the Wesleyan congregation in this town, and many of them children of officers and others belonging to the church. [40]

A similar tendency was observed at St Just in 1831:

In fact it may be conjectured that a large number of the converts of revivals consist of well-disposed persons upon whose minds the Spirit of God has long been operating and who were only waiting the guiding hand of Christian sympathy to become decidedly religious. [40]

Colls has noted a second age cohort as disproportionately represented. This was married people aged 45 upwards. I have not been able to check this for Cornwall, but it could possibly be linked to the re-conversion of 'backsliders', a phenomenon often commented on, for example in the 1824 revival in Redruth, the majority of converts made in the early days were said to have been backsliders. [41]

As well as testifying to the general youth of the converts, the evidence also points to a preceding period of expectation. Of the 'Great Revival' of 1814 it was observed:

...it came not without observation. Indeed for some considerable time past our friends were led to pray earnestly and in faith for a revival of God's work among us, and they felt encouragement by the addition of some members to the classes, by the increasing numbers of our stated hearers, and by the solemn attention which marked all our assemblies. [42]

Prior to its breaking out, 'more than usual seriousness was perceptible among the people and their assemblies were characterised by great solemnity'. [43] Shortly before the revival of 1831-1832, 'a spirit of expectation appeared to come upon the minds of the people'. [44] Once a revival had broken out, the neighbouring societies were naturally put into a state of expectation that they would soon experience it for themselves, or else a state of anxiety that they would not. Either way the necessary emotional state was attained. A miner later recalled of the revival of 1856:

...hearing of revivals around us, and feeling the want of one for ourselves and the people, we agreed three weeks ago, to have special services. We kept them on the first week without any apparent result, and some said, "There will be no revival at Bolingy, they are too dead etc". But God had put it into the hearts of the people to pray and he, by his spirit can quicken, - Blessed be his name! There was more of divine influence in one evening...[and then] it went through the meeting like fire. [45]

At Truro in late 1846, the need to share in a revival was similarly felt:

It was unanimously agreed that the leaders should meet together at half-past five every Sunday evening, to intercede with God for his blessing upon the preaching of the Gospel, and especially on the Sabbath evening service. On the following Sunday this resolution was put into practice, and the spirit of grace and of supplications was abundantly vouchsafed to the brethren present. An unusual degree of life and power attended the preaching of the word, and we were led to hope for better things. [46]

The phenomena of fainting, shrieks and uncontrollable depression which characterised revivals were in part at least produced by a style of preaching which often did amount to the 'terrorism' claimed by Lecky and Southey. [47] A private Methodist letter informs of:

Stout hearted men from the mines come to the prayer meetings and with tears streaming over their faces and in great agony they fall down on their knees and wrestle till they have found mercy. [48]

Although there is a tendency on the part of later Methodist historians to play this down, contemporaries made no bones over accepting this. George Smith, the movement's first full historian, who had experience of Cornish revivals, had no doubts when writing in 1888:

We can only expect as a general rule, to find those extraordinary displays of grace accompanying a clear, distinct and faithful preaching of Gospel truth. We may say even more than this; we have seldom ever seen these signs follow any preaching in which the great practical truths bearing on human salvation - such as men's danger through the guilt of sin, the necessity of instant repentance, justification by faith alone in the atonement of Christ, the privilege and duty of personal holiness, and the like - have not been made exceedingly prominent. [49]

He continued with the observation that the awakened sinner 'trembling in agony' beneath God's frown, could hardly be expected to control his emotions. During the 1814 revival some were said to have been, 'convinced that they are sinful, perishing, helpless creatures…' and to have been 'driven to the throne of mercy by terror'. A witness declared the best impression of this revival he could give was of 'a shipwreck where all are certain of being swallowed up in the waves'. [50]

In 1846 a writer to the evangelical magazine the *Cornish Banner,* faced up to the charges of impropriety which were being levied against revivals concluded:

> *Men possess feeling as well as intellect, and should be judged accordingly. Tell a man that he is in danger every hour of being dragged his beloved wife and children by the officers of the law to be cast into prison and is he not excited? Nor would any Christian think his excitement out of place, but on the contrary would be shocked to perceive apathy under such affecting circumstances. And will he have a man told solemnly and authoritively that he is a rebel against God, and every moment in danger of being cast into the lake which burns with fire and brimstone, and not excited? What! Must a wretched sinner see his sin in its deepest hues, with all its circumstances of aggravation, and his immortal soul on the crumbling verge of Hell and not be excited?* [51]

What is being suggested here is that to a marked extent, revivalism operated in the space between the fully committed membership and those attached but not set signed up for God, rather than in that between the membership and the more distanced community. As early as 1747, the curate at Redruth identified two sorts of Methodists: 'Those that have given in their names and belong to some society and constantly attend all their meetings; and those that attend only sometimes without regularly belonging to them'. [52] One young miner described how in the 1760s he was a firm follower yet never aspired to membership over a period of eight years:

> *I folied the preaching and meetings of the Methides, and Cep up privat prayr. And sometimes in theas Upertuty (sic) I found it good to wait on the Lord, and allwais afraide to put my name among them, for fear I went astray, and for fear I should bring a bad name on the good Coase, for I enjoid every priviledge Among them; and thear rested sining and repenting.* [53]

Samuel Drew, who was born in 1765, recalled that although in his youth he, 'had been in the habit' of attending chapel, yet he had, 'very little serious feeling, and no intention of joining the Methodist body'. [54]

Sometimes this space was within the family. William Carvosso, known as the 'Good Carvosso' records that he 'began to feel a particular concern for the salvation' of his son:

> *His life was quite moral; I could not reprove him for any outward sin. In his leisure hours his delight was in studying different branches of useful knowledge, but this though good in its place, was not religion.* [55]

If it is accepted that an inbuilt necessity for periodic revival can be characteristic of some kinds of religious communities, then actual timing might be attributable to any of a number of things. The 1826 revival at Mousehole broke out at a time when there had been no fish caught for sometime. That of 1848, like that of 1831-1832 was at least intensified by outbreaks of cholera:

> *About this time mighty wonders were wrought by the Holy Ghost. A revival broke out which swayed the people through several circuits with extraordinary power. There had been much prayer and much general preparedness; but the approach of pestilence brought things to a point. A few fatal cases occurred at Illogan, Redruth and at Camborne. The dread name of Cholera seemed to awake the people like the trumpet of doom. Anxiety became deep and general. In many places, such numbers flocked at all hours to the chapels, that their doors could not be closed for days together.* [56]

It should be noted, however that the writer, a Methodist minister, informs of a 'general state of preparedness', existing before the Cholera struck, and in fact a revival had already broken out in Truro ten miles distant before there was any fear of pestilence.

Nor should the fact that periodic revivals provided exciting breaks in the ordinary routines of life be ignored, however serious their purpose. One minister observed that even during the revival of 1814, his Cornish congregation observed some gravity in their conduct:

> *Notwithstanding some disorder and extravagance...there was none of that Ranterism and false fire which have followed the revivals in Yorkshire, Notting-hamshire, Lancashire, Derbyshire etc.*

This minister had no fondness for the Cornish Methodists whom he found as pious as any others, but 'less social, friendly and affectionate'. [57] More generally accounts testify to a high level of excitement. Indeed when William Clowes, the national Primitive Methodist leader, preached in a mining village on a visit to Cornwall in 1825, the 'Ranter' was out-ranted by a group of locals from another Methodist division, the Bible Christians, or Bryanites, as they were more often known:

...several of Mr O'Brien's people were present in the worship to laugh and dance. I was grieved at their conduct, for I knew that many people, who had come to hear the preaching were disappointed by witnessing their noise and actions. [58]

The best-known of all local miner-preachers, Billy Bray, said of people who looked down on his enthusiastic raptures:

They say that there is no need for as much to do as to lepe and dance and make so much noise for the Lord is not deaf, and he knaw harts, and you must know that Devil is not deaf neither and yet his sarvantes make a great noise. [59]

A minister, who had been appointed to West Cornwall in the 1840s recalled of the miners:

They could hardly have too many meetings, and in their meetings shouting and ecstasies were rather the rule than the exception. They had given up the public-house - they had now something better to cheer them than dreams of smuggled spirits -they felt no need and had no thought of theatre or dancing room. All the relief, the refreshment, the congenial excitement of their underground life, they found in the preaching house or in the class-room. There they let themselves go; they shouted, they wept, they groaned, they not seldom laughed aloud with a laugh of intense excitement, a wonderful laugh. [60]

It has been noted that during revivals the old heavy hymns of Charles Wesley could give way to livelier compositions:

> *My Saviour's name I gladly sing,*
> *Who is my Prophet, Priest and King;*

Wher'er I go His name I'll bless;
And praise him all we Methodists.
For Methodist is my name,
I hope to live and die the same,
For pure religion doth increase
And turn the World to Methodist.

That was from 1814. Others could be more millenarial:

King Jesus is riding the white horse afore,
His watchmen close after, the trumpets do roar,
Some shouting, some singing, 'Salvation!' they cry;
In the strength of King Jesus all hell we defy.
The great giant Goliath and Apollyon shall fall,
With the Sword of the Spirit we'll conquer them all;
We'll leave no opposers alive in the field,
And the strength of King Jesus will force them to yield. [61]

If the weekly round of meetings and services was capable of generating emotional excitement, then the great revivals punctuated lives with happenings of greater intensity, wider participation and larger audiences. They had their spectators as well as their participants. One witness of 1814 describes children standing on seats to get a better view. [62] Had they been witnessing one which broke out in a Penwith village in 1882, a time by when as the observer admitted, revivals were, 'less common than formerly', they would have seen excitement indeed:

A young man...fell to his knees and began to hammer the pew with his hands in a violent way, in such a violent way indeed that his hands began to bleed and by and by his face was smeared with the blood. Then swift as a gunshot he rose and darted out of the chapel. In a few minutes he came back, fell on his knees on the sanded floor in front of the little pulpit, shrieked for mercy in a way to alarm sensitive souls. He was soon on his feet again: he had got the blessing; with haste and energy he embraced and kissed his sister (who forthwith burst into tears) and a few other females who were not his sisters. [63]

West Cornwall, even more than Wales was the land of revivals. It directly contradicts Hempton's assertion that by 1820 Wesleyan Methodism had purged itself of revivalism along with radicalism, for it is hard to detect in this respect any distinction between the parent body and its nineteenth century off-shoots. Colls seems to associate the recurrent revivalism of the North East in the nineteenth century specifically with the Primitive Methodists. This was not the case in Cornwall. During a revival in Bodmin in 1835 it was the Wesleyan chapel which was thrown open for a fortnight, with constant prayer meetings from five to seven-thirty in the morning and beginning again at half past seven in the evening continuing until one or two in the morning. [64] What is being suggested here, is that recurrent revivalism in Cornwall is best understood in terms of a dynamic internal to the local religious culture. To do this it has been necessary to look intensely at a particular historical community. However, while there may have been some 'peculiarities' distinguishing Cornwall from other areas, in general these are matters of degree. In communities in which Methodism, generally or in the shape of one of its splinter sects, had reached a certain level of strength, so that it has been made by its adherents into a Volkskirche, whatever the antagonistic sentiments of a distant national leadership, some such dynamic was likely to be at work.

1 E. P. Thompson, 'The Transforming Power of the Cross', Chapter 11 of *The Making of the English Working Class*, first published in 1963. The argument can be placed in the wider context of the debate over the well-known 'Halévy thesis' that Methodism was an effective inhibition on revolution in Britain first put forward by the great French historian in 1906. D. Hempton, *Methodism and Politics in British Society 1750-1850*, 1987, pp. 11-12, 226, 229, 236.

2 A. Gilbert, 'Religion and Political Stability in Early Industrial England', P. O'Brien and R. Quinault (eds), *The Industrial Revolution and British Society*, Cambridge, 1993, p. 91.

3 R. Colls, *The Pitmen of the Northern Coalfield: Work, Culture and Protest, 1790-1850*, Manchester, 1987, pp. 118-189; J. Epstein, 'Some Organisational and Cultural Aspects of the Chartist Movement in Nottingham' in J. Epstein and D. Thompson (eds.), *The Chartist Experience. Studies in Working-Class Radicalism 1830-1860*, 1982, pp. 249-255.

4 For an argument that Methodism generally worked against radicalism and trade unionism among the Cornish miners see: J. Rule, 'A Configuration of Quietism? Attitudes towards Trade Unions and Chartism among Cornish Miners', *Tijdschrift voor sociale geschiedenis*, xviii, 2/3, 1992, pp. 257-260; Republished in this volume, see Chapter 10.

5 J. Baxter, 'The Great Yorkshire Revival 1792-6: A Study of Mass Revival among the Methodists', in *A Sociological Yearbook of Religion in Britain*, No. 7, 1974, p. 68. For Methodist attitudes in the era of the revolutionary wars see also: R. Wells, 'English Society and Revolutionary Politics in the 1790s: The Case for Insurrection', in M. Philip (ed.), *The French Revolution and British Popular Politics*, Cambridge, 1991, pp. 195-203.

6 Report of the Royal Commission on Child Employment, *British Parliamentary Papers*, 1842, XVI, Minutes of Evidence, p. 760; *Old Cornwall*, V, Part 12, 1961, p. 519.

7 T. Shaw, *History of Cornish Methodism*, Truro, 1967, p. 96.

8 ibid, pp. 81-82.

9 ibid, p. 78.

10 Quoted in R. Currie, *Methodism Divided*, 1968, pp. 30-31; Methodist Archives, John Rylands Library, Manchester, Fletcher-Tooth Correspondence, C. Sleep to Mrs Tooth, 4 April 1842 and 30 March 1831.

11 D. Luker, 'Revivalism in Theory and Practice: The Case of Cornish Methodism', in *Journal of Ecclesiastical History*, XXXVII, (4), 1986, pp. 610, 605; W. Ward, 'The Religion of the People and the Problem of Control, 1790-1830', in *Studies in Church History*, VIII, Popular Belief and Practice, Cambridge, 1972, pp. 245-146. In this volume Ward stresses the distinctiveness of Cornwall in persisting in extreme revivalism within Wesleyan Methodism: 'the Cornish people under native impulses were making Methodism a popular establishment, a Volkskirche without parallel in any comparable part of England'. Ward also suggests that the local leaders of Wesleyanism gained, 'an ascendancy which did not bend easily to preachers' pressure'.

12 *Cornwall Gazette*, 23 April 1831.

13 J. Probert, *The Sociology of Cornish Methodism*, Redruth, 1964, p. 40.

14 Figures from Wesleyan Conference Minutes.

15 'Memoir of Mr Rankin', *Methodist Magazine*, 1811, p. 369.

16 R. Treffry, *Memoir of Mr John Edwards Tresize*, 1837, pp.35-36.

17 ibid, pp. 84-85.

18 ibid, p. 91.

19 Fletcher-Tooth Correspondence, C. Sleep to Mrs Tooth, St Agnes, 30 March 1831.

20 Anon, *An Account of the Remarkable Revival of the Work of God in Cornwall*, Dublin, 1814, pp. 12.

21 G. Smith, *History of Wesleyan Methodism*, Vol. 2, 1888, p. 551.

22 Anon, *Account of the Remarkable Revival*, pp. 5-6.

23 A. Hamilton Jenkin, *News from Cornwall*, Bath, 1951, p. 179.

24 Fletcher-Tooth correspondence, George Russell to Issac Clayton, Helston, 7 July 1815.

25 J. Drew, Samuel Drew, M.A., *The Self-Taught Cornishman*, 1861, pp. 271-272.

26 *Weekly Record of the Temperance Movement*, 25 Oct 1856, p. 250.

27 R. Colls, *Pitmen of the Northern Coalfield*, p. 163.

28 *Letters of John Wesley*, Vol. VII, (ed.), J. Telford, 1931, p. 132.

29 The sudden rise in cereal prices in May 1847, which precipitated the food riots of that year happened some weeks after the revival first broke out. However there had been an upward trend in prices over several weeks, so a link cannot be completely ruled out. For the chronology of food rioting in Cornwall see J. Rule, 'Some social aspects of the industrial revolution in Cornwall' in R. Burt, (ed.), *Industry and Society in the South West*, Exeter, 1970, pp. 86-106.

30 Thompson himself accepted that the Cornish revivals had no connection one way or another with political radicalism. See E. P. Thompson, *The Making of the English Working Class*, 1968, p. 920. That is not to say that there were not some Cornish Jacobins, but there is no evidence of a significant impact being made on the miners. Indeed a letter from Truro to the London Corresponding Society gives a striking instance of the lack of interest shown by a crowd of rioting miners: 'I walked by some of them with a few other citizens. Tho' we declared that we were their friends, yet their jealousy and hatred rose to such a height that they threatened us with instant death'. British Library, Add. MSS, Minute Book of the London Corresponding Society, from Truro, 6 April 1796.

31 As well as Colls, for the long history of 'industrial society' on the northern coalfield see D. Levine and K. Wrightson, *The Making of an Industrial Society: Whickham 1560-1765*, Oxford, 1991.

32 R. Colls, *Pitmen of the Northern Coalfield*, p. 155. The major flooding at East Wheal Rose which drowned forty miners took place on 9 July 1846, while the revival of 1847 broke out in the April of that year in the nearby Truro circuit. This gap seems too long for a link.

33 D, Luker, 'Revivalism in Theory and Practice' also argues for an internal dynamic. He does not however take notice of the importance of the age of new converts. Despite having read my 1971 thesis, 'The Labouring Miner in Cornwall c.1740-1870', University of Warwick, Ph.D, 1971, he notes it only in the context of food rioting, surprisingly not advising his readers that it devoted more than a hundred pages to Methodism, including an attempt to explain revivalism.

34 W. Cross, *The Burned-over District*, New York, 1950, p. 41.

35 Anon, *Account of the Remarkable Revival*, p. 11.

36 See above endnote 24.

37 See above endnote 23.

38 Anon, *Letters from West Cornwall*, 1826, p. 74.

39 *Cornish Banner*, 1847, p. 306.

40 R. Treffry, *Memoir of Mr John Edwards Tresize*, p. 87.

41 Methodist Archives, Fletcher-Tooth Correspondence. John Radford to Mrs Tooth, 30 January 1824.

42 Anon, *Account of the Remarkable Revival*, p. 9.

43 G. Smith, *History of Wesleyan Methodism*, pp. 550-551.

44 R. Treffry, *Memoir*, p. 87.

45 W. Tyack, *The Miner of Perranzabuloe*, 1866, p. 81.

46 *Cornish Banner*, 1846, p. 305.

47 Lecky described Methodism thus: 'a more appalling system of religious terrorism, one more fitted to unhinge a tottering intellect and to darken and embitter a sensitive nature has seldom existed'. W. Lecky, *History of England in the Eighteenth Century*, Volume III, 1882, p. 77; see also the observations made throughout Robert Southey, *The Life of Wesley*, (ed.), Atkinson, 1893.

48 Methodist Archives, Fletcher-Tooth Correspondence, Sleep to Mrs Tooth, Helston, 4 April 1842.

49 G. Smith, *History of Wesleyan Methodism*, pp. 604, 607.

50 Anon, *Account of the Remarkable Revival*, p. 12.

51 *Cornish Banner*, 1846, p. 186.

52 J. Probert, *Methodism in Redruth until the death of John Wesley*, Redruth, n.d., p. 4.

53 P. Burall, *Cornwall to America in 1783*, (rep 1932), p. 5.

54 J. Drew, *Samuel Drew*, p. 58.

55 B. Carvosso, *A Memoir of Mr William Carvosso*, 1837, pp. 46-47.

56 ibid, pp. 258-259; S. Coley, *The Life of the Reverend Thomas Collins*, 1871, pp. 302-303.

57 See above endnote 24.

58 T. Shaw, *The Bible Christians*, 1965, pp. 85-86.

59 Methodist Archives, MSS Journal of Billy Bray.

60 J. Rigg, *Wesleyan Methodist Reminiscences Sixty Years Ago*, 1904, pp. 67-68. But note the comment of a minister during a local revival at Perranwell in 1838: '…we had a good time; and some were distressed in mind', H. Williams, *The Life of the Reverend Joseph Wood*, 1871, p. 117.

61 T. Shaw, *History of Cornish Methodism*, p. 67.

62 ibid, p. 65.

63 J. Vickers, (ed.), *New History of the Methodist Church in Great Britain*, Volume IV: Documents and Sources, 1988, p. 559.

64 *Cornish Guardian*, 20 March 1835.

Methodism, Popular Beliefs and Village Culture in Cornwall 1800-1850

The investigation of the social impact of popular religion needs to be localized. Not only did the level of religious observance in nineteenth century England vary significantly from one region to another, but the distribution of the various churches and sects followed different patterns. Regional diversity means that one must treat with caution all attempts to write generally of the influence of religion on the working class. In a critique of recent trends in the history of popular leisure it was suggested that in their attempts to reform traditional recreations evangelicals or temperance reformers were 'purveyors of minority causes'.[1] An historian of the metropolis might well have found that to have been the case, but it would be misleading to approach the social history of many smaller and different kinds of community from the same premise. In the mining villages of Durham or Cornwall, Methodists of one kind or another could often claim majority support, at least so far as influence went if not membership.

The miners of Cornwall formed an occupational community to which Methodism came early and prospered greatly. By the early nineteenth century West Cornwall had become one of the movement's greatest strongholds. By Methodism we mean to embrace both the Wesleyans and the various splits and offshoots from the parent body, giving, by 1851, 16,691 members of whom just under two-thirds lived in the Western mining parts. On Census Sunday in that year 113,510 attendances were recorded at the various connexional chapels and churches. Membership statistics are not convertible by some magic multiplier into a measurement of influence, nor are the badly collected ones of attendance in 1851. They do, however, strongly support the impression of a very strong influence that emerges from a large number of sources. In 1842 Charles Barham produced the most detailed and fully researched survey of the early Victorian mining population we have. He found that the Methodist miners formed a class 'so numerous that its qualities become prominent features of the whole body when it is compared with other communities'.[2] The Anglican clergy would certainly have agreed. 'We have lost the people', complained a vicar in 1833, 'The religion of the mass is become Wesleyan Methodism.' Another, high church, explained his very modest success to Dr Pusey by stressing the difficulties of working in a county, 'wholly given up to dissent and perversity', where there was, 'Methodism in every house'. [3] Two specific aspects of Methodism's influence on the life of the mining communities will be considered in this article. The first is its impact on popular pastimes and the second will be its relationship to popular beliefs. In the first of these areas it will be argued that the temperance and teetotal movements can be viewed in Cornwall as a 'religious' force extending and amplifying already well-established Methodist sanctions. Traditional work in the history of leisure was criticized by Gareth Stedman Jones for concentrating too much on the role of such agencies and thereby producing a misleading orthodoxy. This stresses the advance of a methodical capitalist rationality and the disappearance or decline of traditional recreational forms. Lurking behind this approach he sees the sociologist's concept of social control; a concept which he considers of dubious value. In stressing the concern of the upper and middle classes to impose rational recreation on the working class as part of the process of incorporating it into the capitalist scheme of things, historians of leisure have got things out of perspective. By focusing upon the reforming attempts of evangelicals, Methodists, civic élites and capitalist employers, they have based their analysis only on a reading of the case for the prosecution. [4]

Stedman Jones's strictures are important qualifications and perhaps have already had a deserved modifying effect on the subject. Some recent work shows a degree of dissatisfaction with the simple idea of a successful attack on traditional recreational forms and stresses that the old working class leisure culture may not only have persisted but even expanded during the first half of the nineteenth century. The baby need not, however, be discarded with the bathwater. If historians have put evangelicals, temperance reformers, Methodists, magistrates, the 'new' police and capitalist employers into a 'sharply delineated foreground' perhaps that is where they should be put. The central issue in the history of recreation during this period is the attempt to control and reshape the leisure activities of the working class. Given the stage of development of the entrepreneurial capitalist economy there is no historical mystery

about this. Nor is there any need to employ a metaphor of the 'invisible hand' to explain why second-line forces such as Methodism or temperance reform fought what was fundamentally the cause of capitalist
employers. In the first place such groups were not wholly separable. In
the second, employers' objectives and those motivations of groups like
Methodists meshed with and reinforced each other well enough without
the need to look for hidden string pulling or formal alliance. Confrontation of religion with 'revelry' is not just part of the history of popular recreation; it is central to the understanding of the social history of religion
in industrializing Britain. Dr Harrison has pointed out that it was over
attempts to dominate popular leisure that the churches and the working
classes came most frequently into contact in the nineteenth century.

*Nineteenth century Christians deplored that recreational complex of be-
havior which included gambling, adultery, drinking, cruel sports and Sabbath
breaking and blasphemy - all of which took place together at the race-course, the
drinking place, the theatre, the 'feast' and the fair.* [5]

One difficulty with the 'social control' concept is that it is suggestive
of the imposition of new forms of behavior upon the working class by
external forces. This is evidently the case with capitalist employers and
order-conscious magistrates, but it cannot be wholly so of popular religious movements, for both Methodism and teetotalism elicited significant working-class participation and activity. For all the conservatism of
the Methodist 'establishment' and the 'respectability' of its town-chapel
elites, in the villages Methodism in its Wesleyan, Primitive and Bible
Christian forms had become internalized to a great degree by the beginning of the nineteenth century. In some villages chapel members formed
a clear majority of the mining population.

Wesley's Journal reveals the extent to which, from its earliest days,
Methodism came into conflict with traditional uses of leisure time. He
recorded his disgust at the 'savage ignorance and wickedness' of colliers near Newcastle in 1743 who assembled on Sundays to 'dance, fight,
curse and swear, and play at chuck ball, span farthing, or whatever came
next to hand'. In the town itself he set out to confront the 'crowds of

poor wretches' who passed their Sundays in 'sauntering to and fro on the Sandhill'. In Ireland he outfaced a company of revelers and dancers who had taken over his usual preaching place. At Otiey in 1766 he made his visit on the local feast day and found a town gone mad in 'noise, hurry, drunkenness, rioting, confusion' to the 'shame of a Christian country'. [6] The impact of Methodism on traditional pastimes in Cornwall was reinforced from the late 1830s by the temperance and teetotal movements. Harrison has shown the reluctance of church leaders including the Wesleyans, to become involved with them, but official detachment was not always followed. In Cornwall an uneasy tolerance of teetotal meetings was ended by a Conference ban on their being held in Wesleyan chapels. The immediate reaction was the secession of 250 members to form the separate Teetotal Wesleyan Methodists. Joined by teetotallers from neighbouring places, they numbered 600 by 1842. Teetotallers could reasonably hope for success in a country, which in 1834 had had by far the biggest membership per thousand of the British and Foreign Temperance Society of any county. [7]

Was there a connection between termperance and teetotal success and the pre-existing strength of Methodism? To many working class Methodists, signing the 'pledge' was an extension of their existing attitude towards strong drink rather than a new departure. The 'saved' drunkards may have been the spectacular signatories, but that does not make them typical. James Teare met with a ready-made response when he first visited Cornwall in January 1838. At his first meeting 150 persons signed, and through 1838 to 1839 his success increased. By February 1839 the Ludgvan society was claiming 800 members out of a population of 2,500. By May the 2,700 members of St Ives were equal to half of the town's population. Similar successes came in towns and villages all over West Cornwall. Dr Harrison had suggested that the 'polarization' of pub and temperance society was a predominantly urban phenomenon that spread later to the villages. If this was true of agricultural villages it was not so of Cornish mining ones. John Wesley had remarked of the Redruth Methodists as early as 1788 that they were very willing to 'govern the preachers', a view which was echoed in 1909 when a minister complained that whereas in the towns the minister ruled, 'in the villages the chapel belongs to the people and the people take over the minister as a newcomer attached to them'. The willingness of the local preachers and class leaders to involve themselves in the temperance and teetotal movements was evident, whatever the 'official' views of ministers and church establishment might be. Examples abound in the teetotal newspapers: at St Buryan in 1839 six out of eight class leaders had joined; at Gwennap eighteen and at Germoe the Wesleyan local preachers were reported to have taken up the cause in 'right good earnest'.[8]

The peak of the teetotal agitation in 1839 coincided with the visit to the mining districts of the Chartist missionaries Abraham Duncan and Robert Lowery. They identified teetotalism closely with Methodism as a common enemy. 'The tee-totallers and the Methodists have monopolized the speakers, and their leaders are against us', grumbled Lowery. Duncan remarked that the Methodists had Cornwall 'divided into districts'. 'The tee-totallers keep their division of territory. Between the religious and the tee-total agitation, a considerable amount of enterprise and talent is absorbed. He declared 'Pharisaical cant' omnipotent in every teetotal committee. [9] The link was strengthened by the fact that, in Cornwall, the Bible Christians (Bryanites) were second only to the Wesleyans in number and they were notable enthusiasts for total abstinence. While we can accept Professor Bailey's view that by the 1840s the single most important agency of recreational improvement was the rising Temperance movement, we need to emphasize that in Cornwall by this time, it reinforced and amplified long-standing sanctions and pressures. [10]

Behind the changing pattern of recreations in eighteenth and nineteenth century Cornwall can be discerned pressures broadly divisible into two main categories: the effects of the capitalistic transformation of the mining industry on the amount of leisure time available to miners, and secondly, those pressures which can for convenience be considered as 'evangelical'. This category covers those who condemned the leisure activities of the miners on the grounds of their inhumanity, inherent brutality or general unspecified sinfulness. Such moral reformers usually aimed at substituting 'improving' uses of leisure time for traditional rough ones accordingly they must be considered a counter-attractive as well as a counteractive force. From the mid-eighteenth century humane clergymen had attacked the brutality in many of the amusements of the poor and had been concerned to control the drunkenness, which was associated with popular festivities. The Methodists went further: Their puritanical distrust of enjoyment led them to regard secular amusement as inherently sinful, while their equally rigid abhorrence of idleness made them of similar mind to those employers who for their own reasons condemned time-wasting.

Cornish miners enjoyed many holidays in the eighteenth century that were gradually eroded in the first half of the nineteenth. Holidays not associated with any particular custom were occasions for gatherings at which, apart from sideshows, beer-tents and dancing, the miners indulged in their traditional sports of hurling and wrestling. [11] By the mid-eighteenth century accusations that such gatherings had become characterized by excessive drinking, brawling and rowdyism were frequently leveled. Traditional sports could be arranged for any holiday, but were especially associated with parish feasts. Borlase wrote in 1758:

Every parish has its annual feast, and at such time (however poor at other times of the year) everyone will make a shift to entertain his friends and relations on the Sunday, and on the Monday and Tuesday all business is suspended, and the young men assemble and hurl or wrestle in some part of the parish of the most public resort. [12]

Hurling was not like the modern Irish version, but a traditional form of football played between teams of indeterminate size over several miles of country. Matches were usually promoted by local gentry who rewarded the victors and entertained the players to beer. The object was to carry the silver-encased ball to the goal, often a gentleman's house, in the face of the opposing side seeking to capture it and carry it to their goal several miles in the opposite direction. Sides could number several hundred and contests were rough and bloody:

When this sort of hurling is over, you shall see the Hurlers retire as from a pitched battle, with bloody noses, wounds and bruises and some broken and disjointed limbs, which are all deemed fair play without ever consulting an Attorney, Coroner, or petty lawyer about the matter'. [13]

By the time Borlase wrote in 1758 the game was largely confined to matches between teams from the same parish, inter-parish matches having shown a tendency to develop into local wars. [14]

Wrestling was probably a more frequently indulged pastime. It needed fewer participants and less time and space. In the eighteenth century it was also promoted by gentry who offered prizes and bet on results. Ad hoc contests frequently took place outside inns. The nature of the sport ensured its survival longer than hurling, which by the end of the eighteenth century was claimed to have become almost extinct. Although the same thing was still being said in 1824, Germoe feast in 1822 seems to have been the last at which it was a central feature of the programme. [15] Primarily a holiday sport, it declined because the occasions for its holding were being eroded. This decline was certainly hastened by the reluctance of a more genteel gentry to promote what Defoe had described as a game fit only for barbarians. Polwhele, a clerical magistrate writing in the early nineteenth century, presented a similar explanation.

The discontinuance in frequency of such sports, indeed among the common people, is chiefly to be attributed to a change in the habits and manners of their superiors. In Carew's time [c. 1600] gentlemen used to entertain a numerous peasantry at their mansions and castles in celebration of the two great festivals, or the parish feast or harvest home; when at the same time that our halls re-echoed to the voice of festal merriment, our lawns and downs and woodlands were enlivened by the shouts of wrestling and of hurling. Hospitality is now banished from among us: and so are its attendant sports. [16]

Anglican clergymen did to a degree confront the conduct of popular amusements. William Temple at St Gluvias preached against bull-baiting there in 1796. Borlase of Ludgvan sorrowed that immoderate 'frolicking and immoderate drinking' had made the parish feasts the target of those who would not distinguish between the institution and the 'disorderly observation of it'. The vicar of St Erme was praised for his preaching against wrestling, hurling and other 'robust exercises' which in the 1750s had characterised the parish feast. [17] Methodists altered the tone of condemnation. The sports themselves in their minds had an inherent sinfulness. William Carvosso, a prominent local class-leader, wrote of his youth: 'I was borne down by the prevailing sins of the age; such as cock-fighting, wrestling, card-playing; and Sabbath breaking. Paying tribute to Wesley, a writer in 1814 listed wrestling and hurling along with drunkenness as the vices of the Cornish, while the broadsheet confessions of James Eddy, hanged at Bodmin in 1827 for a rape and robbery he denied, explains that he got into bad habits in his youth 'smuggling, Sabbath breaking, adultery, drinking, pilfering, gaming, wrestling etc. and thus got a bad name'. [18] From their first footholds in the county the Wesleys had condemned wrestling. Charles Wesley noted as early as his second visit in 1744 that the Gwennap men had been unable to raise men enough for a wrestling match, 'all the Gwennap men being struck off the devil's list, and found wrestling against him not for him'. [19] Claims for Methodist success in transforming the behavior of the miners were put forward regularly by the early years of the nineteenth century. In 1802 a writer on the decline of wrestling: 'every old inhabitant of this county can tell you how very much it has declined', argued that although the magistracy had done much to control `assemblages of riot and murder', [20] the contribution of the Methodists had been a substantial one. Six years later an Anglican clergyman gave them the larger share of the credit for the fact that 'desperate wrestling matches, and inhuman cockfights, and riotous revelings' were becoming rarer. [21]

The tone of Methodist condemnation was strong. An advertisement in the *West Briton* in 1821, inserted to dissuade match promoters from endangering the souls of miners, claimed that if converted miners were asked why they did not attend, they would reply that it was because of the commandment: 'Whether ye eat or drink, or whatsoever ye do, do all to the glory of God'. A letter in 1829 asked the miners:

Why do you not go to the wrestling? For eight good reasons. Because I can employ my time better. Because it is throwing my money away. Because I wish not to be seen in bad company. Because I would not encourage idleness, folly and vice. Because I should set a bad example. Because God has forbidden it. 'Abstain from all appearance of evil'. Because I must soon die. [22]

Although regularly denounced from the pulpit, wrestling did survive, but the decline of open patronage drove it into closer alliance with the publicans. [23] Inns and beer shops continued to play a significant role in the recreational life of many miners. It was noted in 1839 that no sooner did mining operations commence in a district than a beer shop was opened to induce the 'honest but thoughtless' miner to spend his money by drawing him into 'haunts of vice', pubs offering skittles, quoits and pitch and toss. Paydays, it was complained, were frequently spent in the beer shops in weekend-long celebrations, and work itself offered customary opportunities for drinking. When a boy first took on a man's work a treat was expected and promotion to sump-man, pit-man or captain carried the like obligation. [24] The view that the second quarter of the nineteenth century was 'bleak age' before a post-1850 reconstruction of popular leisure needs qualification. As Dr Cunningham has pointed out, there were respects in which it was rather a period of vigorous growth of popular leisure.[25] Robert Storch has suggested that one reason that temperance reformers such as Joseph Livesey saw a desperate need for the 'moral improvement' of the masses was the real profusion of pub-centred gambling and sporting activities in early Victorian cities. If there had not been such a variety of other popular indulgences, the counter-attractive side of temperance reform would not have needed so much emphasis.[26] The Reverend Thomas Collins took the children of the Camborne Wesleyan Sunday School on a seaside trip in 1849 to give them pleasure and to remove them from the influence of a 'noisy, revelling' fair. He even composed a special hymn for the occasion:

> We rejoice and, and we have reason
> Though we don't attend the fair;
> Better spend the happy season
> Breathing in the fresh sea air
> Happy Children!
> What a number will be there!

To coincide with another fair he held special evening services to 'guard our young people'.[27] The annual tea-treat for Sunday scholars had become a widespread institution by the 1820s. Teas were followed by recitations of amazing length from prize scholars and there was much flag waving, banner carrying and processioning. In the early days the Methodists had represented a minority culture, distinguished from their neighbours by their attitudes and behavior. Their activities centred on the chapel with its services, revivals, meetings, love feasts, watch-nights and hymn singing. By the nineteenth century it had grown from a minority culture into one, which imparted generally observable traits to the mining community. With growing strength, confrontation between Methodists and 'revelers' became more frequent. Even before the end of the eighteenth century, Sithney Methodists were confident enough to try to drown the noise of the feast by singing psalms and were stoned for their pains. [28] By the early years of the nineteenth century Methodists were strong enough to move from their village strongholds into the towns and the fair as well as the feast became an area of confrontation. The Wesleyan minister at Camborne held services on the fairground in 1840. Nor did the annual games escape. At St Austell the Primitive Methodists held a camp meeting on the site on the Sunday before the games. They offered fervent prayer that God might stay 'the prevalence of vice, and abolish the Sabbath desecrating custom'. One of the intending umpires was actually converted and although the games were held, they were so in a more retired place on the outskirts of the town. [29]

The teetotallers especially used counter-attractive measures. Miners were marched around behind banners and bands, their thirsts quenched with gallons of weak tea and their need for excitement and involvement met by meetings dominated by the passionate oral rendering of hard-won struggles with temptation. The distance between the Methodists and the recreational patterns of the old popular culture widened as gentry patronage had given way to publican promotion. Opposition was now carried to the point of fanaticism. The abstainers' banner at a Penzance rally proclaimed simply: 'Eight thousand drunkards die annually and go to Hell'. [30]

Attempts had been made before to reform the drinking habits of the lower orders. A Society for the Suppression of Drunkenness had been formed at Redruth in 1805 to exert pressure on local officers of the peace to enforce laws against drunkenness and to offer rewards to informers.[31] But this was an attempt by the socially superior to enforce sobriety on their inferiors: Teetotalism enlisted the poor themselves in the campaign against the public house. As Dr Harrison pointed out:

Tee-totallers transformed temperance meetings from occasional gatherings of influential worthies into counter-attractive functions enabling working men to insulate themselves from public-house temptation. [32]

In this way a bond between the middle class and working class 'respectables' was consolidated. In 1838 the teetotallers held a grand field day at Redruth. Following a sermon in the market place the members marched behind a band through the streets with flags, ribbons and banners flying. They returned to the market place where about 300 took tea before leaving once again behind the band for the Methodist chapel where at a large meeting many new members were joined. [33] The observance of the annual feast at Ludgvan in 1839 was a major departure from precedent. It was celebrated by teetotallers who, after meeting in the church-town, marched three miles through the village. The local newspaper recalled the scene twelve months previously:

> ...the parish was one scene of revelry and drunkenness: and it seemed as if destruction had taken hold of the four corners of it. There were four public houses and twelve beer shops: and in these no less than £6000 was annually spent in intoxicating drinks. At present it is a rare tiling to see a man drunk, unless he comes from another parish. Not a quarter part of the money is spent on drink; and those who formerly wasted their time and their earnings in the ale-house, are found decently clothed, with their families in places of religious worship. [34]

The excitement of bands and processions, the encouragement of a sense of direct personal involvement and the invitation to the working man to be a hero (at least for the moment that he signed the pledge or testified to his salvation from drink) were designed to wean workers from traditional recreations and old patterns of living. A mile-long procession of Rechabites through Camborne and Redruth in 1841 was described by a local diarist as 'a very grand sight indeed'. He also commented that a wrestling held at the same time near the Brewery was 'very slightly attended'. [35] Two years later an even longer and more grand procession of Rechabites and teetotallers perambulated Redruth before assembling for an open-air meeting at Plainanguarry, literally 'playing place' in the Cornish language, that is a site for the holding of popular amusements from time immemorial, followed by tea in a local chapel. After the tea a crowded meeting completed a successful day. The diarist could not resist concluding his entry for that day by noting that a drunken miner returning from a spree on the mineral train fell off and had his hand cut off. [36]

A glance at the Whitsun weekend of 1844 is instructive on the extent to which the alternative provision of counter-attractions had succeeded in winning adherents. Whitsun was a traditional holiday period favoured in particular by traveling fairs. It is to be expected that teetotallers would have made a special effort during it. Truro fair was reported ill-attended in comparison with previous years. A local newspaper commented especially on the absence of young people noticeably of the mine girls who from 'time immemorial' had been accustomed to attend the fair in their 'ill-assorted dresses, in every variety of colour'. Camborne fair was also badly attended despite fine weather and as good a supply of amusements as usual. In contrast, the holier side did really well. At Redruth the Rechabites and teetotallers held a festival which was celebrated with 'more than usual gaiety', with large crowds thronging the streets until late evening. At Hayle the abstainers mustered a parade with three bands. [37]

By the early 1850s organized railway excursions added to the counter-attractions. One, in 1852, carrying the Camborne teetotallers to the sands of Hayle in 76 trucks, was celebrated in song:

> Steam is up and we are ready;
> See the engine puffing goes
> Keep your heads cool, and be steady
> Mind your cups and mind your clothes

Apprehension was in order, if a local news report is to be believed, for on the return journey the engine ran out of steam and the excursionists took the chance of raiding an orchard alongside the track. [38]

Building on pre-existing Methodist attitudes the teetotal movement may have had greater success in Cornwall among the miners than it had among most occupational groups. The tightness of the mining villages with those disproportionately large Methodist chapels that are still the visible reminders of a great culture influence suited the hold as well as the spread of religious movements. By 1864 an outsider could describe Cornish parish feasts as a 'sorry sight' where the offerings of drinking, sack races and donkey derbies had ceased to attract the mass of the people. He attributed this to the success of temperance in removing 'the great object of attraction':

The majority derives far more amusement at assisting in the numerous tea drinks connected with the Sunday Dissenting Schools. The drinks are also held on a variety of occasions, thus if a chapel has to be repaired, or a new one built, or a missionary meeting to be held, the same ceremony accompanies it.

Plain fare was compensated for by 'intellectual' plenty, for the speakers were many and their orations lengthy. [39] Others commented in similar vein. 'Wrestling is almost discontinued, except as a publican's speculation', remarked one, 'but the spirit of aggregation rather finds a vent in camp-meetings, temperance parties, and monster tea-drinkings'. [40] The assessment of success of religious and temperance reformers in their contest with 'revelry' must be impressionistic; influences of this kind cannot be measured easily. Probably the initial 'novelty' element of teetotalism wore off to an extent, and people went back to old ways to join again those who had never left them. It is not easy to judge how rapidly this happened, for as the novelty wore off so too did the inclination of the local press to report temperance activities. Perhaps we can balance the picture we have so far given with examples of revelers inflicting the bitter taste of failure on abstainers. In 1845 Thomas Trevaskis, a Bible Christian known as the 'Temperance Father of the West' was defeated by the forces of revelry at Padstow. In the previous year he had spoken against the oldest of all the Cornish festivals, the Padstow Hobby-horse. He had described its celebration as a scene of 'riot, debauchery and general licentiousness, a perfect nuisance to all the respectable inhabitants of the place', and backed his condemnation with the public offer to substitute a fat bullock to be roasted on the day for the next seven years:

To the Proprietors of the Hobby Horse of Padstow. This is to give notice that on or about the end of the month, I shall offer you the bullock, according to promise. It is for you to consult against that time, whether you will give up your vain practice of the Hobby for the more rational amusement of eating roast beef.

On the first day of May he drove his bullock into town. The people persisted in their preference for irrational amusement and, with a hail of stones, drove him out of town, bullock and all. [41]

Trevaskis was not the only Bible Christian to confront the celebrators of the 'hoss'. In 1846 some members of that sect bound for Canada as missionaries were much disturbed when some Padstow men among the crew rigged up their own 'hoss' from canvas. The rider and his helpers galloped about the deck in the time-honored tradition of the ceremony and endeavored to blacken the faces of all who had not prudently retired below decks. One of the missionaries stood his ground, but received a blackened face despite the poker, which he brandished in defiance of such satanic revelry. [42]

In 1843 the teetotal societies of East Cornwall had arranged a meeting on the slopes of Roughtor on the Bodmin Moor. Despite damp, misty weather 3,000 persons attended. The following year they tried to repeat their success. This time 10,000 attended, but the increase was not entirely accounted for by teetotallers, far from it. The publicans of the neighbouring parishes, who had been impressed with the size of the last crowd, seized the opportunity. They attracted many people by promising that they too would come to Roughtor with booths, stalls, donkey riding and other amusements. A day which was to have been a great demonstration of strength by the abstainers instead earned for itself the unlikely name for a teetotal rally of the 'Roughtor Revels'. It was small consolation that one of the publicans was subsequently fined for selling outside the area of his licence. [43]

Such setbacks show the incompleteness of teetotal success, but they should not be allowed to detract too much from the very real impact that the movement had. Many of the moral reformers may seem quaint; many of the incidents of confrontation amusing, but it should not be forgotten that the recreational reformers were in deadly earnest. If we shift our focus from the community to the individual we enter a realm of internal mental conflict; the hard and painful balancing of enjoyment against damnation. The struggle was for more than the leisure time of the miner. It was for commitment to a changed style of life. An account of the religious revival of 1824 notes: 'Among the vile and profane tinners that have been subdued…is a noted wrestler…[he] thanks God that among all the prizes which he has won he has now the best'. [44]

The second aspect of the influence of religion on the life of the mining communities to be considered is the relationship of Methodism to pre-existing popular beliefs and attitudes. Certainly there is much to support Dr Harrison's suggestion that Christian attempts to dominate their leisure brought the working classes most clearly into contact with the churches. But there is a danger in this approach to popular culture. Gareth Stedman Jones has, as we have noted, stressed the dangers of a 'social control' perspective, which neglects to consider the class expression of the workers themselves. [45] Labour historians, already accustomed to see Methodism as an inhibition on the growth of popular radicalism and as a carrier of the work disciplines of industrialism, tend to view it as an external force attempting to shape the working class into respectability. This is not an incorrect perspective, but it is not a complete one. Whatever, it was in the towns that village Methodism was not completely dominated by the middle class. Teetotalism was not new in many aspects of its working class activism. Village Methodism through its local preachers and class leaders had from its formative years gloried in the participation of working people. Those who impressed the virtues of sobriety and industry on the Sunday scholars and those who contested with the ale-houses were as likely to be neighbours and work fellows as they were social superiors. It has already been argued that the enormous success of teetotalism in Cornwall was in greatest measure due to the fact that the county had long been a great Methodist stronghold.

If the reasons for Methodism's success among the miners are examined, then it appears that with its dark areas of superstition and its anti-intellectualism it was less in conflict with many traditional forms of belief and action than a self-reliant rationalism would have been. A traditional Methodist historiography which offers a universal-panacea theory of the movement's success in West Cornwall distorts the true picture. According to this tradition the 'depraved' tinners lived without fear of God and without the benefit of 'experimental religion': swearing, fornicating, drinking, fighting, wrecking, smuggling, profaning the Sabbath with an unconcerned regularity and in general living a life of unchecked sinfulness. [46] Then came John Wesley, whose teaching filled every moral, spiritual and social need of the hitherto deprived Cornish. Such explanations are, to say the least, partial. Even had the Anglican church really been inadequate in every way since the Reformation, it would be difficult to believe that the common people of West Cornwall lived for two centuries in a moral and cultural vacuum, facing the changes of fortune and harsh demands of the world with a self-reliance and certainty out of keeping with their level of sophistication and the narrowness of their intellectual horizons, or else living in unsupported misery, reeling from a fate they could not begin to understand and finding oblivion only in alcohol or relief in mindless violence. They were not, of course, without religion. Village people living to a large extent outside the culture of literacy came to possess a background of beliefs, partly religious, partly magic, against which they sought to understand the realities of existence: both the ups and downs of life and those calamities like fire, flood, fever or storm which pressed so heavily on people living close to the margins of subsistence. Dr Obelkevich has shown how the "religious realm' of the labourers of South Lincolnshire in the nineteenth century reached beyond Christianity to 'encompass an abundance of pagan magic and superstition'. In addition, popular religion included conceptions of Christian doctrine that was adapted and transformed as they passed from the church to the cottage. [47] In Cornwall the miners and fishermen among whom Methodism grew so rapidly both pursued occupations in which the role of luck was considerable. Fishermen were not only dependent upon wind and tide, but in some seasons the migrating shoals on which their livelihood depended failed to appear in their usual abundance. Miners paid under the tribute system were remunerated according to the value of the mineral ore, which they raised, and chance played a large part in determining whether their place in the mine was a good or bad one. [48] Both miners and fishermen faced unusually high risks of death or injury. Small wonder that they attributed power over the sea or the mine to other agencies than those, which ruled on land or above ground. Fishermen would not put to sea, if a clergyman were seen near their boats, and miners would not permit the sign of the cross to be made underground.[49] Underground spirits were known as 'knockers'. Related to the piskey (pixie) they were said to be in the spirits of Jews who had worked the mines in Roman times. Morally neutral, they brought good or bad fortune according to the treatment they received. They could indicate the location of good ores by knocking with their hammers, but they could bring injury or death to those who treated them with hostility or skepticism. Above ground in the everyday life of the community, chances in fortune could be explained by the struggle of good with evil spirits, Sometimes a human agency, the witch, was involved, especially in small communities in which a personal relationship between the bewitcher and the bewitched could be identified. A clergyman of considerable local standing and literary reputation claimed in 1826 that within his memory there had been conjuring persons and cunning clerks. Every blacksmith had been a doctor, every old woman a witch. In short all nature had been united in 'sympathizing with human credulity; in predicting or in averting, in relieving or in aggravating misfortune'. He went further to claim that some of the rusticated clergy reinforced popular superstition by pretending to the power of laying hosts and hinted that he could name some whose influence over their flocks was largely attributable to this pretence. Well into the nineteenth century Curate Richards of Camborne was reputedly seen by miners attempting to lay the ghost of the recently dead squire with a whip. Some saw utility in popular superstition, fearing that when finally removed from the popular mind 'religion would languish if not expire'. 'The decline of superstition', one remarked, 'has made the people very irreligious.' [50]

More sophisticated clergymen had little sympathy. They could not, as Obelkevich has pointed out, avoid being hostile to what they regarded as 'a mass of dimly perceived beliefs that were deviant at best and heathen at worst'. [51] The Reverend William Borlase reprimanded a parishioner who claimed to be able to recover lost or stolen goods by conjuration. He warned him not to meddle with the 'dangerous mysteries of the lower world' and to refuse all intercourse with the devil. While Methodists tended to confine their attribution of powers to God and the devil, and were said in 1817 to be under their 'soul-subduing' power emancipating the miners from the 'terrors of imagination', much evidence suggests that not only did that 'emancipation' take a long time, but while it was being pursued many elements from Methodism itself were being taken up and absorbed into the very popular culture with which it was contesting. [52]

Methodism did not so much replace folk-beliefs as translate them into a religious idiom. Neither witchcraft nor spirit-agency as an explanation of events precludes commonsense empirical observation. Men die because they happen to be at a moment in time under a fall of rock. What needs explaining is why that man was in that place at that time. Witchcraft, as Max Gluckman has observed, explains that singularity of misfortune, which the agnostic or scientific mind prefers to see as 'chance'.[53] In modern British history no church of comparable weight has allowed a greater degree of comprehensiveness or frequency to divine or satanic intervention than did early Methodism. The idea of an omnipotent deity and a malicious devil can explain singularity of misfortune as well as can witches or evil spirits. The retributive anger of God can explain the most widespread of disasters.

The credulousness of the miners was an essential feature of their ready acceptance of the teachings of John Wesley. They could be responsive to his message not because he demanded a new and rational view of the world, but because he did not. Methodism did not ask that a man fully understand his environment. He need only realise that what was incomprehensible to him had purpose for a God who owed him no explanation. Not that good fortune necessarily followed the good, for the tests of faith could be very stiff. After all, the rewards that the wicked might reap in this world were as nothing compared with the retribution awaiting them after death. The hand of God was seen in everything from bee stings to earthquakes: 'That God is himself the author and sin the moral cause of earthquakes; (whatever the natural cause may be,) cannot be denied', wrote John Wesley. Preaching once at St Just, he was troubled by the sun in his eyes, but a cloud suddenly appeared from nowhere and covered the sun. 'Is anything', he remarked, 'too small for the providence of him by whom our very hairs are numbered?' The evangelical *Cornish Banner* published an account of the East Wheal Rose mine flood of 1846. Among the 1,260 persons employed there it concluded, many surely had been of 'a very wicked and abandoned character'. The flooding of the mine was viewed as 'a judgment', and as 'a loud appeal' to other miners: 'Be ye also ready; for in such an hour as ye think not, the Son of man cometh?' [54]

The hand of God could be seen in the varying fortunes of the miner working on tribute. If he did well it was Providence, which blessed his labours; if not, then it was his faith, which was being tested. In matters such as disputes over the siting of chapels the wishes of the Lord were ascertained by the casting of lots. Divine intervention was never more dramatic than when the Lord's people were safeguarded. The Helston class was meeting when one of its members had a premonition of danger. They left straightaway, just before a spark ignited some gunpowder stored in an adjacent room. 'So', Wesley concluded, 'did God preserve those who trusted in him'. Conversely the suffering or demise of an adversary also showed God's power. With no small degree of satisfaction Wesley recorded the suicide of a Cornish clergyman who had opposed the Methodists and in his journal for 1757 we find:

His wife promised Mr P. before he died that she would always receive the preachers. But she soon changed her mind. God has just taken her only son, suddenly killed by a pit falling upon him, and on Tuesday last a young strong man, riding to his burial dropped of his horse stone dead. The concurrence of these awful providences added considerably to our congregation. [55]

Such attitudes prevailed into the nineteenth century. In 1839 a Primitive Methodist minister entered in his diary a blow-by-blow account of God's dealings with his opposers:

Looking over the way God has lead me it is mysterious. I have been here four years. My opposers have so far been put down. When I came into the circuit 264 members, now 970; Enemies put down and others that opposed suffered. Bromsle ill Penzance Coulson gone out of his mind. Elias wife ill two years. Moon ill Penzance. Mr Blazey died suddenly June 24th 1838, the day should be removed he wrote against me. He was Mayor of St Ives. Strange mother died, sister died, brother in law drowned. Mary Pollard lost 6/-. Cheel married old woman... [56]

A book published in 1837 relates a tradition that when Charles Wesley visited the society at St Just it was suffering severe persecution from the local squire. Wesley is said to have declared, 'The man who has troubled you this day shall trouble you no more for ever.' Shortly after the Squire died insane. The impression made on the popular mind was obviously a strong one. The memory however differs from what Wesley himself recorded. In his journal he wrote that he had asked that: 'the door might again be opened, and that he who hinders might be taken out of the way as God knew best'. The Squire did indeed die soon after, and it is not hard to see how Charles Wesley's rather guarded intercession became transformed over time into the unequivocal pronouncement attributed to him in the popular tradition. [57]

The starkness of many aspects of Methodism's popular theology enabled it to be woven into existing folk-beliefs; the more especially since its regular interpreters were not the educated Wesleyan ministry, but the local preachers and class leaders. These men could be regarded as the interpreters or even agency of God's will, just as witches and conjurers were the agencies through which darker powers operated. At the simplest level the powers of intercession attributed to a local preacher might be no more than the belief that his directed prayer could secure fine weather for feast days. [58]

Such inter-minglings were especially evident in the nineteenth century in those rural areas being freshly evangelised by the Bible Christians. In one village the bullock of a local farmer-preacher died. Suspecting an old woman of ill-wishing it he roasted its heart and had his suspicions confirmed when the old woman woke up screaming. Both he and the woman were members of the Bible Christians and the burning of the heart was accompanied by a reading from the Bible. A miner from the same sect who was thought to have powers of conjuration was reprimanded by a fellow miner whose pig he had failed to find: 'Ah William, you are not so pious as you used to be, or you could have instantly told me where to find my pig'. A folklorist of the late nineteenth century records an ill-wishing in 1870, which is remarkable not so much for its lateness as for the fact that the woman regarded as responsible was a 'backslider'. Since marriage she had ceased to attend chapel. In a village where Methodists were dominant, it is not surprising that a woman who reacted against their influence, she had called them a 'set of duffans and back-biting and undermining hypocrites', was regarded as having at least some link with the forces of evil. [59]

Obelkevich has remarked on the central role of the devil in popular culture, and certainly in Cornwall the influence of Methodism gave him a special importance. The holder of a Cornish living in the 1850s noted the frequency with which his parishioners reported dreams of Jesus and

Billy Bray.

the devil: 'these are real persons to the Cornish mind, and their power is respectively acknowledged. [60] Although physical manifestations of God, Father or Son, were rarely reported (though one convert at a Bodmin revival did see Christ no less than three times with his naked eye), sightings of the devil were frequent. Even sophisticated Methodists, like the distinguished philosopher Samuel Drew. believed they had seen the devil, or at least his messenger. Satan or his agent was usually bestial in form, described as resembling a large shaggy dog or bear, always hairy and with eyes that glowed fiercely red. [61]

Billy Bray was the best-known miner-preacher of the Victorian era. Once passing a shaft where some miners had been recently killed, he became convinced they would materialize from the invisible world. They did not, but approaching a second shaft, which had to be crossed on a narrow bridge, he became even more convinced that the devil awaited him on the bridge. He exclaimed:

The devil! Who is he? what can he do? The devil is a fallen angel! thrown out of Heaven by God? He is held in chains! I am Billy Bray! God is my heavenly Father! Why should I fear the devil? Come on, then thou devil; I fear thee not? Come on Lucifer and all demons! Come on, old ones and young ones, black ones and blue ones, fiery and red-hot ones; come on devil and all thy ugly hosts!

Bray got so used to the devil's attempts to frighten him or lead him astray that he familiarly referred to him as 'Old smutty face'.[62]

John Wesley himself believed in ghosts and witches. By substituting the devil and his bestial messenger for 'knockers' and piskeys, Methodism did not substitute reason for superstition. By and large it successfully translated that superstition, but the triumph of the religious idiom came only after a period of intermingling of Methodist and folk-beliefs. Methodist superstition matched the indigenous superstition of the common people. Perhaps it was not intended, but the match in Cornwall was sufficient to contribute to the consolidation of one of their strongest congregations. [63]

A folklorist found in the late nineteenth century that the circles of standing stones, relics of Cornwall's stone-age culture, had come to be regarded as petrified young people who had sported on the Sabbath. Here we have together, superstition, divine retribution and condemnation of sport. [64]

1 G. Stedman Jones, 'Class expression versus Social Control? A critique of recent trends in the social history of "leisure"', in *History Workshop*, No. 4, Autumn 1977, p. 165.
2 Report of the Royal Commission on Child Employment, *British Parliamentary Publications*, 1842, Vol. 16, Report of Charles Barham, p. 760; H. Miles Brown, 'Methodism and the Church of England in Cornwall 1738-1838', unpublished Ph.D thesis, University of London, 1947, p. 70; *Old Cornwall*, Vol. 5, Part 12, 1961, p. 519.
3 G. Stedman Jones, 'Class expression versus Social Control', pp.162-163.
4 For a useful survey see H. Cunningham, *Leisure in the Industrial Revolution*, London, 1980; G. Stedman Jones, 'Class Expression versus Social Control', p. 165.
5 B. Harrison, 'Religion and Recreation in Nineteenth-century England', Papers presented to a Past and Present Conference on Popular Religion, 7 July 1966, p. 2.
6 John Wesley, *Journal*, Vol. 1, (Everyman edition), 1906, pp. 420, 425, Vol. 2, pp. 99, 265 (entries dated 1 April 1743, 10 July 1743, 15 May 1749 and 4 August 1766).
7 B. Harrison, *Drink and the Victorians. The Temperance Question in England 1815 to 1872*, London, 1971, p. 180; M. Edwards, 'The Tee-total Wesleyan Methodists', in *Proceedings of the Wesleyan Historical Society*, 1961, pp. 66-67; B. Harrison, *Drink and the Victorians*, p. 109.
8 H. Douch, *Old Cornish Inns*, Truro, 1967, pp. 108-9; T. Shaw, *History of Cornish Methodism*, Truro, 1967, p. 78; R. Currie, *Methodism Divided*, London, 1968, pp. 30-31; *Cornwall Tee-total Journal*, February, April and May 1839; B. Harrison, 'Pubs', in H. Dyos and M. Wolff, (eds.), *The Victorian City. Images and Realities*, Vol. 1, London, 1976; *Past and Present: Numbers of People*, pp. 161-162.
9 British Museum, Add MSS, Vol. A, 34, 245, f. 148; B. Harrison, *Drink and the Victorians*, p. 180.
10 P. Bailey, *Leisure and Class in Victorian England. Rational Recreation and the Contest/ or Control*, 1830-1885, London, 1978, p. 47.
11 I discussed the pressures stemming from the new disciplines imposed by the mines in 'Some Social Aspects of the Industrial Revolution in Cornwall', in R. Burt, (ed.), *Industry and Society in the South West*, Exeter, 1970, pp. 71-106.
12 W. Borlase, *Natural History of Cornwall*, Oxford, 1758, pp. 300-301.
13 R. Heath, *A Natural and Historical Account of the Islands of Scilly and Lastly a General Account of Cornwall*, London, 1750, pp. 437, 41.
14 W. Borlase, *Natural History*, p. 300.

15 ibid, p. 304; R. Polwhele, *The Old English Gentleman*, London, 1797,
p. 114, footnote; H. Douch, *Cornish Inns*, p. 50; R. Polwhele (ed.), *Lavington's enthu-siasm of Methodists and Papists Compared*, London, 1833, pp. cxxi-cxxii. For a general argument see the section, 'The Withdrawal of the Upper Classes' in P. Burke, *Popular Culture in Early Modern Europe*, London, 1978, pp. 270-281.

17 L. Bettany (ed.), *Diaries of William Johnstone Temple*, Oxford, 1929, p. 187; W. Borlase, *Natural History*, p. 300; 'Account of a Tour in Cornwall', Pendarvis MSS, CRO; R. Pococke, *Travels through England*, (ed.), J. Cartwright for Camden Society, London, 1888, (reprinted 1965), p. 136.

18 B. Carvosso, *A Memoir of Mr. William Carvosso*, London, 1837, p. 32.
Cornwall Gazette, 19 March 1814; Broadsheet in County Record Office, Truro.

19 Charles Wesley, Journal entry for 4 August 1744, reprinted in J. Pearce, *The Wesleys in Cornwall*, Truro, 1964, p. 49.

20 *Cornwall Gazette*, 11 September 1802.

21 R. Warner, *A Tour through Cornwall in 1808*, London, 1809, pp. 300-301.

22 *West Briton*, 2 November 1821, 24 July 1829.

23 Anon, *Letters from West Cornwall written in 1826*, London, 1861, p. 71.

24 'Drinking Customs of the Cornish Miners', *Cornwall Teetotal Journal*, Vol. I, No. 9, Supplement, August 1839.

25 H. Cunningham, *Leisure in the Industrial Revolution*, p. 9.

26 R. Storch, 'The Problem of Working-class Leisure. Some Roots of Middle-class Reform in the Industrial North', in A. Donajgrodskj (ed.), *Social Control in Nineteenth Century Britain*, London, 1977, p. 153.

27 S. Coley, *Life of the Reverend Thomas Collins*, London, 1871, pp. 297-299.

28 R. Polwhele, *Anecdotes of Methodism*, London, 1801, pp. 28-29.

29 *West Briton*, 3 July 1840; J. Petty, *History of the Primitive Methodist Connexion*, London, 1880, pp. 28-29.

30 H. Douch, *Cornish Inns*, p. 109.

31 R. Polwhele, *History of Cornwall*, Vol. 7, London, 1806, p. 100.

32 B. Harrison, 'Religion and Recreation in Nineteenth Century England', in *Past and Present*, No. 38, 1967, p. 106.

33 'A Redruth Diary', *Old Cornwall*, Vol. 5, p. 178.

34 *Cornwall Gazette*, 1 February 1839.

35 'Redruth Diary', p. 103.

36 Cornwall County Record Office, MSS, Diary of Thomas Nicholl, June 1843.

37 *West Briton*, 31 May 1844.

38 D. St J. Thomas, *A Regional History of the Railways of Great Britain*, London, 1960, Vol. 1, *The West Country*, p.104. Mr Thomas and other popular historians of the railway like to claim that the refrain was: 'Happy Camborne/Happy Camborne/Where the railway is so near/And the engine shows how water/Can accomplish more than beer'. Sadly it was not so sung. The last two lines of the refrain are an added parody. See *Old Cornwall*, Vol. 2, Part 5, p. 42. On the thin line separating 'respectability' from 'unrespectability' among the working class see P. Bailey, "Will the Real Bill Banks Please Stand Up?" Towards a Role Analysis of Mid-Victorian Working-class Respectability', *Journal of Social History*, Vol. 12, 1979, pp. 336-353.

39 'Social Condition of the Cornish Miner', in *Western Morning News*, 10 August 1864.

40 *Quarterly Review*, 1857, p. 34.

41 *West Briton*, 31 May 1844; L. Maker, *Cob and Moorston*e, London, 1935, p. 48.

42 Shaw, *Cornish Methodism*, p. 69.

43 H. Douch, *Cornish Inns*, p. 111.

44 Methodist Archives, Fletcher-Tooth Correspondence, John Radford to Mrs Tooth, 31 January 1824.

45 G. Stedman Jones, 'Class Expression versus Social Control'. For an evaluation of the concept and its relevance to nineteenth century Britain see introduction by A. Donajgrodzki to *Social Control in Nineteenth Century Britain*.

46 For example: 'There is no more splendid page in the Methodist annals than the transformation of Cornwall. Quite apart from the viciousness and lawlessness which prevailed; there was almost a total ignorance of religion. Churches were un-attended, and the very phraseology of religion had become obsolete'. M. Edwards, *John Wesley and the Eighteenth Century*, London, 1935, p. 160.

47 I researched this subject area in my post-graduate days (see my unpublished thesis, 'The Labouring miner in Cornwall, c. 1740-1870: a Study in Social History', University of Warwick, 1971, pp. 240-607). The systematic and perceptive study of Obelkevich seems to suggest that I was on the right lines and that a more thorough investigation of Cornwall would produce conclusions generally in line with his. J. Obelkevich, *Religion and Rural Society: South Lindsey 1825-75*, Oxford, 1976, pp. 258-261. A leading historian has described his work on South Lincolnshire as a 'vindica-tion' of mine. See D. Hempton, *Methodism and Politics in British Society 1750-1850*, 1987 p. 27.

48 For a detailed account of the tribute system see J. Rule, thesis, pp. 34-71 and See above chapter 4.

49 R. Hunt, *Popular Romances of the West of England*, London, 1881, p. 349.

50 R. Polwhele, *Traditions and Recollections*, Vol. 2, London, 1826, p. 605; *Old Corn-wall*, Vol. 2, No. 2, 1931, p. 3; MSS, Journal of Christopher Wallis, 7 November 1795, *County Museum*, Truro.

51 J. Obelkevich, *Religion and Rural Society*, p. 262.

52 P. Pool, 'William Borlase'. *Journal of the Royal Institute of Cornwall*, New Series, Vol. 5, Part 2, 1966, p. 151; C. Gilbert, *Historical Survey of Cornwall*, Vol. 1, Plymouth, 1817, pp. 104-105.

53 M. Gluckman, *Custom and Conflict in Africa*, Oxford, 1955, pp. 83-84.

54 J. Wesley, *Works*, London, 1830-1831, Vol. 7, p. 386; *Journal*, 6 September 1755, see J. Pearce, *Wesleys in Cornwall*, p. 123; *Cornish Banner*, 1846, p. 57.

55 J. Wesley, *Journal*, 7, 13 September 1755, 5 September 1757; See also J. Pearce, *Wesleys in Cornwall*, pp. 124, 126-127.

56 J. Prohert, *Primitive Methodism in Cornwall*, Redruth, 1966, p. 68.

57 R. Treffry, *Memoirs of Mr John Edwards Tresize*, London, 1837, p. 31; J. Pearce, *Wes-leys in Cornwall*, 21 July 1746, p. 55.

58 *Cornish Magazine*, Vol. 2, 1898, p. 224.

59 'Social Condition of the Cornish Miner', *Western Morning News*, 16 June 1865; W.

Bottrell, *Traditions and Hearthside Stories of West Cornwall*, Penzance, 1873, pp. 285-286.

60 J. Obelkevich, *Religion and Rural Society*, pp. 276-279; W. Haslam, *From Death into Life*, London, n.d., pp. 52-53.

61 *Cornish Guardian*, 30 March 1853; J. Drew, *Samuel Drew. The Self-taught Cornishman*, London, 1861, pp. 33-34.

62 F. Bourne, *The King's Son. A Memoir of Billy Bray*, London, 1898, p. 70.

63 On Wesleyanism and superstition see E. Thompson, 'Anthropology and the Discipline of Historical Context', *Midland History*, Vol.1, Part 1, 1971, pp. 54-55, and especially on Methodism and witchcraft see O. Davies, 'Methodism, the Clergy and the Popular Belief in Witchcraft and Magic', *History*, Vol. 82, No. 266, 1997, pp. 252-265.

64 R. Hunt, *Popular Romances of the West of England*, p. 177.

8 Richard Spurr of Truro:
Small Town Radical

Richard Spurr was a cabinet-maker occupying premises in Truro's Pyder Street. Like many others of the small tradesmen of the town he was a Methodist, quite possibly a Bible Christian. Truro had grown and prospered with the growth of the Cornish mining industry. It had done so as the commercial and financial centre. Truro drew its wealth from the mines without being itself inhabited by miners. Trouble with the miners came in the form of pay night drinking or incursions into the corn market when food was hardly available at affordable prices. The lower orders in such towns were typically made up of people like Spurr, the lower classes of shopkeepers, journeymen, store men, apprentices and casual labourers of various kinds. It is among such people that any evidence of radical politics must be sought.

Spurr was thirty-eight years old when the local press first began to report his activities in detail in March 1838. The Mayor had called a public meeting for the purpose of approving the sending of an address to Lord Melbourne declaring approval of his Administration's general policy and expressing confidence in its future policies. Spurr addressed the meeting at great length on, it was reported, matters not at all relevant to the object of the meeting. He concluded by proposing an amendment to a proposal of an active local liberal calling for the abolition of slavery in the West Indies. Spurr wished to add, 'something about the liberation of white slaves also being insured'. Sadly the *West Briton* reported only this fragment of his speech.[1]

A few weeks later, on the 8 May, Spurr played a prominent part in the Church Rate Riot, and was one of five persons charged with its incite-

ment. The disturbances were unquestionably organised by the defendants. That is to say that they adopted a course of action explicitly designed
to stir up the populace of the town. The five were Richard Barrett, draper,
Jacob Corin Edwards, ironmonger, Samuel Randall, pipe-maker, William
Ball, watchmaker, and Spurr himself. Barrett, Edwards and Randall were
dissenters. Edwards was in fact a preacher of the Bryanite or Bible Christian Connexion who had refused to pay church rates for two years past.
Consequently, an officer was sent to make a distress on their goods. It
was here that what seems to have been a well-organised attempt to gain
popular support began. Randall insisted on the officer taking a Bible, and
the other defendants gave some other articles, all of which were taken to
the saleroom of William Oke, an auctioneer, and a time for the sale of the
seized property was announced. A handbill subsequently appeared in
the town signed by the three men:

This is to inform the public that the summonses that have been so frequently
served on us during the past month (21 in number), have this day been carried
into execution, by the distraining of our property to a very considerable amount
so as to form a complete bazaar of plunder. The prosecution against us is insti-
gated by Mr. John Ferris, currier and tanner, and Mr. William Warren, attorney,
the impartial church wardens for this town, no doubt through the instigation of
a party who covet their neighbour's goods and anything that is his. The mock
sale will take place at Mr Oke's Pyder Street (he being once a rigid dissenter,
now a churchman; what he will be time will tell), on Tuesday 8th May instant,
at ten o'clock precisely, probably that the church party may have a better opportunity of dividing it among themselves, as has been generally practiced towards
the society of friends for three centuries past; but we give this information for the
satisfaction of our friends, and to assure those persons who may be disposed to
become possessed of those goods, we shall notice their part also in this religious
persecution, by handing down their names as family memorials in connexion
with this religious crusade against us, inflicted because we deem it right to be
dissenters.

The articles are very appropriate viz:

One Bible, three japan waiters, containing good likenesses of the Rev. John Wesley and three ditto of Mr Samuel Drew, and one with a church in the centre, and several others with interesting representations, together with a general assortment of linen drapery, household furniture etc.

We shall be in attendance for the purpose of informing strangers of the particulars and articles of sale.

On the same day Richard Barrett inserted the following advertisement in the *West Briton*:

Taken by the constable of Truro, this day from Richard Barrett, London House, to support Holy Mother Church, and to provide sacramental wine for the ladies and gentlemen of this town, the following goods to pay £1.0s.10d. demanded for what the churchwardens, Mr Ferris and Mr Warren, called church rate.

It was on the morning of the sale that the two men, later to become locally notorious as Chartists, Spurr and William Rowe, began to become involved. Rowe blew a bugle at 10 a.m., playing a call known as the 'General Assembly', promptly to summon people to the sale. At ten, Edwards, Barrett and Randall entered the sale room with a crowd at their heels. Among the crowd, Ball, Spurr and Rowe were especially noticed. Spurr, claimed one witness, although another claimed it was Ball, cried out, 'Oke, how can you sell people's goods to support a d—d bloody church?' The crowd began hissing and hooting, and to cry out, 'Put up the Bible'. Oke said that it was not intended to be sold. He told Miners, the constable, to show the Bible. Miners accused, 'You know Randall, you forced me to take the Bible'; an assertion, which was not contradicted. At ten in the morning Oke commenced the sale by putting up a hat which was knocked down amidst uproar, a waiter was then knocked down, and when Oke asked for the money, he was told that it had already been passed to him via William Rowe, who claimed, 'I believe Oke have got the money'. There followed complete uproar. Rowe called out, 'Oke adjourn for six months, you will never carry out the sale'. At this point Oke's window was broken and several of his shop fittings smashed, and he announced an adjournment to 2.30 p.m. Barrett now denied he had the power to adjourn, to which Oke replied that he would accept the responsibility. What happened next is best described in Oke's own words:

There was a sort of groan, I can hardly describe it for I was in such terror. The crowd rushed upon me and broke the counter to pieces before me; and I being a little higher than the people, threw myself towards the kitchen door. They then layed hold of me and tore my coat in pieces. The crowd tried to hold him, but aided by friends he managed his escape to the kitchen. Just before two in the afternoon, Barrett and Edwards came to the shop and broke their way in with a crowd of people. Oke escaped, but does not seem to have lacked the courage to return and recommence the sale, although by now there were upwards of 600 hundred persons in the street. He knocked down all of Barrett's goods from an upstairs window, through which a stone was immediately thrown. At this moment the mayor arrived with the town constables, cleared the shop and nailed it up. The crowd did not yet go home, however, for all evening they paraded the town behind a band of music, and when they came opposite Oke's shop they stoned it. [2]

The five men were to be found guilty, but the trial was not held until the Lent Assize of 1839, leaving some eleven months intervening for Spurr to continue to build up his growing reputation as the town's most outspoken radical. On 22 June 1838, the mayor called a public meeting to consider the best means of celebrating Her Majesty's coronation. Here at least, he must have thought, was a subject for a fair degree of consensus. He was wrong. Proposing a beef distribution to the poor he announced that two bullocks had already been earmarked for the purpose. William Rowe with strong support from the floor pointed out that two would hardly be sufficient. Ten at least would be needed. At this point Spurr intervened. The *West Briton* continues the account:

…he said as he had anticipated certain resolutions would be proposed to which he should have objected, he had prepared an amendment. But since he had heard what had fallen from the chair, he would now propose his amendment as a resolution, first premising it by a few observations.

By now Spurr was notorious and the mayor interrupted:

Mayor: Before you go on, I must tell, you Mr Spurr that if you mean to begin any political harangue I will not listen to it.

Mr Spurr: It is not a political harangue - but it is a matter connected with the subject.

Mayor: If you confine yourself to the subject we will listen but not else.

Spurr, after reminding the mayor that he ought to be impartial, read his resolution, which was simply that the best way of testifying loyalty to the Queen was 'everyman attending to his business'. This was greeted with a loud hiss, as Spurr amplified his resolution by explaining that any money expended in celebration would come out of the pockets of the labourers. He continued in similar vein until interrupted by the mayor, who to the accompaniment of loud cheers threatened to close the meeting if Spurr did not choose to confine himself to the business of the meeting:

There is no need of such nonsensical haranguing that you are now always bringing forward. Whenever the people are gatherer together; they are doomed to listen to such nonsense as this.

The meeting then proceeded in a more orderly manner and the first propositions were agreed to. [3]

When Spurr's political activities were next reported, the meeting was occasioned by a matter more serious than celebrating the coronation of the Queen. For some time complaints of hooliganism and drunken crime had increased in Truro, and it had been proposed to form a police force to maintain order in the city. A meeting was called for the purpose of opposing this intention, and a motion to this effect was put by a Mr Tealor and seconded by Mr Concanen. The motion was passed and Spurr ascended the platform proposing a vote of thanks to those who had called the meeting for their resistance to, 'so oppressive a scheme'. This meeting held in December 1838, not surprisingly did nothing to stop the force being formed and, in January 1839, five subalterns and an inspector commenced their duties. [4]

The 8 May 1838, day of the Truro riots, was also one of the most significant dates in the nineteenth century history of the British working class.
On that day the People's Charter was published. Drawn up by the New-
lyn-born William Lovett, who was then Secretary of the London Working-
men's Association, it set out the principles of reform on which Chartism,
the first really national labour movement, was to be based. The principles
were equal representation (200 electoral districts of equal size); universal
adult male suffrage; annual parliaments; no property qualification for
members of parliament; vote by ballot, and payment of members.

It was some months before the Charter began to provide a fresh im-
petus for radicalism in a town so distant from the main centres of political activity as Truro. But on 1 February 1839 the *West Briton* was reporting local Chartist activities for the first time. To established radicals like
Spurr, the clear formulation of principles in the Charter gave a new core
to radicalism, and it is not surprising to find him taking the lead in establishing a local Chartist group. The first meeting was held at the Truro
Institute. The room was half full and there were only three persons on
the platform: Spurr, a Mr Longmaid, and one other whom the paper does
not name. There were loud calls for Mr Tealor to take the chair. Tealor
was the man who had called the meeting to protest against the police
force, but it became apparent that acceptance of the clear principles of the
Charter was to separate Spurr and a few others from men who had made
common cause with them on past issues. Tealor asked Spurr the purpose
of the meeting. Spurr outlined the principles of the Charter and said the
purpose of the meeting was to adopt the national petition for the Charter,
a petition already signed by, 'two million Britons determined to be free'.
Tealor declined the chair. He felt such power should not be conferred
upon the multitude until they had been fitted for them by previous education. He was hissed until he resumed his seat. Spurr stood up and was
soon in full stride denouncing Tealor, the 'sham' Whigs, the Tories, the
Poor Law Bill and the 'blue devil' police force of Truro. Tealor attempted
to support the Poor Law bill, but the meeting would not hear him, and
passed on to conclude by adopting resolutions put to it by Spurr and
Longmaid. [5]

The emergence of Chartism clearly had the effect locally of throwing into sharp relief the different political groupings in the town. Around Spurr had collected a small group of radicals who had accepted the principles of the Charter. Among them were certainly William Rowe, the butcher prominent in the Church Rate riot, and John Longmaid, who had shared the platform with Spurr at the first Chartist meeting, and who was to chair a meeting addressed by the Chartist missionaries when they came to Cornwall later in 1839. Spurr was clearly the group's leader and its most articulate speaker. The first meeting had shown that one man, Tealor, from whom they had hoped for support, neither believed in immediate universal suffrage, nor shared their opposition to the new Poor Law. A further split was revealed by a public meeting called on 15 February 1839 to adopt a petition for the repeal of the Corn Laws. A Mr Stokes proposed the petition and after he had spoken, Spurr stood up to give one of his longest and most emphatically radical of speeches. He agreed with Stokes but he wished to go a good deal further. Besides the Corn Law delegates, there was also sitting in London the People's Parliament, who aimed at getting them not just a cheap loaf, but a little bit of beef with it. He would put the Corn Law reformers to the test to see how far their support for the workingman really went. Would they support this amendment?

That in order to avert the ruin with which our country is threatened, it is not only necessary that the Corn Laws, should be immediately and unconditionally repealed but that the exclusive mode of electing the House of Commons should be changed so that the productive millions may be fairly represented, that being the best way of repealing those odious, oppressive and starving imposts... There were two ways of getting rid of a thing - by lopping off the branches by degrees, and by tearing up the roots. He was for tearing up the roots. They might be continually agitating the country first to get rid of the Corn Laws, and then of some other law equally objectionable. But give the people their rights - they asked for no more and they would accept nothing less. The time was when the people were told they had nothing to do with the laws but to obey them; but in 1839 the people entertained a different opinion - they now thought that they had a right to a voice in the making of them. The people were oppressed but they would make themselves heard.

He continued until the mayor interrupted by telling him to keep to the question:

Mr Spurr: I am proving to you that the best way of getting these Corn Laws repealed is by enfranchising the people.
Mayor: That we cannot listen to (uproar).

Spurr continued saying he would keep as close as possible to the question but before he did that he would say that Cornishmen should not want a workingman to support their claims. As to the question, he was opposed to petitioning the House of Commons, because it would amount to a trial before an unjust judge and a packed jury. The Corn Laws had existed for the last twenty years, and he swore, 'by the God who made him and by the Redeemer who he hoped would save him', that he would sign no petition but the National Petition of the Chartists for Parliamentary reform.

Stokes tried to patch the rent by pointing out that over the country Chartists had signed the petition for the repeal of the Corn Laws, quoting the famous radical poet Ebenezer Elliot who had signed on the grounds that he was not prepared to starve while waiting for the Charter. Stokes thought there must be many present who would be happy to sign both petitions. Spurr was adamant:

I will have no compromise…The Cornish motto is, "one and all", and let us all go together on this occasion. Let us either have our rights, or let us be content till we can get them.

This, the mayor, thought 'rather too rash'. Mr Heath, described as an operative, stood up to say, 'I cordially, willingly and gladly second neighbour Spurr's resolution'. (Heath joins Spurr, Longmaid and Rowe to provide our fourth named Chartist in the town). Concanen, one of the town's best-known moderate reformers, begged the agitators not to wreck, 'a rational cause' by their intemperance. He would not go side-by-side with

such men as Fergus O'Connor, Mr Stephens, and Mr Oastler, whose conduct would go to make the home of everyman unsafe. He called upon the
meeting not to be misled by men whose proceedings could only result 'in
the destruction of property, the disjointing of society, and the endangering of life'. Spurr described Concanen's speech as 'humbug' and refused
all demands to withdraw his amendment: 'I will never withdraw it. I
stand up for the working classes of this country, and I will have it put'.
The eventual outcome of the meeting was that the proposal for petitioning for the repeal of the Corn Laws was carried by an overwhelming majority, and greeted with hearty and long-continued applause. The *West
Briton* headed its report: 'Defeat of the Chartists'. [6]

This account has been given at some length because it is the fullest
account we have from which to see something of the nature of Spurr's
oratory, and because it shows how uncompromising his radicalism had
by now become. In the spring of 1839 the Chartist National Convention
sent two missionaries, Abraham Duncan and Robert Lowery, to seek
support for the Charter in Cornwall. They held meetings in the towns
and addressed open-air meetings in the mining districts. At their Truro
meeting, the chair was taken by Heath, the operative who had supported
Spurr at the Corn Law meeting; and Spurr, seconded by Rowe, proposed
the adoption of the National Petition. [7]

This meeting was held in mid-March and was Spurr's last public
meeting for a while. On 1 April the Lent Assizes began, and the bound-
over defendants on the Church Rate riot charges were tried. Spurr, with
the others, received sentence of a month's imprisonment. [8] When their
sentences had run their course, the five were released to demonstrations
of enthusiastic support from the populace. They were drawn into Truro
in a chaise and four preceded by flags and music and followed by a body
of Chartists and others. After parading the streets they went to the Institute, where a dinner was held. Probably the mass support was for the
opposition to church rates rather than for the principles of the Charter,
for at the dinner the most significant speaker was Edwards, the Bible
Christian preacher, who spoke of the law under which he had been sentenced as, 'a pagan law fraught with Popish bigotry'. [9]

Spurr's time in Truro was now drawing to an end. His business had suffered badly. Presumably a month in gaol had not helped, but his political activities had almost certainly lost him the patronage of wealthy customers. In June 1839 he pleaded want of work for many weeks when charged with not having paid his shop rates since 1835. This clearly contributed to his decision to leave Truro for London, although, on the Mayor of Truro's own admission, so closely was he being watched by the police (the very force whose institution he had so vehemently opposed), that circumstances were combining to make life in Truro difficult for him. Out of work, on the verge of being prosecuted for rates he was in no position to pay, and bothered by the close attentions of police, he went to London and ended his career as a small-town radical. [10]

It was not, however, Spurr's career as a radical, but only the small town period of it which ended. In London he quickly established himself in the Chartist movement, becoming involved with the more extreme 'physical force' wing, and has been described by one authority as an advocate of insurrection, and opponent of the moderate William Lovett. In January 1840 while addressing a meeting he was arrested with other Chartists, and charged with sedition. Reading of his arrest in the papers, the Mayor of Truro took it upon himself to inform the Home Office of Spurr's earlier activities in Truro. He described him as, 'a most violent declaimer at public meetings', 'a suspicious and dangerous person', and further claimed that he had not ceased to trouble his native town, for he was sending Chartist literature for his wife to distribute. With his leadership lacking, however, there seemed to have been no regular Chartist meetings in Truro after his departure. [11] The further details of Spurr's London activities are for the historian of London Chartism, but it would appear that for reasons either of a change of heart, or simply for tactical reasons, he was expressing a more moderate line by the end of 1841 when he rejoined hands with William Lovett and actively supported his National Association for the peaceful securing of the aims of the Charter. [12]

There may yet be a chapter of Spurr's life in the 1840s to be uncovered by scholars of London radicalism, but what is known is that he left Britain in 1850 and emigrated to Australia with his family.

Perhaps Richard Spurr represents others like him: radical artisans in small towns over England, who living outside of the more strongly supported radicalism of industrial areas and some of the decaying traditional centres of manufacturing, nevertheless, as minority voices kept the great radical issues of the day alive in towns where many would have been happy to ignore them. At the same time the frequency of opportunities for public debate that Spurr so eagerly took up testify to the existence of an active political culture in small town England. [13]

1 *West Briton*, 23 March 1838.

2 This account of the riot is based on a supplement issued with the *West Briton*, 5 April 1838.

3 ibid, 22 June 1838.

4 ibid, 21 December 1838, 1 February 1839.

5 ibid, 1 February 1839. John Longmaid was to remain one of Cornwall's leading Chartists down to 1848. He then disappears from local newspapers, but is most probably the John Longmaid who was active later in London alongside Karl Marx on the Committee of the First International in 1864 and who was also active as a trade unionist on the Reform League in the agitation for the Second Reform Act.

6 ibid, 22 February 1839.

7 ibid, 15 March 1839. For a full account of the mission see below Chapter 9.

8 *West Briton*, Supplement to 5 April 1839.

9 *Royal Cornwall Gazette*, 3, 10 May 1839.

10 ibid, 28 June 1839; Public Record Office, HO, 40/54 from Mayor of Truro, 'Respecting an Individual named Richard Spurr, a speaker at Chartist meetings', 12 January 1840.

11 Howell, *The Chartist Movement*, Manchester, 1918, p. 209; PRO, HO, 40/54; R. Gammage, *History of the Chartist Movement*, 1894, p. 172.

12 Howell, *The Chartist Movement*; See William Lovett, *My Life and Struggles in Pursuit of Bread, Knowledge and Freedom*, (reprinted 1967),p. 214.

13 In earlier versions of this essay I did not know of Spurr's emigration. But following a chance finding of the essay the information was sent to me from Australia by his great-great grandson, Mr Noel Spurr.

To some of the fifty-three delegates who assembled in London in February 1839 to form the first Chartist General Convention of the Industrious Classes, that body represented an alternative to Westminster, a true People's Parliament. But whatever it symbolized, the Convention had immediate practical matters to organize. Paramount among these was the collection of signatures for the national metition for the six points of the People's Charter. To this end it was determined in March to send missionaries to parts of the country as yet unrepresented in the movement. Among them were the mining districts of West Cornwall, to whose unenlightened condition they had just been alerted. Two men, Robert Lowery, an experienced radical from the coal-mining area of the North East, and a Scotsman, Abram Duncan were accordingly sent there:

> We, the delegates of the industrious classes assembled, having appointed you as missionaries, do hereby instruct you to explain the People's Charter to obtain signatures to the National Petition for Universal Suffrage - to collect subscriptions of Rent, and by every legal and constitutional means, to extend political information among the people, and in the prosecution of the above objects, we hereby charge you not to hold communication with any associated body, not to infringe the laws in any manner by word or deed. [1]

They were cautioned to be as economical as possible with their allocation of funds, and were then dispatched into a county neither had previously visited nor had any personal contacts in. Their well documented experiences, however, provide a chapter interesting not only in the general history of the Chartist movement, but also for the significant contribution which it makes to the controversial question of the role of Methodism in early nineteenth century working class politics.

The two missionaries travelled by ship from London to Falmouth (the railway was not to cross the Tamar for another twenty years) arriving there on the evening of 4 March. The town did not much impress them. They reported it full of drunken sailors and prostitutes, with a large number of shops, which profited by their expenditure. The scene did not seem propitious for the opening meeting of their mission, so they contented themselves with circulating copies of the National Petition. [2]

Next day they set out for Truro, where they proposed to hold the first meeting. Unable to book a hall, they decided to hold an open-air meeting in High Cross, and employed the town crier to announce it. Interest was certainly aroused, for a thousand people attended and it lasted for two-and-a-half hours. [3] The interest of the local press was also aroused. The *West Briton* reported:

They harangued the populace for a considerable time...Their addresses evinced considerable talent, but were highly inflammatory. We hope the good sense of Cornishmen will prevent them from being tainted with notions so wild and visionary as those of the Chartists. [4]

The following day they went to Redruth in the heart of the mining district. Here, despite a warning from a magistrate that they would be arrested if there was a disturbance, they held a well attended meeting. Returning to Truro on the next day, they held a second meeting; this time, in the Town Hall. Resolutions adopting the Petition and in support of the National Convention were passed. This outcome was perhaps not surprising, for a group of Chartists had already established themselves in the town. In his report of the meeting, Lowery wrote: 'We got a working man Mr Heath to take the chair, Mr Spurr and Mr Rowe proposed and seconded the acceptance of the National Petition'. [5] Neither here nor elsewhere in his reports, nor in his autobiography does he make any formal mention of these men. Duncan is similarly silent. Spurr in fact had presided over a named Chartist meeting in Truro five weeks before the arrival of the missionaries. He had had an active career as a local radical and continued an active Chartist after moving to London, where he was arrested on a sedition charge in 1840. For some reason the missionaries did not inform the Convention that they had met an existing group of committed Chartists. [6]

After this meeting the two men went back among the miners, holding meetings in the open air, despite snow, at the large village of Chacewater and at the town of Camborne. At the latter, the 'Whigs', they complained, had bribed the crier not to advertise the meeting, and they had to resort to having handbills printed and distributed around the mines.

At this point they seem to have conceived the idea of holding a grand, final meeting at nearby Gwen nap Pit, a natural amphitheatre, which had been one of John Wesley's favourite preaching places on his many visits to the county. It was very much considered a 'holy place' by the local Methodists. The attempted implementation of this intent was later to provide one of the key moments of the mission.[7] The next day being a Sunday, they decided against holding a meeting, and went to the local Wesleyan chapel, where Lowery remarked on the custom of the women and men sitting on opposite sides of the aisle, with the men, of course hatless, allowing Duncan to notice something which dimmed his hopes of success in the far South West:

My Scotch friend, being a phrenologist, observed emphatically, "the development of the women is splendid, but did ye ever see such a set of bad heads as the men have?"

Duncan never did overcome his poor impression of Cornishmen. At St Ives he complained that the 'working men' lifted their hats to him as they passed by: 'It could only be because I had a good coat on. I cannot bear such servility to the appearance of wealth'. The women, however, were another matter: 'Duncan says the Cornwall girls have almost tempted him to marry, would the Convention allow anything for a woman?'[8]

From Camborne they had moved west to Hayle and then onto St Ives and Penzance. From there they returned again to Falmouth where this time, despite the attentions of small boys 'gratuitously armed with fireworks by the Whigs', they did hold a meeting.[9] Here they were heard by a local Quaker, who noted in his diary that both Lowery and Duncan were eloquent, but inflammatory, not to say seditious, shrewd designing scamps, misguiding honest men with a blaze of enthusiasm. He feared little, however, for although hearty cheers seemed to indicate that a flame was lit he knew enough of Falmouth to feel pretty sure of its going out unless well fanned.[10] Fanning the flame was a huge task. By now the missionaries had been more than two weeks in the county, and were due to return. They asked for an

William Lovett.

extension of their time 'two months would be too little to agitate this county, the people being so scattered'. [11]

From Falmouth they went on to neighbouring Penryn and again to Penzance, and then to a meeting in the old tin mining centre of St Just-in-Penwith. From there, there was nowhere further to go except for the empty cliffs of Lands End, and they retraced their steps back up the county, through the village Goldsithney and on to Camborne again. They then returned to St Ives where, for reasons that will be explained below they failed to attract a crowd. All that remained now was the planned final meeting at Gwennap Pit. [12]

From the foregoing narrative it can be seen that the missionaries concentrated their agitation on the mining districts, and further that they visited the larger settlements twice. This was a tactical decision. The scattered nature of the population among the mining villages and hamlets made it the best course to hold large central meetings, trusting that the spread of the news of the first meeting would bring the miners into the second in larger numbers. [13] Some of the reports they sent back to the movement's general secretary, William Lovett, conveyed a qualified optimism. Thus, on 12 March, Lovett read to the Convention a letter, giving a most cheering account of their reception in Cornwall and of the effect of their agitation. Their mission had proved that nothing was wanting to rouse the community to a sense of their wrongs and obtain their co-operation, than a little trouble on the part of the Convention [13] Lowery wrote:

Our meetings are well attended, they come from curiosity, they are Radicals and do not know it, they are poor and oppressed and the moment they hear our expositions they adopt them. [14]

With the hindsight of historians, we could add, 'and then they go home and forget them', for, despite Lowery's optimism Chartism did not take root among the Cornish miners. From his letters and those of Duncan we can see the real nature of the huge difficulties that faced them, which weighed more heavily in the scales than even the large crowds assembled for the moment. By the end of their first week in the county, they realized that they were addressing a labouring people to whom the great political awakening was yet to come. Duncan lamented bitterly that the Convention might as well have sent missionaries to the South Sea Islands, to instruct the natives there in the principles of a free government, as to Cornwall.[15.]

Lowery, typically was a little less dramatic in his assessment, but it was cautionary enough:

The people here have never heard Politics, nor had any agitation on that question, when we enter a place we know no one, and if we ask if there are any Radicals, they don't seem to seem to know or when they answer in the affirmative it turns out the persons are mere Whigs or Anti-Corn Law men.

So unused to political agitation were the miners that they appeared, thunderstruck at anyone talking so boldly of authority they have thought was unassailable. [16] Some years later he recalled the response he had got from an old man at St Ives when he had inquired if there were any radicals in that town:

"A what, Master?" said he, with a vacant stare. "Any Radicals or Chartists?" said I. I shall never forget the vacuity and bewilderment of his countenance. "No", answered he, "they catch nothing but pilchards and mackerel". [17]

Lowery drew some comfort from his familiarity with the Northern pitmen, pointing out that they too had been ignorant of politics until their great struggle with the coal owners in 1831. Cornwall might yet become: 'A rich mine of Radical ore which if skilful miners bring it forth may be fashioned into weapons that will do fearful execution on the host of misgovernment'. [18] Things were not to turn out that way. Instead, significant numbers of Cornish miners were to go to the North in the great coal strike of 1844 as strike breakers. [19]

The missionaries encountered active opposition from a number of sources. 'The magistrates had condemned, the parsonocracy had preached, and the tyrant masters threatened', wrote Lowery. [20] Among the Chartist documents in the British Library is one that was not written by the missionaries. Entitled 'Address of the Radical Reformers of the Western Division of the County of Cornwall, in Public Meeting Assembled at Gwennap Pit to the General Convention of the Industrious Classes' its purpose was to appoint Lowery and Duncan as the Cornish delegates to the Convention. After describing their good work in the county, it went on to say that the Chartist cause would have been still furtherer advanced:

Had it not been for the interference and false intimidations held out by the Magistracy Clergy and Employers, (who we feel proud to say are not the most intelligent men in our county). The Magistrates in many places have threatened to issue warrants for the apprehension of the missionaries. The Clergy, who are always timid of any alterations in our glorious constitution as it fits to term it, employ themselves instead watching over their flocks in going to every cottage door, and declaring to the women if their husbands sign the National Petition, they would subject themselves to the penalty of transportation. The employers intimating to the men that worked under them, if they attended the meeting or signed the National Petition, they would directly discharge them. [21]

Such efforts were not always successful. The vicar at Falmouth forbade the town crier from announcing the meeting, but he was a sympathizer and went around to all the houses saying at each that he was not allowed to tell them about it. [22] The mayor of Penzance was thrown into such consternation by the arrival of the missionaries, that he wrote straight away to Lord John Russell at the Home Office, asking how to proceed:

I write to your Lordship from a part of her Majesty's Dominions in which there is no clashing of interests between the agriculturalist and the manufacturer in which the labouring classes are in constant employment, where absolute poverty is unknown, where loyalty is proverbial and contentment almost universal - But all this desirable order of things threatened to be overturned and society disjointed by a party of itinerant politicians who style themselves Chartists and profess to be Missionary Delegates from the National Convention and who held their first meeting in this town last evening - at which the most seditious inflammatory language was fearlessly made use of. Her Majesty the Queen was insulted, the Ministers were grossly abused, all the established institutions of the country ridiculed and the working classes were called upon to arm themselves and obtain by force redress from some alleged grievances and to sign a National Petition to be presented to Parliament insisting on many unconstitutional arrangements. [23]

The report is alarmist but, if they were preaching the use of force and using seditious language so overtly, the missionaries were certainly exceeding their instructions, and it is unlikely that they would have received only threats from the magistrates. One of Lowery's favourite oratorical methods may have contributed. If he noticed any gentry at the back of the crowd, he would look directly at them and in a loud voice announce, 'Fellow countrymen, I stand here to preach revolution' and would pause to enjoy their startled reaction before continuing:

But mark my words and do not misconstrue them. Revolution simply means change, and the Revolution I advocate is a change from bad to good, from corrupt and extravagant government to a real representation, retrenchment and reform. [24]

The Mayor of Penzance's comment on the general prosperity of the county in 1839 was echoed by a Falmouth observer: 'Can't do much harm here, I think, People too well off to kick up a row'. [25] This was a sentiment shared by the vicar of Gwennap who wrote to the Home Secretary, assuring him that a 'more complete mistake never was committed by the Chartists, than in supposing they could make converts here'. Any sensation their language had caused had soon died away and, despite large crowds, few converts had been made. [26] Neither was the Whig *West Briton* any more alarmed when it congratulated the mining population on the good sense they have shown in giving no encouragement to the Chartist Missionaries. [27]

It is probable, however that had Lowery and Duncan been asked to nominate the group whose opposition they regarded as most significant, then, despite the efforts of gentry and clergy, they would have indicated the Methodists. Duncan, especially was emphatic on this:

I don't think there can be much love of liberty here; it's too full of Methodist Chapels and they are too Priest ridden to like freedom. [28]

Lowery came to share this view, although as usual he was a little more reflective than his colleague:

The working classes in general were a simple primitive people with strong religious feelings of an excitable temperament...the Methodist style of preaching, however good to work upon their feelings, wanted some of the Presbyterian reasoning to cultivate their understandings. [29]

From the opponents of Chartism too there was recognition of Methodist counter-influence. 'What,' asked the *West Briton*, 'but our religious light is it that has kept our working classes at peace and free from Chartism?' [30]

The relationship of Methodism to the Chartist movement has often been discussed. The hostile attitude of the Wesleyan Methodist national leadership is undeniable, but so too is the sympathy of sects like Primitive Methodism to the movement and to trade unionism in some parts of the country. The work of R. F. Wearmouth in this regard is now more than forty years old. More recently Epstein, for the framework-knitters of Nottinghamshire, and Colls and Jaffe, for the pitmen of the North-Eastern coalfield, have indicated an input of leadership and organizational skills from Primitive Methodism into early trade unionism and Chartism. [31] So far as Cornwall is concerned, such an input is hard to find.

In an influential survey article, Hobsbawm concluded that it was probably wisest to put the lack of interest in and feebleness of Cornish Chartism down to factors unconnected with the religion of the Cornish, although Brian Harrison in a review of his essay pointed out that this was not the view of Lowery and Duncan. [32] Analysis of the local relationship in the county must begin with an assessment of Methodism's overall influence and strength. Cornwall was the most Methodist of English counties. The Religious Census of 1851 showed that 49% of the population attended services on census day; Methodist attendees were 32% of the population and Anglican 13.2%. The parent body of the Wesleyans themselves accounted for 20.5%, the revivalist Bible Christians and the Primitive Methodists for 6% and 2% respectively.

In so far as historians have stressed the positive role of the last named in early radical movements, then it is clear that it was too weak in Cornwall to have had any significance. The percentages for the county as a whole disguise the fact that Methodism generally was much stronger in the western mining half, where three quarters of all the county's Wesleyans lived. They were numerically the significant body and their influence was strong. Local Wesleyan leaders of the time were not necessarily conservative. [33] Men like Thomas Garland were liberal, even reformist, but while they might see manhood suffrage as a longer-term goal, they believed it should await the general educational improvement of the working class. Garland described Chartism as, 'one of the noxious weeds that spring from the ground where no care has been taken that it should produce healthful fruits'. [34] The effects of Methodism on Cornish Chartism can be examined under three headings: 'Positive Opposition'; 'Competitive Opposition', and 'Negative Effect', meaning by the last any effect which the dominant Methodist culture had on the miner's attitude of mind and outlook on life, which might to some degree have contributed to his observed political apathy. The clearest example of 'Positive Opposition' in 1839 came over the intended final Chartist meeting at Gwennap Pit, a place to which local Methodists were historically and sentimentally attached as the favoured preaching location of the great John Wesley himself. Although the *West Briton* reported that the meeting took place as planned, it is clear that there was confrontation. The *Cornwall Gazette* provided a more detailed account of what actually happened on the day, swallowing its usual Tory line to approve of Wesleyan doings:

> It will scarcely be credited that these fellows had the assurance to advertise their meeting to be held at the PIT at Gwennap, a place - as most of our readers know consecrated by the ministrations of the venerable founder of Methodism, and still retained by his followers for periodical religious worship. The Methodists, however, knew better what was due to their own character, and to the memory of Wesley than to suffer this profanation; the senior minister of the circuit very properly repaired to the spot with the parish constables, and kept the gates against all intrusion. [35]

Lowery's own account is interestingly different. He mentions the refusal of the Methodists to allow the use of the Pit, but suggests that, thanks to Duncan's oratorical skill, this did not work to the Chartist's disadvantage:

> The Conference had been written to and had refused the use of the Pit, but all would not do. Although it commenced to rain long before the hour of meeting and continued to rain heavily, yet for four long hours did the thousands of people stand drenched to the skin, and urged the speaker to go on for they did not mind the wet. There were upwards of 15,000 people on the ground and not a place near to shelter them Mr Duncan then came forward amid great cheering and addressed the people with great energy for an hour and a half. He denounced the aristocracy's plundering of the people, and with withering sarcasm he pointed out the hypocrisy of the bigots who would not let them have the Pit to meet in, though erected by the people's labour. (Here there was a cry of "To the Pit" and in

three minutes though holding upwards of 6,000 people it was filled - The Speaker refused to go) No they would show them they had the power, but would not use it…[36]

The meeting then proceeded to appoint Lowery and Duncan, the county's delegates to the Convention. In a letter to the Home Secretary, the vicar of Gwennap passed on an approving mention of the Methodists' action: 'The leaders consulted with me and cooperated in the most effectual manner to prevent any outbreak, and also to discourage the intruders'.[37]

The element of 'Competitive Opposition' was also strong. Despite attracting large crowds, the missionaries realised that if a permanent basis for the movement were to be established, leaders would have to be forthcoming from among the miners themselves. 'The spirit is raised in the People', wrote Lowery to Lovett, 'but they want leaders to organize them'. It was through Methodist and Teetotal competition that he despaired of finding leaders: 'The Teetotallers and the Methodists have monopolized the speakers, and their leaders are against us'. [38] Duncan was even more specific:

They have been taught to be, believe that tee-totalism is the only cure for all the ills that the flesh is subject to; that all other reforms are idle - that it is a sin to attend to any other. The Methodists have all Cornwall divided into districts. The tee-totallers keep their division of territory; in each of them they have from three to six speakers. They keep up an interchange of these agitators throughout the various districts. Between the religious and teetotal agitation, a considerable amount of enterprise and talent is absorbed. I could have no objection in young men devoting themselves to both; but it is a fact of which I have ample proof, that were any of these young men to give the mission the smallest countenance, they would never again be permitted to address a religious or teetotal meeting. Toryism and Pharisaical cant is omnipotent in every teetotal committee in Cornwall. These things have been obstructions and hindrance in our way. [39]

It was a view that was held within the county and, to many, a matter for congratulation. Looking back over the social history of the mining population almost three decades later, a local journalist remarked on the weakness of radical politics in the area: 'We have few turbulent demagogues in Cornwall. A miner who has any rhetorical powers and strong lungs prefers the pulpit to the platform'[40].

Chartism's most immediate and direct competition came from the co-incidence of the mission with the early heady days of teetotalism. James Teare had first visited the county in 1838 and his impact had been great. In the competition for signatures the National Petition was hugely out scored by the pledge. At Teare's first meeting at St Austell 150 people signified their renunciation of the 'demon drink'. Through 1838 and 1839 the progress of the total abstinence movement was sustained at a high level. By February 1839 the society at Ludgvan claimed a membership of 800 from a village population of 2500, while in May of the same year the 2500 members of St Ives added up to half of the town's population. During the week the Chartists visited Truro, a further 150 of its citizens signed the pledge. [41] At national level, Wesleyan Methodism was hostile to teetotalism as it was to Chartism, but it was not until 1841 that the Wesleyan Conference closed its chapels to teetotal meetings. Over the previous three years, however, the teetotal movement had built on the already strong temperance inclination of many Cornish Methodists in a county that by 1834 had by far the biggest membership per thousand of the British and Foreign Temperance Society of any county. To many Wesleyan miners, signing the pledge was an extension of their normal attitude towards strong drink, rather than a conversion from the ways of the devil. The local leaders of chapel society rapidly embraced the new movement. Examples proliferate in the teetotal press: at St Buryan in 1839 six of the eight class leaders had joined; in the more populous Gwennap eighteen, while at Germoe the local preachers were said to have taken up the cause in right good earnest. [42] When there was an attempt at St Ives to enforce the ban of 1841 on the use of chapels, the outcome was the se-cession of 250 chapel members from the parent body to form the Teeto-tal Wesleyan Methodists. [43] Tension between Chartism and teetotalism existed beyond Cornwall. Chartists found themselves unwelcome in the teetotal societies, leading to the establishment of a distinct Teetotal Chartist movement. As the Chartist Circular explained:

The true mode of killing drunkenness, and the equally mischievous habit of moderate tippling is the adoption of the teetotal pledge. The Chartists, we have reason to believe, are generally in favour of testing the good to be derived from total abstinence But many of them object to take the pledge from the present organizational societies in consequence of their exclusive or sectarian tendency. Many a man has said to the writer of this, I cannot join our Tee-total Society, for while its rules pretend to exclude all discussions on all political matters I am constantly insulted and my Chartist principles derided. [44]

However, it was not only in respect of teetotalism that local independence was a characteristic of Cornish Methodism. No national attempts at propriety, for example, could dampen the miners' extreme revivalism. Lowery and Duncan were to find this too for themselves when they returned to St Ives for a second meeting, having held what they judged a successful one there a week before. This time they could not get an audience. A revival had broken out. There were no people for a Chartist meeting, while the chapels were full night and day for three days, during which most of the people ceased work and the shops closed. Frustrated, the missionaries went themselves to the chapel to witness events. Lowery was familiar with such scenes of religious excitement, having observed similar happenings among the Primitive Methodists in the pit villages of Northumberland and Durham. He later offered an explanation for such outbreaks:

The population possesses all the materials for such explosions, being full of warm religious feeling, which overrules knowledge. Their daily language and the religious services they attend are replete with rapturous exclamations. Perhaps the mother is out on some errand she has left the children to play with those of a neighbour until she returns. Bye and bye in imitation of their elders, they begin singing a hymn and uttering the expressions, which they have heard at chapel. In the midst of this the mother returns. Her paternal feelings are delighted, and she exclaims, "Bless the Lord!" She joins the hymn and calls on her neighbours, who become similarly affected, and the enthusiasm spreads from house to house, then the chapel is sought and the whole neighbourhood are infected. [45]

As well as offering this plausible view of recurrent revivalism in a community with a strong chapel culture, Lowery recorded his disgust at the raw emotion of the scenes he witnessed in the chapel. Insight into the causes of revivalism and distaste at the phenomenon are well enough, but the essential fact remains that: in competing with a revival for an audience, the Chartists were not simply losers. They were non-starters.

The underlying 'Negative Effect' of Methodism on the outlook of Cornish miners is more difficult to evaluate. Clearly they had some tendency towards fatalism, which was a not unexpected consequence of working at such a dangerous occupation. There is, however, a difference between a habitual fatalism and the passive acceptance of this world's trials, which too much emphasis on the world to come can generate. The reporter on the mining districts to the parliamentary inquiry into child labour, in 1842, thought that:

> *Nothing can indeed be more admirable than the cheerful confidence with which in the trust of a future life, the miner contemplates that termination, often an early one, of his labours.* [46]

The system of wage payment at the mines even made it possible for attitudes of resignation to extend into this area. It is difficult in most circumstances for a labour force to see poor earnings as the work of God, but under the tribute system this was often the perception. The miners contracted in small groups to work a pitch that is a defined part of the mine for the percent-age of the value of the tin or copper ore, which they raised from it. They offered to work at rates, which they judged would give them good wages from the quality and quantity of ore they considered to be in the pitch. They had experience enough in making this estimation, but the best of judgments can err. Lodes can unexpectedly disappear, narrow or worsen in quality and it was common enough for miners to find that they had poor or even no wages at all to come at the end of a month's hard work. The opposite too could happen, lodes could improve in quality or quantity after the rate had been agreed and bring, on occasion, very good earning indeed. Under such a system, Methodist ministers could see the hand of God, testing, punishing or rewarding. In

1846, a local evangelical journal carried an article entitled, 'The Cornish Miner: Or the Blessed Effects of Piety in Humble Life'. This portrayed a miner who claimed to be representative. After a disastrous tribute agreement, the man and his family had been brought to the edge of destitution, yet:

No rankling ill will to those whom Providence had placed in easier circumstances, arose in their minds. No hatred to their employers, or rebellious thoughts against the government of the country, for a moment found a place in their hearts. They laboured, they sorrowed, they suffered; but they patiently endured. [47]

The writer was anxious that readers unfamiliar with the Cornish miners should accept this case as typical:

We are fully persuaded, that we have brought into notice that which contributes very greatly to give a character to the mining population of Cornwall. Great numbers of them are truly converted to God, and walk in the light of his countenance; and to the same extent that they are influenced by this holy religion, are they made sober, industrious, and patient in their temporal calling. Philosophy may extend its researches and give us beautiful pictures of moral life. Philanthropy may search out cases of suffering, and labour after means of relief. But while we rejoice in the operations of each, we cannot forget that this religion is the remedy which God has provided for the ruin of a world; and that it is the only agent on which we can certainly rely for teaching, guiding, raising and saving, fallen men. [48]

Max Weber described a 'theodicy of suffering' in which the effect of religious teaching is to turn the experience of deprivation and suffering from finding expression in social discontent into a vehicle of personal redemption. It was something of the kind that John Longmaid one of the few known Chartists active in the county around the time of the mission, had in mind when he wrote to the *Northern Star* in 1841:

The Wesleyans are the people's bitterest enemies. They preach peace and contentment as the only true test of their being in the right road to heavenly bliss. [49]

It should be as evident to historians, as it was to Lowery and Duncan that the role of Methodism cannot be ignored in any discussion of the proclivities and responses of the Cornish mining community. Hobsbawm however, pointed to other factors that, he suggests, contributed more to the weakness of Cornish Chartism. He described the county as having an industrial and social structure that was in many respects archaic. Archaic is perhaps suggestive of a deceptive continuity. [50] The organization of the mining industry represented, in fact, a high degree of specialized adaptation to the productive needs of a high (and increasing) level of capital investment in what remained a risky enterprise. It is correct to point out that the feeling that workers as a class opposed employers as a class developed slow and late. But this was less the direct result of the tribute system than of the fact that, to spread risk, the mines were financed under the cost book system with its plurality of absent shareholders. The classic owner/entrepreneur of the industrial revolution did not figure in the Cornish experience. There was no equivalent of the factory-master and no direct one of the coal owners. Hobsbawm further suggests that being paid under the tribute system, and not seeing a class of employers opposed to them, the miners continued to see the grain-hoarding middleman, or profiteering farmer, as the enemy when high food prices brought hunger. Accordingly they continued to express their discontent in the traditional form of food rioting down to 1847. Duncan learned of one such incident, presumably the 1831 riot at Penzance, but failed to put the right interpretation on it:

The men of Cornwall relied now as they ever had done more upon physical than moral force, instancing two examples of their determination on former occasions. The one when a vessel was laden with corn in scarce times, for transportation upon which the miners and fishermen rose, released the cargo sold it for the real value and paid the receipts to the owners. [51]

Food rioting, however, revealed the miners' conservatism and commitment to a prior political economy, rather than their potential for political radicalism. There are other reasons too which contribute to explaining the observed political apathy of the miners, including the geographical remoteness of West Cornwall. The writer has surveyed these factors elsewhere in considering whether there was a configuration of quietism. [52] Close study, however, of the Chartist Mission of 1839, suggests that it is not possible to offer an adequate explanation if the religious culture of the mining community is not taken into account.

Chartism in Cornwall did not end in 1839. Groups of Chartists continued to attract notice from time to time in the local press and activities were reported occasionally in the *Northern Star* through the 1840s. Camborne, Falmouth, Helston. Hayle, Falmouth, Truro and Penzance all experienced some level of activity. Groups of tradesmen in these towns ensured a persistent, but small, radical presence. Dorothy Thompson has stressed the importance of such artisans to the movement, [53] but the real failure of 1839 was that it built no bridge to the 20,000 miners. At a tee-total meeting in the large mining parish of Gwennap in 1840, a visiting speaker told a crowded meeting that he had had opportunities of knowing that the Chartists were habitual takers of intoxicating liquors, and that but for this they would not have been led into violent acts. At the end of the meeting, forty-eight people signed the pledge. [54]

1 For a succinct account of the Convention see E. Royle, *Chartism*, 1980, pp. 22-25; *Northern Star*, 2 March 1839. The historiography of Methodism and its relation to radical politics revolves around the so-called 'Halévy Thesis' after the French author of the monumental *History of the English People in the Eighteenth Century*, published between 1913 and 1932, who argued that Methodism was significant in preventing revolution in England. Interest was revived, with the hostile view of Methodism taken by E. P. Thompson in his classic *The Making of the English Working Class*, in 1963. For a recent overview which forwards a thesis of its own see A. Gilbert, 'Religion and Political Stability in Early Industrial England', in P. O'Brien, and R. Quinault, *The Industrial Revolution and British Society*, Cambridge, 1993, pp. 79-99.

2 *The Weekly Record of the Temperance Movement*, 11 October 1856, p. 234. Lowery's autobiography was serialised in this journal. It has now been edited by B. Harrison and P. Hollis as *Robert Lowery. Radical and Chartist*, London, 1979. Some letters from Lowery were sent directly to the *Northern Liberator*, a North Eastern-based newspaper with which he had regional links. As well as the Chartist Letter books in the British Library; there is some reporting of the mission in the *Northern Star*. Duncan also wrote a few letters to the *True Scotsman*.

3 British Library, MS Add. 34245, Vol. A, Folio 120.

4 *West Briton*, 5 March 1839.

5 *Northern Liberator*, 16 March 1839. See above Chapter 8.

6 BL, MS Add. 34245, Vol. A, Folio 120. for Spurr see below Chapter 8.

7 BL, MS Add. 34245, Vol. A, Folio 120.

8 *Weekly Record*, 25 Oct 1856, p. 250; BL, MS Add. 34245, Folio 120.

9 BL, MS Add. 34245, Folio 148.

10 Cited in A. Jenkin, 'The Cornish Chartists', *Journal of the Royal Institute of Cornwall*, 9, 1982, p. 57.

11 BL, MS Add. 34245, Vol. A, Folio 169.

12 BL, MS Add. 34245, Folio 148.

13 *Northern Star*, 16 March 1839. William Lovett was the best known of Cornish Chartists, born in Newlyn in 1800 and migrated to London in 1821. He was General Secretary of the Chartist Convention in 1839 in which capacity he was the addressee of the letters sent by Lowery and Duncan. Released from Warwick gaol in 1840 he returned to Cornwall to recuperate; on the coach he engaged in conversation with a gentleman who learning his name exclaimed, 'What William Lovett the Chartist? You don't look like one!' This gentleman proved to be the Superintendent of the Wesleyan Ministers of that district.

14 BL, MS Add. 34245, Vol. A, Folio 148.

15 Cited A. Jenkin, 'Cornish Chartists', p. 58.

16 BL, MS Add. 34245, Vol. A, Folios 120, 148.

17 *Weekly Record*, 25 Oct 1839, p. 250.

18 *Northern Liberator*, 16 March 1839; BL, MS Add. 34245, Vol. A, Folio 120.

19 The coal mining unions sent delegates to dissuade the Cornish from 'Blacklegging', but were unable to prevent many from going North. See *Northern Star*, 8 June, 17, 31 August, 14 September 1844; R. Fynes, *The Miners of Northumberland and Durham*, Sunderland, 1873, p. 91.

20 *Northern Liberator*, 6 April 1839.

21 BL, MS Add. 34245, Vol. A, Folio 178.

22 *Weekly Record*, 11 October 1856, p. 254.

23 PRO, HO 40/41.

24 *Weekly Record*, 25 October 1856, p. 250.

25 A. Jenkin, 'Cornish Chartists', p. 57.

26 PRO, HO 40/41.

27 *West Briton*, 5 April 1839.

28 *Weekly Record*, 25 October 1856, p. 250.

29 ibid.

30 *West Briton*, 14 February 1840.

31 R. Wearmouth, *Some Working Class Movements of the Nineteenth Century*, London, 1948; R. Colls, *The Pitmen of the Northern Coalfield. Work, Culture and Protest 1790-1850*, Manchester, 1987; J. Epstein, 'Some Organisational and Cultural Aspects of the Chartist Movement in Nottingham', in J. Epstein, and D. Thompson, (eds.), *The Chartist Experience*, London, 1982, pp. 221-268; See also D. Hempton, *Methodism and Politics in British Society 1750-1950*, London, 1884, p. 179.

32 E. Hobsbawm, 'Methodism and the Threat of Revolution in Britain', in his *Labouring Men*, London, 1964, p. 30; B. Harrison, review in *Economic History Review*, 10, 1967, p. 179.

33 T. Shaw, *History of Cornish Methodism*, Truro, 1967, p. 96; R. Currie, 'A Micro Theory of Methodist Growth', in *Proceedings of the Wesleyan Historical Society*, 36, 1957, p. 72.

34 T. Garland, *Memorials Literary and Religious*, 1868, p. 398.

35 M.Edwards, 'Communication', in *Journal of the Cornish Methodist Historical Association*, 2, May 1966, p. 109.

36 *Northern Liberator*, 6 April 1839.

37 PRO, HO 40/41.

38 BL, MS Add. 34245, Vol. A, Folio 148.

39 B. Harrison, *Drink and the Victorians: The Temperance Question in England 1815-1872*, London, 1971, p. 180.

40 *Western Morning News*, 10 January 1865.

41 H Douch, *Old Cornish Inns*, Truro, 1967, pp. 108-109.

42 On the close connection between Methodism and tee-totalism see J. Rule, 'Methodism, Popular Beliefs and Village Culture in Cornwall 1800-1850', in R. Storch, (ed.), *Popular Culture and Custom in Nineteenth Century England*, London, 1982, p. 51.

43 M. Edwards, 'The Tee-Total Wesleyan Methodists', in *Proceedings of the Wesleyan Historical Society*, 30, Parts 3 & 4, September-December 1961, pp. 66, 68.

44 *Chartist Circular*, 1, No. 1.

45 *Weekly Record*, 25 October 1856, p. 250.

46 *British Parliamentary Publications*, 1842, XVI, p. 759.

47 *Cornish Banner*, 1846, p. 22.

48 ibid, p. 24.

49 A. Jenkin, 'Cornish Chartists', p. 64.

50 E. Hobsbawm, 'Methodism and the Threat of Revolution', p. 30, 51.

51 *Northern Star*, 18 April 1838.

52 J. Rule,"A Configuration of Quietism. Attitudes towards Trade Unionism among the Cornish Miners" *Tijdschift voor sociale geshiedenis*, 18,1992; *Regional Implementation of the Labour Movement in Britain and the Netherlands*, pp. 248-262. See also below Chapter 10.

53 See A. Jenkin, 'Cornish Chartists'; D. Thompson, *The Chartists: Popular Politics in the Industrial Revolution*, Aldershot, 1984, p. 203. The places listed are taken from Thompson's appendix of Chartist locations, except for Hayle for which there is evidence in HO 40/4154.

10 Configuration of Quietism? Attitudes towards Trade Unionism and Chartism among Cornish Miners

At a conference of the Society for the Study of Labour History in 1970, I presented a paper on the role of Methodism in explaining the weakness of Chartism among the tin and copper miners of Cornwall.[1] I concluded by suggesting that although Methodism can be seen as inhibiting the implantation of Chartism, on its own it had only a limited explanatory value. It was among several significant factors making up a 'configuration of quietism'. That Cornish miners were hardly involved in the working-class industrial and political movements of the first half of the nineteenth century was widely noted by contemporaries and has been confirmed by historians.

In the first place some of the separate factors were also present in other areas among working groups where either trade unionism or political radicalism or both were much stronger and where they seem to have had a different impact. The positive contribution generally allowed to Primitive Methodism by historians of the North Eastern coalfield is an obvious example. If the factors offered in explanation of political quietism are in themselves separately insufficient, or even contradictory, can a useful explanation of the lack of political and industrial conflict be readied by combining them?

Recently, after a long period of writing labour history at the national rather then local level, I returned to re-examine my argument. We hardly expect single or even 'main' cause explanations these days, but it may not be unrealistic to work towards constructing configurations, where the interrelations and interactions of various factors have some explanatory value, even when some of whose factors can be shown to have had a dif-

ferent impact in the particular context of another occupational community. Perhaps what is being suggested is no more than that a combined or
cumulative effect could be the outcome of an environment unpropitious
for the growth of trade unionism and popular political radicalism of the
kind exemplified by the Chartists. This essay considers the range of explanations offered by contemporaries for the low interest shown by the
Cornish miners in early labour movements.

In 1838 there were around 160 mines in Cornwall employing 27,028
persons of whom 17,898 were adult males. By 1851 the labour force had
reached 36.284 with a proportionate increase in the number of adult
males. They were employed in enterprises of varying size. In 1838 there
were five concerns employing more than 1000 persons each and a further
five employing between 500 and 999. Fifty-four mines employed between
100 and 499, the rest of the miners being scattered around smaller workings. The mines were fairly concentrated geographically for although
miners made up a quarter of the adult (20+) male labour force in the
county as a whole, in the central copper mining district around Redruth
in 1851 they accounted for more than half. [2]

The working miners received a 'good press' from nineteenth century
observers. The novelist Wilkie Collins, who toured Cornwall in 1850,
found them a 'cheerful, contented race', with 'remarkably moderate and
sensible' views. To a *Quarterly Reviewer* in 1857, the miners made up, 'one
of the most orderly and civilized societies in the world'. L. L. Price who
published a thorough study of the organization of the mining industry
in 1888 concluded that it had, despite its rapid growth and capitalization,
'escaped the disturbing influences of the industrial revolution'. When
the Webbs came at that time to write their pioneering history of British trade unionism, they afforded the Cornish miners a single sentence:
'Among the tin, lead and copper miners Trade Unionism is, as far as we
can ascertain, absolutely unknown'. [3]

The tribute system

Most favoured among contemporary explanations, was the peculiar
method of wage payment used in the mines. An impressive list of writers

on economic and social matters praised the system and recommended its extension to other industries. Henry Mayhew, Charles Babbage and John Stuart Mill were among them. Babbage wanted the system to become more general because:

No other mode of payment affords to the workmen a measure of success so directly proportioned to the industry, the integrity and the talent which they exert.

Mill first wrote of the tribute system in 1845 in *The Claims of Labour*, where he stated that miners were 'invariably' joint-adventurers in the mines, along with the share-owners, and concluded that for:

...intelligence, independence and good conduct as well as prosperous circumstances, no labouring population in the island is understood to be comparable to the Cornish miners.

In the *Principles of Political Economy* he returned to the theme under the heading: 'Examples of the association of labourers with capitalists'; and again commended the system as producing a level of intelligence, independence and 'moral elevation' which ranked the Cornish miners 'far above' the 'generality of the labouring class'[41].

Lesser-known commentators wrote similarly and so regularly that the 'strike-free' Cornish mining industry became a cliché as one writer picked up from the account of another. One claimed in 1834 of the tribute system: 'so admirably does it reconcile all conflicting interests, that strikes among the miners are there unknown'. The greatest advocate was the mining engineer turned manager John Taylor who tried to introduce tributing into the lead mines of Derbyshire. He wrote:

No one has heard of disagreements between the Cornish miners and their employers, no combinations or unions on the one side or the other exist; nor have turnouts or strikes been contemplated or attempted. [5]

It was a view shared by a Birmingham employer appearing before a Parliamentary inquiry in 1824. As a manufacturer of steam pumping engines, he probably did have some first hand knowledge of the industry. He was of the opinion that the tribute system so 'perfectly prevented' strikes that its extension would remove the necessity for any laws against combinations. [6]

The tribute system was peculiar in the way it combined payment by results with individual wage bargaining. Tributers undertook to work measured portions of the mine for an agreed share of the price the ore they raised fetched when sold. The contract known as the 'bargain', usually ran for two months and was expressed in terms of a rate in the pound, which varied from a shilling or less (5p) to as much as fifteen shillings (75p). The variation was due to the fact that 'pitches' would contain not only different quantities of ore, but different grades. Tributers had in fact to estimate the rate at which they could make good wages. If a pitch contained abundant and/or high grade ore, then they would accept a bargain at a lower rate than if prospective yields were low. The speculative dimension is evident. The final selling price of the copper or tin was subject to fluctuation and remuneration was tied to it. Luck played a part. Lodes could turn out thinner or poorer than the first signs had indicated. They could, as a result of geological faulting, simply disappear. The skill and judgment of the tributer in assessing the potential was critical, for the distinctive feature of the system was that places in the mine were not allocated by lot as in the coalmines of the North East, nor were they distributed by management. They were bid for at a form of 'dutch auction'. The pitches were put up one by one and the team of miners (usually consisting of two or four men and known as a 'pare'), who offered to work it for the lowest rate took it for the next two month contract period.

It is not hard to see why the system appealed to those nurtured in the axioms of political economy. It suggested a high degree of task-application because tile miners were paid by results. It associated labour with capital in the risk of the enterprise and was commonly presented as a form of joint speculation. A premium was put on 'intelligence'. It was the antithesis of collective bargaining and it 'naturally' regulated wages by supply and demand, for when work was scarce fiercer competition would have the direct effect of the miners bidding down their own wages. [7] Certainly a system which involved a miner in periodic competition with his comrades for work which was to go to the lowest bidder was hardly a propitious one for collective action on the wage front. The speculative element was considerable. The tributer was not offered constant high earnings comparable with those of skilled labour, but the chance of a sudden windfall and the risk of poverty. Although estimation was brought to a fine art by both sides - mine captains as the managers were known and the experienced miners - there were always times when the unexpected happened and one side or the other was substantially favoured. A letter from 1804 illustrates this:

...within the last six or seven days two poor men were working in a part of the mine where lode was very hard and poor, they suddenly cut into a bunch of rich copper ore very suit and consequently easy to break. The poor fellows having by their contract 12s. (60p) out of the pound...Their time expires at the end of the month and if the lode continues so good...I expect they will get £100 each for themselves for two weeks labour, and that same piece of ground will be taken next month for less than one shilling in the pound. [8]

Such 'starts', as they were called, might happen once or twice in a lifetime and were rarely so high as £100 a man, but they help explain the miners' attachment to a system which more often denied them a good wage and sometimes left them with nothing. Significantly there is evidence that miners' wives preferred their husbands to work on other tasks in the mine than raising ore, for example sinking shafts or driving adits and levels. This 'dead' groundwork, known as 'tutwork' was paid by the fathom and produced usually lower but much more constant wages. In writing of the generally 'prosperous circumstances' of the miners, Mill in common with the other advocates of tributing, based his account on propagandist descriptions. Only a few with real experience of the county bothered to point out that speculation produces losers as well as gainers and for a working man with only his labour to venture the opposite to fortune can he destitution. One mine engineer with close knowledge remarked of the bargaining system that while it gave every man a chance of competing for well-paid work, it did not give to every one, 'the means of purchasing the necessaries of life'. [9] John Harris, a miner who became a poet, did not need reminding of this:

A month had nearly ended
and he severe had wrought,
Day after day in darkness
And it was all for nought.
The mineral vein had faded
And now all hope was fled,
Tomorrow should be pay day
His children have no bread. [10]

There is no doubt who gained most. The capitalist investors did not mind the paying of occasional large sums to miners, for as Taylor pointed out they were rare enough and when they did happen, they served to, 'animate ill the others who increase their exertion in the hopes of similar discovery'. They encouraged competition at the next bidding and served to bring neglected parts of the mine into working. In 1805 it was remarked that following a 'bonanza', a pitch was taken for as little as 5d (2p) in the pound, when the captain's estimation was that 5p was the lowest rate at which good earnings were possible, but 'there was no stopping them in the survey so eager were they to have that pitch'. [11]

As well as ignoring its darker side, the system's advocates tended to write as if all Cornish miners were tributers. In fact the proportion varied from time to time and may in some mines have been little more than half of the adult miners at times. In a sense they were a 'labour aristocracy' whose values and attitudes tended to predominate. But not in a very full sense. As the men who raised the actual ore, they were regarded as the miners proper: 'He was a tributer and tributers look with as great a contempt upon the tutman, as the tutmen do upon the surface labourers'. [12] In fact there is evidence that if some men only worked as tributers, others took work under both forms of contract as employment opportunities dictated, for the distribution of work available between ore-raising and dead ground driving obviously varied over time and between mines. In an expansive phase new sinkings would increase the need for tutworkers. Advocates also tended to be a little sanguine in their belief that tributing involved completely free bargaining. In many mines management clearly favoured trusted and established pares, leading to a practice known as taking 'farthing pitches', when newcomers worked an initial contract period for a nominal rate, with a view to getting established at a good mine. More significant was the convention among the workforce in the older mining districts of not bidding against the 'old pare', that is allowing the pare working a pitch the first chance of agreeing terms at its re-setting. More attention to this detail might have modified some views, for it could be described as a tacit combination. On one occasion in 1853, the tributers at a mine felt that the current high price of copper ore was not being reflected in the tribute rates that the management was prepared to accept. They met and agreed that no one would undertake to work a pitch where the previous pare considered the terms of renewal too low. This produced a showdown; a strike which spread to other mines in the district and lasted for several weeks. At a mass meeting the miners spoke of the need to end, 'some bad customs amongst themselves', meaning the extent to which they were competing with each other. This was an isolated event, which although it qualifies the view that the tribute system invariably precluded strikes, hardly denies the very low incidence of disputes in the industry. I have discovered only seven strikes between 1793 and 1859, two of which were not over wages. All were local. None were long lasting and, significantly, none seem to have been connected with the activities of a pre-existing trade union, nor to have led to the establishment of even a temporary one. [13]

It is not to being argued that payment by results in itself diminished strike or trade union activity. Piece-rates were the basis of the payment systems used in most mines, coal as well as metal. It has recently been argued that the 'bargaining' involved on the North Eastern coalfield was the basis of the development of a collective labour consciousness. [14] It has also been shown that a deliberate restriction of output per shift was the main strategy of the early pitmens' union. [15] But the pitmen worked at a rate which applied to all those working in similar conditions. Their working places were allocated by lot ('cavilling') at quarterly intervals. Under the bond system they bargained as a group once a year with the agents of the coal owners, although more often on a local basis in respect of particular working conditions. Until the later adoption in some areas of the 'sliding scale', their wages were not directly tied to the market value of their output. If the tribute system was to any degree responsible for the absence of trade unionism among the Cornish miners, then the emphasis should be on its core component; short term, competitive and, especially, individual wage bargaining.

The Organization of the Industry

Price, in his detailed study of work and wages in the industry asked why there were no strikes, and why the relations between miners and mine-owners seemed to adjust themselves so peacefully. He did not, however, think that the divergent interest of miners bidding against each other was the best explanation of the lack of a collective labour consciousness. His answer was that, 'the workman is in a sense his own employer'. [16] He suggested: 'The comparative absence of strife is due, not to the elimination of the capitalist, but due to the practical disappearance of the employer'.

Tributers, and to some extent tutworkers, could regard themselves as independently contracting with the shareholders through the medium of the captains. Indeed, by mid-nineteenth century the term 'captain' to describe the face-to-face managers of mines was in larger mines giving way to 'agent'. Accordingly the miners were slow to exhibit the solidarity of a wage-earning class. Since earnings were determined by individual estimating and bargaining skills, by luck and directly by the fluctuations of the market, management did not normally directly confront labour with wage cuts or with lay-offs in times of recession. Increased competition at the setting did this for them. This practical disappearance of the employer was in part due to the tribute system. To spread risk most mines were run on the cost-book system. They were controlled not by owner-entrepreneurs but by a plurality of shareholders ('adventurers'). Day-to-day financial management was entrusted to a purser, and man-management to the captains. The representative capitalist was a financier not entrepreneur. Nor were there any mine-owners in the way that there were on some of the coalfields. Cornish landlords made fortunes but they almost always leased their mineral rights. As the writer of an official report in 1842 put it:

> The mine adventurers, the real employers are not brought into conduct in any way as masters with the working miners, so that the agents, men taken for the most part from their own ranks, are the only superiors with whom they have to do. [17]

He thought there to be 'something American' in the system. Social advancement was possible through the achievement of responsible positions and hopes of a substantial gain on tribute for tributers meant that some at least achieved the material means to rise out of their class. Had not the grandfather of Sir William Lemon, the County M.P. in the 1830s begun his family's rise in this way? [18]

With no employer class in face-to-face contact, the feeling, as Professor Hobsbawm has expressed it, that 'workers as a class opposed employers as a class developed slow and late'. Hobsbawm was incorrect in indicating that a labour dispute in 1831 was the only known one, but significantly it was the nearest to a typical strike and it took place at the one considerable mine which was owned and managed by a single capitalist. [19]

Paternalism: Lords and Masters

In 1857 a writer remarked on the great local influence exercised in the mining districts by individual 'gentlemen'. Paternalism has become much used as a hold-all explanation of social relations between classes [20] and there were features of the mining districts which enhanced the influence of some landowners. The owners of the lands under which tin and copper lodes ran, were known as the 'lords' and received dues from the profits of the companies to whom they leased mining rights. A profitable mine in the mid-nineteenth century could bring in as much as £1000 an acre. Some of the 'lords' were actually peers, others were titled country gentlemen, many were neither. Several began as one and, aided by their mining fortunes, ended as another. Some were old-established, but newly enriched. Others were *parvenu* in both respects, when rich min-

'The Gentleman and the Miner', John Opie.

eral discoveries brought them fortunes from inconsiderable landhold-
ings. Whether new or old, they shared social attitudes. It was of Sir William Lemon, the miner's grandson, that the historian Richard Polwhele
wrote:

> In him we see the old country gentleman, faithful to his King without ser-
> vility, attached to the people without democracy'. [21]

As landlords and frequently, as magistrates the 'lords' presented
themselves in paternalist rhetoric and actions. Sometimes they referred
to themselves as 'fathers of the people', but saw themselves as strict parents. Charity and patronage was expected from them and in return they
expected deference and order. A number made a practice of granting
smallholdings from their wastes to working miners on generous terms.

They hoped that moral improvement would stem from a purposeful use of non-work time and, as actual landlords, their influence became even greater. The most influential from the 1790s to the third decade of the nineteenth century, was Sir Francis Basset of Tehidy near Redruth. In conversation in 1810, he remarked that the problem of carrying on mining operations by bodies of absent shareholders was that they were hardly ever 'liberal'. He was not thinking of politics, but of charity. He did not supply reasons, but they can be suggested. The out-adventurers were not justices, so the threat to order posed by hungry miners was not their concern. They were not local landowners and so not bothered by the poor rate. They had no social position to maintain in the locality, which depended on respect and gratitude. Out-adventurers might be rich but largess is not expected from the distant. It is expected from those who accept the deference of the local poor. [22] In the very hungry year 1801, an estate steward wrote to his employer:

> My neighbour has just communicated to me...a letter from J Buller Esq., inclosing a draft for £100 towards a fund for procuring corn for the poor. Sir John St Aubyn, who has but a very small estate here, gave £5. 5s [23].

The implication was not only that his employer was expected to contribute, but to do so in relation to the extent of her influence. Similar implications derive from another letter in 1847 from a steward to his employer:

> Wheal Prosper is not your property, neither are you at present receiving any dues of inconsequence, but merely on Halvana...I do not think you can be expected to subscribe to anything more than the relief fund of the Parish which I consider they are in great want of.

Charity was hardly ever casual. This steward wrote on another occasion informing his employer that he was withholding a contribution to a relief fund because some of the other landowners had not yet come forward. [24] Stewards linked lords with miners. They fixed, collected and on occasion remitted the rents for cottages and smallholdings. They generally managed the lord's charity. When the steward of the Basset estates died in 1841, a newspaper obituary described him as:

...a gentleman who for fifty years has proved himself the constant friend of the tenantry as well as of the miners and labourers...while besides most zealously carrying into effect the benevolent designs of his noble patrons, he has been careful to bring under their consideration every case, in which they might with advantage to deserving persons...do good. [25]

In the depression of copper prices in the 1780s, out-adventurers (non-local shareholders) pressed for the closure of loss-making mines. They were surprised to find themselves opposed by the lords, who were as prepared to sink their money in employing the poor as to maintain them without working. The lords, who were prepared to give up their royalties to enable marginal concerns to continue, were resentful that distant investors took a different view about losing money. In later depressions reactions were similar. In 1847 a steward suggested that his employer give up his dues: 'as should the mines stop, it will be ruinous to many of the inhabitants, in that neighbourhood, the greater part of whom are your tenants'. In 1854 he was urging not just that dues be forgone, but that the lord consider taking up shares in a mine in danger of closing. [26]

Charity wove a web of dependence and deference that was as much the cement of the social system as patronage was of the political. It was assisted by ceremony. The social leaders had to be seen to be such. The gentry sought to identify tenants and dependents with their families. They provided largesse and entertainment on family occasions such as weddings and christenings. They involved the poorer sort in elaborate processional pomp at patrician funerals. When the Basset family won an important lawsuit, they treated the entire labour force of one of their larger mines to ale. There was patronage of local cottage gardening societies, and of schools for the poor. [27] With no manifest employer class contending for influence, their domination of the mining villages was unchallenged. Tied to the labour force by complex strings of patronage, landlordship, traditional authority and deference (the relationship was more subtle than the wage-nexus), but at bottom it rested just as much on the labour of the working miner. A steward reminded his employer in 1795 that he owed a 'bounty' to the poor inhabitants of a neighbourhood from which his 'great fortune' was considerably augmented by 'some mines wrought by the labour of these very poor people.[28]

Methodism

Quietism is properly applied to a passivity originating in religious attitudes, and we now return to the question to which I gave priority in my attempt at explanation: To what extent was Methodism an inhibiting influence on the development of political and industrial protest in nineteenth century Cornwall? Quantification of religious influence is always difficult. There are figures for society membership, but no way of converting these into one for wider attendance at chapel, still less of more peripheral attachment. Many years of researching the subject has led me to accept the opinion of the author of an official report on the mining population in 1842 that while not all miners were Methodists, sufficient numbers were to determine important characteristics of the community as a whole. [29] Did contemporaries either with approval or with complaint, claim quietistic effects for Methodism? 'What but our religious light is it that has kept our working classes at peace and free from Chartism?' asked a writer in 1840, while an evangelical periodical observed that to the extent that the miners became converted so were they made 'sober, industrious and patient in their temporal calling'. [30] Coming from middle class evangelical sources, such expressed opinions do not in themselves justify a reconsideration of Hobsbawm's view that it is probably wisest to attribute the weakness of Cornish Chartism to factors unconnected with religion. [31] There is, however, evidence from the Chartist side. Two 'missionaries', Abraham Duncan and Robert Lowery were sent in 1839 to interest the miners in the movement. They placed the Methodists at the top of their list of opponents. Duncan wrote: 'I do not think there can be much love of liberty here; it is too full of Methodist chapels'. [32]

It is convenient to discuss the relationship of Methodism to Chartism under three headings.

Positive opposition

Methodist leaders were hostile to Chartism, which one of them described as one of the 'noxious weeds' that sprang from, 'carelessly cultivated or neglected ground'. This hostility was evident when the Methodists sought to prevent the missionaries from holding a public meeting in a natural amphitheatre that had been much used by John Wesley, and was the major shrine of Methodism in the county. Local newspaper reports poured high praise on the Methodists for their action, as did the Vicar of the parish in a letter to the Home Secretary. [33]

Competitive opposition

Methodism can be considered as an organizational rival to Chartism, which had been long established in terms of the allegiance of actual and potential talent as well as of numbers. Cornish Methodists were strong advocates of temperance and the teetotal agitation was taking place at the same time as the Chartist one. Duncan reported:

The Methodists have all Cornwall divided into districts. The tee-totallers keep their division of territory; in each of these they have from six to twelve speakers. They keep up an interchange of these agitators through the various districts. Between the religious and the tee-total agitation, a considerable amount of enterprise and talent is absorbed. These things have been obstructions and hindrances in our way.

It was for audiences and attention as well as for leadership that the Chartists had to compete. Lowery had to cancel a meeting planned for St Ives because a religious revival was filling the chapels and preoccupying the population. [34]

Negative effect

The pioneer of sociology, Max Weber, used the concept of a 'theodicy of suffering' to explain the effect of religious teaching in turning the experience of deprivation suffering from finding expression in social discontent into a vehicle of personal redemption. An article on the Cornish miner in the *Cornish Banner* in the difficult years of the 1840s provides almost an ideal illustration of this claimed effect:

> *No rankling ill will to those whom Providence had placed in easier circumstances arose in their minds. No hatred to their employers. Or rebellious thoughts against the government of the country, for a moment found a place in their hearts. They laboured, they sorrowed, they suffered, but they patiently endured.* [35]

However, Methodism was a strong cultural influence in areas other than Cornwall and in some of these places more positive effects have been claimed, in particular in respect of Chartism. Epstein's study of the framework knitting districts of Nottinghamshire shows a relationship that is complex and in some respects contradictory. Methodism, especially in its Primitive Methodist form, developed leadership and organizational skills that were of 'inestimable value'. In contrast to Weber's negativity, Epstein points to the possibility of religion offering a moral basis for the aims of the Charter, quoting a local preacher and Chartist's remark, 'we endeavor to prove to them that our principles are those advocated in the Bible'. A marriage between Methodism and Chartism could never be so complete. The former constituted a community, which to a large degree had turned in upon itself, separated and sheltered from the working class at large through a sense of moral superiority, whereas Chartism was a 'non-sectarian inclusive movement, which sought to appeal to a larger sense of class solidarity'. Further, Methodism was sternly opposed to some aspects of popular culture and life with which Chartism wished to connect, especially tavern culture and recreational forms. Of a Nottinghamshire Primitive Methodist preacher expelled in 1841, it was said that he was a 'bad man, fond of ale, a desperate tobacco smoker, and a great Chartist'. [36]

It is perhaps significant that Primitive Methodism was comparatively weak in Cornwall; behind the Bible Christians as well as the parent Wesleyans to which most Methodist miners belonged. [37] As well as Nottinghamshire the coal mining areas of the North East of England also reveal a complex relationship between Methodism and radical politics. Robert Colls has stressed that Primitive Methodism was an essential component of the same sense of community, which gave colliers' unions their strength. It was, he argues, through the opportunities offered in and around the chapel that Methodists acquired the confidence and ability to hold places of influence in local unions out of proportion to their numbers. James Jaffe has argued similarly about the importance of the Primitives for labour leadership. [38] Robert More has argued further that this leadership was of a kind, which worked against any very class-conscious forms of political radicalism or trade unionism. [39] Methodists did not see the world in that way. They divided it between the saved and the unsaved; the serious and the light; the good and the evil. What is clear is that whatever common theological and organizational forms it took Methodism could play different roles in different communities. To put it briefly, communities formed their own 'methodisms' in an interactive way with other dimensions and structures of their local situations. There was no single Methodism imposed as a uniform external force. Methodism was received and accommodated in different ways. [40]

Traditional versus Modern Protest

Following the work of the Tillys and others, [41] popular protest is sometimes presented as going through a linear modernisation process over the nineteenth century taking its concerns, motivations and repertoire of actions away from the protective mentality of the traditional community. Trade unions organized for collective bargaining and deploying industrial strategies to that end are 'modern'. Luddites opposing new technologies or forms of work organization are not. Food rioters legitimating their seizures of grain by selling it at just prices are perhaps the most traditional form of popular protest. If this over-simplified categorisation has any value, then the persistence of food rioting down to 1847 in Cornwall can be at least considered as a symptom of the non-availability of more modern wage-oriented protest forms, if not as an inhibition on their development. Not seeing a class of employers opposed to their interests, the hungry miners continued to see the profiteering corn factor or the grain-hoarding farmer as their enemy in hard times. It is too simple. Food riots were directed at shortages in supply and those who were viewed as aggravating them. In 1801, 1812, 1817, 1831 or 1847 it would hardly have altered the situation if significant wage increases had been sought and given. The actions taken by mine adventurers and those concerned with relief of seeking out and buying in grain and flour supplies and selling them on to the workforce at reduced prices was more appropriate and effective. [42]

Distance and Isolation

In 1857 a writer after expressing surprise that 'so hot-blooded a people' who had in the past something of a reputation for riotous protest, were displaying only indifference to radical politics:

Leagues and unions, and Chartist gatherings have had small attraction for them, nor has any purely political cause found numerous and sanguine adherents in Cornwall.

He thought that the county's geographical situation had much to do with this by isolating it from the 'contagion of foreign zeal'. [43] This probably also contributed to the featuring of Cornish miners as strike breakers in several coalfield strikes including the great Northumberland and Durham dispute of 1844. The Chartist missionaries, who had traveled to the county by boat in 1839, found: 'The people have heard nothing of the agitation, and know nothing of political principles'. The miners appeared 'thunderstruck' at any one talking so boldly against an authority they had thought unassailable. At St Ives, when Lowery asked if there were any radicals or chartists among the miners and fishermen, he got the reply that there were not for, 'They catch nothing here but pilchards and mackerel'. [44]

Isolation can however be easily exaggerated. If the mining villages were politically unengaged, this was not true of the Cornish towns in general. The evidence of the local newspapers is conclusive that national political matters were discussed regularly by the townspeople, both professional and artisan. At Truro, for example, a small group of Chartist artisans was formed ahead of the mission and seems to have been both committed and noisy. [45]

The explanations discussed in this paper were all offered either singly or in combination by contemporaries. To a degree they are re-enforcing. Landowners in the west would have had great influence anyway, but involved in a mining industry without an identifiable employing class, they had no rivals in the exercise of influence. If under the tribute system, luck played a not inconsiderable role in the determination of earnings, then the Methodist could accept instead the role of Providence rewarding or testing faith. [46] I prefer to stress the cumulative importance of a number of factors, of which the method of wage payment was the most important, co-existing at a time when very little was working in the other direction.

1 For a summary of the paper and the discussion see *Bulletin of the Society for the Study of Labour History*, 22, 1971, pp. 8-11.
2 Data from the Population Census 1851, and Sir Charles Lemon. 'Statistics of the Copper Mines of Cornwall', *Journal of the Statistical Society of London*, 1, 1838.
3 W. Collins, *Rambles Beyond Railways*, 1852, p. 78; *Quarterly Review*, 1857, p. 321-322; L. Price, 'West Barbary; or Notes on the System of Work and Wages in the Cornish Mines', in *Journal of the Statistical Society*, (50), 1888, p. 498; S. & B. Webb, *History of Trade Unionism*, 1911, p. 421.
4 For a collection of contemporary writings on the: tribute system see R. Burt, (ed), *Cornish Mining: Essays on the Organization of the Cornish Mines and the Cornish Mining Economy*, Newton Abbot, 1969. Mayhew briefly alluded to the system in *Low Wages: their causes, consequences and remedies*, 1851; Charles Babbage lauded it in *On the Economy of Machinery and Manufactures*, 1832, p. 177. J. S. Mill expressed firm approval of the system in *The Claims of Labour*, Vol. 4, 1845, Toronto University Press, and in *Principles of Political Economy*, 1917, p. 765.
5 *Penny Magazine*, 27 December 1834, in R. Burt, (ed), *Cornish Mining*, pp. 38-39.
6 *British Parliamentary Papers*, Fourth Report of the Select Committee on Artisans and Machinery, Vol. V, 51, 1824, pp. 323-324.
7 Except for Taylor the advocates had little or no first hand experience of the system. None for example, seemed aware of the existence of ore stealing and wage fraud, which were associated with it. See J. Rule, 'The Perfect Wage System? Tributing in the Cornish Mines' in J. Rule and R. Wells, *Crime, Protest and Popular Politics in Southern England*, 1996, pp. 53-65. See also above Chapter 4.

8 Royal Institution of Cornwall, Truro, Jenkin MSS, Jenkin to Hunt, 24 November 1804.

9 Cited in R. Burt, (ed), *Cornish Mining*, p. 10.

10 J, Harris, *Wayside Pictures. Hymns and Poems*, 1874, p. 158.

11 Jenkin MSS, Jenkin to Colewell, 25 February 1805.

12 *Morning Chronicle*, 24 November 1849.

13 *West Briton*, 15 April 1853.

14 This is the argument of J. Jaffe, *The Struggle for Market Power. Industrial Relations in the British Coal Industry 1800 to 1849*, Cambridge, 1991.

15 See R, Colls, *The Pitmen of the Northern Coalfield, Work, Culture and Protest 1790-1850*, Manchester, 1987, pp. 246-250, 285-290.

16 L. Price, '*West Barbary'; or notes on the system of work and wages in the Cornish Mines'*, p. 533.

17 *BPP*, Report of the Royal Commission on Child Employment, 1842, XVI, p. 759.

18 L. Namier and J Brooke, *History of Parliament: the House of Commons 1751-1790*, III, HMSO, 1964, p. 34.

19 E. Hobsbawm, 'Methodism and the threat of Revolution in Britain', in Labouring Men, 1964, p. 30; J. Rowe, *Cornwall in the Age of the Industrial Revolution*, Liverpool, 1953, p. 144.

20 For example see Patrick Joyce's extension of the concept to the early factory system in *Work, Society and Politics. The Culture of the Factory in later Victorian England*, 1980. For some trenchant criticisms see E. Thompson, 'Eighteenth-Century English Society. Class Struggle without Class', in *Social History*, 3, 2, 1978, p. 134 ff.

21 Namier and Brooke, *History of Parliament*, III, p. 34.

22 J. Grieg (ed.), *Farrington Diaries*, VI, 1926, p. 134.

23 Jenkin MSS, Jenkin to A. Hunt, 29 April 1801.

24 Cornwall Record Office, DDJ1227, Hawkins MSS, Letter book of Henry Trethewey, 7 and 12 June 1847.

25 *Cornwall Gazette*, 2 July 1841.

26 Birmingham Central Library, Boulton and Watt MSS, Boulton to Watt, Truro, 11 October 1787; Hawkins MSS, Trethewey to Hawkins, 13 August 1842.

27 Jenkin MSS, Jenkin to George Hunt, 22 June 1798; 1200 miners were formally involved at a ceremony dedicating a monument to Francis Basset.

28 Jenkin MSS, Jenkin to George Hunt, 23 January 1795.

29 Report on Child Employment, 1842, p. 760.

30 *West Briton*, 14 February 1840; *Cornish Banner*, 1846, p. 22.

31 E. Hobsbawm, 'Methodism and the Threat of Revolution' p. 30.

32 *Weekly Record of the Temperance Movement*, 25 October 1856, p. 250.

33 PRO, HO 40/41, from the Vicar of Gwennap.

34 *Weekly Record*, 25 Oct 1856, p. 250.

35 *Cornish Banner*, 1846, p. 22.

36 See generally D. Hempton, *Methodism and Politics in British Society 1750-1850*, 1984, pp. 211-216. For Nottingham see J. Epstein, 'Some organization and cultural aspects of the Chartist movement in Nottingham' in J. Epstein and D. Thompson (eds.), *The Chartist Experience*, 1982, pp. 221-268.

37 See the analysis of baptismal records in J. Probert, *The Sociology of Cornish Methodism*, Redruth, (n.d).
38 See R. Colls, *Pitmen*, Parts II and III; Jaffe, *Struggle for Market Power*, pp. 120-148.
39 R. Moore, *Pitmen, Preachers and Politics. The Effects of Methodism in a Durham Mining Community*, Cambridge, 1974.
40 I have argued elsewhere in this anthology for the local shaping of Methodism. See above Chapters 6 and 7.
41 For example see C. and R. Tilly, *The Rebellious Century 1830-1930*, 1975.
42 For a full account of food rioting in Cornwall see J. Rule, 'The Labouring Miner in Cornwall 1740-1870', Ph.D, University of Warwick, 1971, pp. 119-180 and above Chapter 2
43 *Quarterly Review*, 1857, p. 312.
44 BM, Add MSS, 34245, Vol. A, f. 120; *Weekly Record*, 25 Oct. 1856, p. 250.
45 See J. Rule, 'Richard Spurr of Truro. Small-town Radical' in J. Rule and R. Wells, *Crime, Protest and Popular Politics*, pp 81-90, reprinted above as Chapter 8 and A. Jenkin, 'The Cornish Chartists', in *Journal of the Royal Institute of Cornwall*, NS, IX, 1, 1982, pp. 53-80.
46 See for example: 'I feel thankful to say the Lord has greatly prospered me at the mine lately more than £95 per man, the two months', W. Tyack, *The Miner of Perranzabuloe*, 1866, pp. 54-55, and J. Harris, *Autobiography*, 1882, p. 60: 'Providence… blest my labours'.

The South Western Deep-Sea Fisheries and their Markets in the Nineteenth Century

11

Before the coming of the railway brought the necessary means of rapid distribution fresh sea fish were hardly consumed away from the coast. Only prime varieties repaid the cost and complications of transport, and these were consumed only by the well-to-do. After the mid-nineteenth century this situation changed rapidly with fish becoming a dietary staple even in inland urban Britain. The deep-sea fishing industry expanded hugely, most dramatically at the great East coast ports of Hull, Grimsby and Yarmouth. The fisheries of the South West also grew significantly, although their response to the enlarging of the market has been less studied. This essay looks at their nineteenth century experience in selling their catch before and after the arrival of rail transport.

Early nineteenth century writers on the British food supply regularly condemned the neglect of sea fish and particularly denounced the up-market orientation of the fish trade. Fresh sea fish they believed were capable of becoming a significant item in the support of Britain's growing and increasingly urban population. In the second half of the century the astonishing spread of the fried fish shop was of course to realise this hope. That revolution in working class diet was still, however, in the future when a writer surveyed the fish trade for a leading periodical in 1813. While butchers' meat, he commented, had become 'beyond the reach of the great mass of the people; the labouring poor can scarce hope to taste it', the harvest of Britain's seas was neglected and misdirected to the extent that fresh fish was 'a prohibited article, even to the middling ranks of life'. Even London, where water transport could take fish directly to Billingsgate was no exception. It suited those who monopolized its trade to concentrate on the premium priced, up-market varieties of sole and turbot for the tables of the wealthy. The mass of the City's inhabitants never visited a fishmonger: 'They would as soon think of going into a shop to ask the price of a pineapple as ask that of cod, turbot or salmon'. [1] While it reflected a widely held view, the article undoubtedly underestimated the consumption of sea fish by London's poorer classes, and the efforts, which distant fishermen would make to supply it. Poorer consumers did not in fact buy from fishmongers but from the barrows of costermongers or the baskets of female fish-hawkers. Herrings were the most consumed variety fresh, or in one of their preserved forms. Of fresh fish, mackerel were the most significant. Two thirds of the 23,520,000 sold through Billingsgate in 1850 reached the consumer through hawkers and costermongers. The first-caught prime mackerel of the early season were capable of fetching premium prices, but for most of the year fresh mackerel was widely consumed. It became unavailable in the early summer, although that was the very time when the shoals on their migration up the English Channel were being caught at their closest to London. At that season the costermongers and basket women ceased visiting Billingsgate and turned their attention instead to deal in soft fruits. For this reason the large Cornish mackerel fleets never followed the fish up channel beyond Plymouth, leaving the early summer fishery off Brighton to the local boats. [2]

Little had changed by 1842 when another survey was published. As in 1817 the inhabitants of many inland towns 'know not the taste of fresh sea fish'. Everywhere apart from sprats, mackerel and herring, fish was still looked upon as a luxury by most classes of the populace. There was, however, an indication that things were about to alter. Billingsgate was becoming more than just a London market and taking on the role of a distribution centre for a much wider trade:

Over the last few years fish is being increasingly sent by rail from Billingsgate at the expense of the market women who are in the habit of hawking their wares about the Over the last few years [fish is] being increasingly sent by different parts of the Metropolis. [3]

By the 1860s there was scarcely an inland town of any significance, which was not receiving a regular supply of fish, and Billingsgate was now one of several inland distribution centres. The railway was not the unaided agency of this change. The increasing use of ice-kept fish fresh over its journey and the discovery of the huge potential of the North Sea fishing grounds had resulted in the expansion of trawling. Trawling the bottom brought to mass consumption a variety previously considered 'offal' fish fit only for local consumption. The survey of 1842 noted that plaice had only just become plentiful, but by 1850 33,600,000 were sold at Billingsgate. The costermongers and hawkers took seven-eighths. By then plaice had displaced mackerel as the most purchased fresh fish, largely because it was much less subject to fluctuations in supply, but while the latter no longer headed the list, take-up by the capital city still experienced a railway related increase. [4]

By 1881 the 58,000 fishermen in England and Wales was more than double the 24,000 recorded in the 1841 census. This was a peak, by 1891 there been a fall to 53,000, but thereafter numbers remained consistent until from 1921 there began the long decline which has lasted to the present day. The major centres of the expansion were the North Sea ports, especially Hull, Grimsby and Yarmouth, the last a traditional centre of the herring fishery entering a new period of expansion as a trawling port. The 'floating population' of the North Sea fleets in the 1880s numbered around 15,000 souls at any one time. A third of all the fishermen of England and Wales sailed from these ports along with Lowestoft in 1883. By 1904 the two Humber ports were receiving as much fish as all the others put together. Such an expansion clearly overshadowed developments in Cornwall and Devon. The ports of the South West had a good year in 1879 when the Great Western, and the London and South Western Railways together conveyed 10,047 tonnes of fish to London, in the same year the Great Northern, and the Great Eastern brought in 60,009 tonnes. But the fisheries of Cornwall and Devon continued to constitute a fishing district of national importance, second only in England and Wales to the North Sea fishery. The railway brought change to them too, even if did not produce such a spectacular expansion as it did in the trawling ports of the North and East. Even though the industry was carried on in a multitude of small ports, it still had its major centres. A sixth of the fishermen of Cornwall and Devon in 1883 sailed from the registration ports of Penzance, Fowey, Plymouth and Dartmouth (Brixham). As late as 1904 Brixham was still the fifth largest trawling port in England and Wales, while Plymouth was eighth and at that time still ahead of Fleetwood. In the drift fishery, Cornwall's Mounts Bay fleet was the most important after Yarmouth. [5]

Although both Cornwall and Devon possessed a wide range of line fishing and inshore fishing from small boats, their major fisheries went separate ways. In Devon deep-sea fishing meant trawling: in Cornwall it meant drifting. Brixham's pride was its fleet of ketch-rigged trawling smacks, of around 30 to 40 tonnes, although tending to become larger later in the century. They were fast-sailing. In addition there were at the port a number of smaller trawling vessels known as 'mumble bees', which fished only local waters. Large smacks registered in Devon probably numbered around 100 at the end of the eighteenth century and 150 by the 1830s. Later in the century many smacks had migrated to the North Sea ports, but there were still at least 120 operating from Brixham in 1883 and even an increase to 150 by 1904. The port kept to sailing trawlers never going over to steam vessels. An estimate of 159 sailing from it in 1887 can be compared with the 839 at Grimsby. However, at the latter port there were only 34 smacks operating in 1903 steam trawling having almost completely taken over. In 1900 Brixham smacks were crewed by around 1000 men and boys. Plymouth was the only other South West trawling port of significance. Trawling began here around the beginning of the nineteenth century with 30 smacks operating by the 1820s. The 50 to 60 there by the 1880s were generally twice the size. There were around 100 by the 1890s, but by the beginning of the next century they were a mixed fleet of steam and sail. [6] By the end of the century larger smacks of between 60 to 80 tonnes were operated from the North Sea ports. Their greater drawing power - greater still with the arrival of steam - allowed them to replace the traditional beam trawl with the otter trawl that considerably increased catching capacity. At Brixham the beam trawl persisted into the next century in line with the general smack size of from 30 to 60 tonnes. Plymouth too persisted with the smaller smacks. As will be shown below, the Brixham smacks fished from other ports for much of the year, but when fishing from home, they usually trawled from six to eight miles off shore and landed their catches daily. The Plymouth boats usually trawled in daylight twelve to nine miles west of the Eddystone returning each evening. Days were often lost in the summer to too light winds, while in winter gales often kept them in port. Catches accordingly fluctuated more at Plymouth than at other major ports. [7]

The Cornish drift fishery employed two main types of boat: the larger luggers in the offshore mackerel fishery and smaller vessels known as drivers fishing closer inshore for pilchards. The largest centre was Mounts Bay, withy Newlyn its main port St Ives on the North coast was next in importance, followed by the South coast port of Mevagissey in St Austell Bay. These were followed by a large number of village ports, like Polperro, which had around 30 drifters in 1871, and the still smaller Portloe which had 53 fishermen according to the Census of 1891. However, well over half of the Cornish mackerel fleet of around 400 in 1883 came from Mounts Bay. St Ives had 70 luggers in 1874 and Mevagissey 60 in 1904. In the era on the eve of the railway, an estmate put the Mounts Bay mackerel fleet at 140 drifters in 1850 which employed around 850 fishermen. By 1883, well into the railway age the men and boys employed numbered around 1000. [8]

None of the fisheries of the South West was a new creation in the manner of Grimsby, purpose built by a railway company. But only the railway allowed them to operate other than marginally in the developing inland trade in fresh sea fish. The best known and most often described of the Cornish fisheries was the seine netting of pilchards when the shoals came close in shore. For centuries huge quantities of fish were taken and salted for export chiefly to Italy. This fishery, because it exported a preserved product, is not within the scope of this chapter but fresh pilchards in their season were much consumed as well as being bought for home salting. These were not the pilchards from seine fishing, but those netted a little offshore by drifters. This is clearly indicated in evidence before a Parliamentary commission in 1866: 'The fish taken by the drift boats is used for the support of the population':

Last year Mr Fox's seines caught pilchards at Mevagissey, but he would not let his men sell one to the poor of the country. All of them were salted and exported, you will see therefore that if the drivers don't catch fish to supply a quantity the poor people hereabout would starve. [9]

Before the railway transformed the market changes had already been taking place, the most significant of which was the increasing tendency for fishermen to migrate seasonally to fish from other than their home-ports for part of the year. Shortly after the end of the Napoleonic War, two important migrations began. The first was the movement of Brixham trawlers up the Channel and into the North Sea. The second was the annual participation of the Cornish drifters in the Irish herring fishery. The first was to have huge consequences for British deep-sea fishing, for from it was eventually to develop the North Sea trawling industry.

About 1820 Brixham fishermen, still seeking prime fish for the luxury market, found that fishing from Dover not only enabled them to profit from the rich sole and turbot grounds of the Ridge and Varne banks, but also to land their catches at a shorter van distance from London. There began a seasonal migration from Brixham to Dover and later to Ramsgate for winter fishing, returning to Brixham at the beginning of May. They continued to do this for around twenty years, during which period a further boost was given, when an opening for plaice developed. Van transport from the Kentish ports to London was at a premium, and plaice could only be carried when space was to spare. When it did get to Billingsgate it could, if in sound and fresh condition, fetch good prices, but if sole and turbot catches were good enough to take up fully the available van space, then the dealers on the quayside had little interest in plaice and much remained unsold. About 1830, however, French boats from Boulanger and Dunkirk began to cross over and take up the surplus plaice. At about the same time the trawler men, who had not previously ventured further east than the Galloper Light vessel, began to fish as much as 30 miles east and found such an abundance of soles that they prospered for seven years before dwindling catches drove them even further into the North Sea. Again fortune blessed them and in 1843, sixty miles from the mouth of the Humber, they discovered the very rich Great Silver Pits, which confirmed the shift of attention to the North Sea.

Some Brixham fishermen from Ramsgate and Dover moved on to settle permanently at Hull or Grimsby. Others remained domiciled in Brixham but continued for some time to make a seasonal migration to fish in the summer alongside the growing fleets of the eastern ports. Few followed this pattern, however, after the railway reached Brixham in 1870 and through the 1880s attention turned back to the home fishing grounds by those who had not made a permanent move to the Humber. With London only four hours away, fish could be on sale at Billingsgate in five or six hours from the quayside, with trawlers landing their catches at Brixham the year round. Markets as much as fish supplies had driven the move further into the North Sea, with the wealthy summer visitors to the fashionable bathing resort of Scarborough providing the demand. After the 1880s, as local fish stocks began to lessen, another migration began. This time the larger trawlers began to move around into the Bristol Channel, landing their fish at Tenby, from where newly developed rail links took it to a number of urban markets. At first the Tenby season lasted from April to September, but by the early years of the twentieth century Brixham smacks were working the Bristol Channel from January to August traditionally returning for the annual regatta. By then their catches were being landed at Milford Haven, with the smacks coming in every five or six days. Hence for eight months of the year Brixham itself was getting only the fish caught by the smaller 'mumble bees'. Good catches in the Bristol Channel could make smack owners prosperous, but for local fish salesmen and tradesmen, the best memories were of the 1870s and 1880s. [10]

About 1820 at the end of the home mackerel fishery, Cornish luggers from Mounts Bay and St Ives began to move annually to the Irish herring fishery. This fishery lasted for several weeks from mid-July. Considerable numbers made the trip. In 1839 the Cornish fleet so engaged amounted to 250 boats and a similar number was still making the trip in 1885.

The Irish herring fishery began to fail towards the end of the nineteenth century, but it was increasingly substituted for by either the Irish mackerel fishery, a new development centred on Kinsale, or by the North Sea herring fishery. Some Cornish drifters were fishing for herring off Scotland and in the North Sea by 1850. A newspaper account from 1848 describes the St Ives boats as leaving at the end of June for either Whitby or for the Irish herring fishery. It is not recorded why some chose one and some the other. Past experience and family traditions probably played a part. Until the 1880s and 1890s the Irish fishery seems to have been the more important, but from then increasing numbers were going either to Scotland or the Yorkshire coast, favouring Whitby or Scarborough. Sometime after the discovery of the Irish fishery, Cornish fishermen found - nearer to home - the potential of fishing for herrings off Plymouth, a resource not exploited by the bottom-fishing trawlers of that port. It came to play an annual role filling in from the late autumn until just after Christmas. Only the larger luggers from Mounts Bay and St Ives made the long migrations. Apart from the Plymouth herring season, even the fishermen from the next ranked port of Mevagissey pursued a purely local fishery, as did the fishermen from the many smaller ports. In Mounts Bay too the smaller boats remained at home to engage in pilchard drifting or pick up the smaller amounts of mackerel that could still be caught out of the main season. For the crews of the larger luggers, however, the season followed this pattern: the local mackerel fishery occupied them from around February to May or June. They then refitted for the Irish or North Sea fisheries. Returning in late summer, they would leave again towards the end of the year for Plymouth, to return after Christmas to refit again for the coming home mackerel season. [11]

Even on the home fishery, as the nineteenth century progressed the Mounts Bay luggers based themselves for part of the time on Scilly when the shoals were closer to those islands. There was of course little point in landing cargoes, on St Mary's, but even by 1850 the boats had developed a system of fishing in groups with each taking its turn to act as carriers. An informed account from that year records these boats as absent from the fleet for two to four days, carrying the fish to 'some distant market', so their likely destination was Bristol or South Wales. Two developments at the end of the 1850s combined to permit the landing of fish in Scilly itself. The first steamer link to Penzance began in 1858 and that town was linked to the mainline railway to London through Plymouth from 1859. By the 1880s two steamers were sailing daily and the Mounts Bay fleet was landing fish each morning at St Mary's. As a local poet expressed it:

> *And the men were all glad*
> *For the fish they had*
> *Will be at Penzance before night*

When the boats did come in
The work did begin
The buyers came down from the town,
All the packers they had
Put the fish in the pads;
That day to go the same round.

A further verse is clear on the length of this fishery:

It was one afternoon
In the middle of June
The fishing boats all sailed away
They have all left the shore
To come back no more
Till next year in April or May. [12]

Although the Mounts Bay fishermen probably regarded the Scilly interlude of around six weeks as part of the home fishery, it is clear that even before the coming of the railway, the fishermen of the South West were making their economy work only by landing their catches for much of the year at other than their home ports. It is a main concern of this study to examine further what was happening to the catches landed at home, both before and after the railway and in particular to examine the extent to which the market transcended the local. It would not, however be correct to be overly dismissive of the sustaining importance of the local market throughout the period. In Cornwall in particular the immediate hinterland was made up of well-populated mining districts and the miners probably consumed more fish per head than any other industrial population. Accordingly many traders were involved in the local distribution of fish. When it was heard that a large catch of mackerel was being landed at St Ives in 1836, 400 carts came to the beach from Redruth, Camborne, Crowan, Gwinnear, Phillack, Ludgvan, Marazion, Zennor, St Just and other parishes, a list which includes most of the leading mining parishes in that part of the county. [13] Catches were bought by local dealers known as 'jowsters' who hawked the fish around the

towns and villages. The more successful had carts. A miner told an inquiry in 1842, that as soon as he had saved enough, he would buy a cart
and give up his underground employment to become a fish hawker. His
wife was already selling fish, presumably without the benefit of a cart;
she was one of the colourful community of women fish sellers who were
not always the wives of fishermen. Popular tradition represents them as
formidable indeed. A Mousehole fisherman recalled how in the 1840s
his great-grandmother would take half a cowl of fish on her back, with
20 pounds of salt on each side in large pockets and visit nine parishes as
her usual round. Nancy Humphries supplied the parishes around St Ives
for many years in the early nineteenth century and reputedly carried as
much as a hundredweight of fish on her head, and it was gin rather than
this exertion to which her death at 54 was attributed. Not all women fish
sellers hawked their fish around the villages as the market towns had
designated selling areas for fish. [14]

In 1817 a claim that all the low ranks of society in South Devon subsisted on fish is probably an exaggeration, but as in Cornwall the local consumption of fish was considerable. A large proportion of the Brixham catch was sold locally through hawkers. It was reported in 1786 that in addition to the van loads of soles and turbot being sent to London, Bath and Bristol, a vast quantity was carried on horses 'into every market town and village in the county'. Prime fish fetched good prices by being dispatched over considerable distances to market, but throughout the nineteenth century large quantities of smaller fish and less esteemed varieties such as plaice, hake and sprats continued to depend on local sale. At Plymouth a large proportion of the total catch consisted of such varieties, and these were consumed in the city or taken by hawkers into the country districts. [15] Torbay soles and turbot, however, were esteemed in London long before the coming of the railway, as they were in Bath and Bristol. Bristol and Exeter were described in 1837 as the two great markets for prime fish in the West; both supplied trawled fish for the London market by land carriage. As early as 1786 an annual 500 van loads were sent to London from Brixham and a like quantity to Bath and Bristol. Several Brixham fishermen giving evidence to the Sea Fisheries Committee of 1866 recalled the methods of sending fish before the railway.

A 66 year-old speaking of his days as a boy remembered that most of the best fish was sent to the capital: 'The greatest part we sent from here to Exeter, and it was taken from Exeter to London'. The second leg of the journey was by coach. It took three days and the old fisherman admitted that in summer the fish sometimes went 'queer', but pointed out that the risk was the merchant's not the fisherman's. Another witness whose memory went back to the mid-1830s recalled that then the fish went from Brixham by packhorse to catch the Exeter coach, but that later carts were introduced charging 3 shillings a hundredweight. By then although Exeter was still supplying London, it was sending yet more to Bath and to Bristol. A Plymouth witness recalling the 1820s similarly rated the important markets for prime fish. He recalled two carts taking away a ton of fish a week, some of it to go as far as London, but most destined for Bath and Bristol. In the early nineteenth century some Brixham smacks were landing their catches at Portsmouth to take advantage of that port's first class road to London. [16]

The mackerel is a fish which changes in size and flavour over the year, the early caught fish from Cornwall were esteemed in London and fetching premium prices well before the railway age. Many of these reached Billingsgate through the intervention of the Brixham smacks.

Mounts Bay luggers.

These could make much better speed than could the lugger-rigged Cornish boats, and by the beginning of the nineteenth century some of them were sailing to Mounts Bay at the beginning of the mackerel season, not to fish themselves, they were not rigged for drifting, but to purchase fresh mackerel from the Cornish boats and carry it to Portsmouth from where it went overland to London. Local newspapers refer to Torbay craft waiting at Penzance as early as 1802 and two Brixham witnesses to the inquiry of 1817 spoke of it as an annual practice for many of the smacks to make the early spring trip to Cornwall for this purpose. It is not clear when the practice ceased. Presumably it did so soon after 1820 when the smacks began their annual migration up the English Channel and were north rather than west of Torbay in the spring. [17]

By the 1820s Cornish mackerel were reaching London by another route. The Luggers themselves when catches were good and winds suitable were sailing them directly to Bristol, or less commonly to South Wales. Some of those taken to Bristol were bought by 'regular dealers' who conveyed them by light van to London. In 1827 such fish in early season were said to reach Billingsgate on the third day from catching. Several St Ives luggers finding the winds strong enough and from the right direction sailed their catches to Bristol in 1830, but the fact that the local newspaper reported it as an event, suggests that it was not an everyday occurrence. Luggers were not fast sailing enough to take mackerel reliably over such distances and in most seasons faster sailing skiffs came to St Ives and to Mounts Bay to buy mackerel for the Bristol and London markets. These had a large impact on prices. In 1837 fish, which had been fetching £3 the hundred (of 120 fish), dropped to 6s. 6d, adverse winds meant that only the local jowsters were buying. [18] By the 1840s it was no longer necessary to sail the fish to Bristol as regular steamer links were in being between that port and Hayle. Two rival ships were providing a service by 1843, and when they raced each other as a challenge in that year the winner did the journey in fourteen hours. A third steamer was operating by 1850 each making four voyages a month. From Bristol the fish could be sent on to London after 1841 by rail. [19] Steamer sailings were regular, but not daily, so missing its departure could be costly with such a perishable commodity. A Penzance historian writing in the 1880s recalled the urgency often generated: when 'great catches' were taken in Mounts Bay:

On the night before, or early morning of the day [of sailing] all the carts and horses in Penzance and its neighbourhood were pressed into service, and the road to Hayle was almost like a French race-course, with the number of vehicles on it all striving to outstrip each other in the race to Hayle. [20]

Even though the ship sometimes delayed its departure by an hour or two while the baskets of fish were piled like 'small mountains' on the deck, there was always some too late and left, 'lamenting on the quay, to curse their fate and to sell their fish in the neighbourhood for what they would fetch'. When no fishing boats returned to St Ives in 1859, the local newspaper concluded that they must have been unsuccessful as they would otherwise have made every effort to come in: 'This being the day for the steamer leaving for Bristol'. It was not to matter for much longer, for that was the year in which the rail link from Penzance to London was finally made. [21]

The railway introduced reliability as well as reach to the British fish trade. One by one the fishing ports were linked by it to the inland markets: As a writer noted in 1874:

The quick delivery of the fish is becoming an important object, as the demand for it increases all over the country; and the smacks may daily be seen racing back to the great trawling stations to land their fish, each one endeavouring with the help of balloon canvas, to bring her catch early to market, where the buyers are waiting with orders to purchase from all parts of the country. [22]

Nine years later he wrote again of wholesalers attending the arrival of the boats at all the fishing ports of 'the slightest consequence'. The railway did not extend into Brixham itself until 1868, but before then fish were taken by light van the short distances to Torquay or Paignton. In 1860 the railway took 248 tonnes from the former and 600 tonnes from the latter. [23] The extension of the railway into the port itself brought something of a speculative boom:

Those who had been doing an ordinary living trade in fish suddenly found themselves in a position to dispose of all they could catch at good round London prices.

A fishing fever resulted. Householders sold their properties and tradesmen borrowed all that they could to invest in smacks costing from £800 to £1000. The fever lasted around three years before fishing returned to the hands of the practical fishermen and Brixham then settled down to enjoy a prosperous twenty years.[24] By the early 1880s 2,000 tonnes of fish were being annually dispatched by rail. The fish were sold to the dealers by auction and the fishwives preserved at least part of their traditional role by acting as auctioneers. Much rail-moved Brixham fish did not go directly to London. Bristol was still favoured as a distribution centre for forwarding to inland towns, with instructions being wired from Brixham.[25] Turbot, for so long the most prized of all fish, did not travel well by rail, which probably explains why one local witness in 1866 did not think the railway had had much effect on prices. In any case it of all varieties could still repay the higher transport cost of vans. When they were available selling them in London and other luxury markets had never been a problem. One Billingsgate salesman boasted of having received between 200 and 300 on a single day in 1839. Soles, however, were suited to rail transportation and along with them a regular supply of whiting developed, which compensated for the difficulty in expanding the trade in turbot. The Brixham fish market did undergo something of a decline towards the end of the century. That was the result of the increasing tendency of its smacks to fish in the Bristol Channel and land their catch at Milford Haven from where the Great Western Railway was able to get fish loaded by four in the afternoon to Paddington by two the following morning in time for the early sales at Billingsgate. [26]

Plymouth got its rail link in 1849 and found it a means of conveyance ideally suited to the transport in quantity of the coarser varieties in which its trawlers had tended to specialize. If prime varieties were landed they were sent as before to Billingsgate, Bristol and Bath. Other varieties went not only to those centres, but also directly to towns in the

south west such as Taunton, Bridgewater and Weston-super-Mare; as a
salesman put it in 1866: 'We send fish to all the towns down the Great
Western Line'. The downward social extension of the fish market in London seems to have allowed a regular dispatch of hake to develop. The
railway reached Plymouth ten years before it did Penzance and, as did
Bristol, the Devonshire port functioned as a railhead for Cornish catches.
Obviously the herrings caught by the Cornish drifters in the Plymouth
herring season were landed and moved from that port, but in the 1850s
mackerel from the Mounts Bay fishery was also frequently sailed to Plymouth, although not matching the volume still making the previously
mentioned combined steamer and rail journey via Bristol. A review
of the food supply of London in 1854 referred to the Great Western as
bringing annually 'the harvests of the Cornish and Devonshire coasts to
the amount of 1,560 tonnes in a year'. These were mostly pilchards and
mackerel but given that that there was only a very limited market for
fresh pilchards outside Cornwall - they do not figure at all in Mayhew's
table of varieties sold at Billingsgate - we can assume that mackerel made
up most of those carried. Even after the opening of the rail link with
Penzance several boats from the smaller and nearer Cornish ports, not
themselves on the railway, continued to find it more convenient to land
their fish at Plymouth. [27]

In 1861, within two years of the Great Western mainline crossing
the Tamar, the railway was already dispatching more than 1,000 tonnes
of fresh fish from Cornwall, with the most intense traffic coming from
Penzance in the mackerel season. Those fish would have had a broken
journey at Truro. Brunel was still committed to the seven-foot gauge and
the line to Truro was that broad. However, there it met the existing Cornwall Railway, which had been built to the later standard narrower gauge.
Welcoming in 1866 the laying of the broad gauge from Truro down, the
West Briton particularly stressed the importance to the fish trade, claiming that the transfer had been adding a day to the time a cargo reached
London from Penzance. From that year the mackerel, which on Friday
morning swam in shoals seven or eight miles south west of the dreaded
Wolf Rock, were sold in Billingsgate early on Saturday morning. [28]

On days when heavy catches were being landed, fish were rushed from Newlyn to Penzance station in carts all day long, keeping roads and streets busy and causing some discomfort to those who were at that time trying to turn the newly connected town into a fashionable holiday resort. On a notable day in 1868 it took three special trains as well as the mail train to get the catch to London. In all 135 tonnes of mackerel were carried mostly from Penzance station, but with some being loaded at Hayle. The fish trade from Cornwall became substantially a monopoly of the Great Western Railway, although not without some competition. It was challenged for example in 1871 when the London and South Western attempted to introduce steamer links between St Ives and Bideford, and between Penzance and Exmouth to by-pass the Great Western by bringing Cornish fish directly to its own Devonshire railheads. The venture was not successful and by the end of the century there were many complaints of the GWR's monopoly pricing. A steamboat service direct from Penzance to Billingsgate was introduced in the 1890s carrying fish at £2 the ton. This was about half of the normal GWR rate, but as the journey took around three days and there was only a weekly sailing, the fish can hardly have commanded premium prices and hardly represented a serious challenge to the railway. [29]

The impact of the railways on the Cornish trade is hard to establish in quantitative terms. Not only, as this study has shown, is it impossible to give other than an impression of its size and scope before the railway but even for the rail era itself there are only scattered statistics available. As railway historians so often lament, detailed reconstructions of particular freight traffic are hardly possible. In broad terms, however, a very significant impact is indicated. An authoritative article in 1850 put the annual catch from the spring and summer mackerel fishery around that time at about 2,000 tonnes. Mackerel were then, the only variety sent fresh from the county in significant amounts. Between 1890 and 1895 the port of St Ives on its own sent an average of 4,401 tonnes via the GWR. The trade would seem to have increased very substantially over the early railway era, for between 1865 and 1880 the Company had conveyed in total an annual average of 5,001 tonnes to Billingsgate. Except for

Milford Haven, the GWR had no major connection with fish landing ports outside of Cornwall and South Devon, and in the latter it was in competition, as it was to a small extent in North East Cornwall, with the LSWR. Even if the fish carried by the latter were added, this would to a relatively small share of the 74,439 tonnes delivered annually on average by all the rail companies together. The importance of the East coast trawler ports is evident, but in their own terms the fisheries of the South West clearly benefited from the opportunities the railway brought. [30]

There were however some criticisms of the railway. The GWR was often criticized for charging excessive freight rates for fish. Many contemporaries also commented on the depletion of local fish supplies:

Persons who formerly had their choice of soles, cod or other kinds of fish are in these times frequently obliged to send to some large market inland, and perhaps pay a high price for such fish as used to be regularly brought for sale to their own doors. [31]

Even an Exeter fish salesman complained in 1866 that he could get fish cheaper from London than from Brixham. [32] In the 1880s fish from nearby Mevagissey were brought in carts to St Austell station, when that town itself had no fishmonger. More serious was the complaint that by opening up new markets for higher priced fish, the railways diverted fishermen from catching the cheaper kinds, which were so important in the diet of the Cornish poor. There was perhaps a tendency to exaggerate this effect on local consumption. St Austell may have had no fishmonger in the 1880s, but it was still visited regularly by a jowster's cart from Mevagissey. Indeed that small fishing port continued to depend on the local market throughout the nineteenth century. Much of the catch of its small drifters consisted of pilchards, which were bought on the quays directly from the fishermen by hawkers and sold in the villages and towns around as far as Bodmin. Even here, however, mackerel, if they were not sailed directly to Plymouth, were only sold to dealers through the auctioneers and dispatched from St Austell station. Polperro, another port with mostly small drifters also had a considerable local trade in fresh pilchards as well as sending cartloads of coarser varieties of fish two or three times a week to the nearby mining towns of Liskeard, Tavistock and Callington. Some jowsters specialized in such fish. One, known as 'Blind Dick', regularly brought a donkey-cart of pollack from the Land's End district into Penzance in the 1850s and 1860s. [33] What the railways did enable was the transport of exceptionally large catches of fish, a large proportion of which would previously had to have been sold locally at very low prices. In 1897 150 tonnes of herring were sent from Port Isaac station, an event considered newsworthy by the local newspaper. All the fish were brought to the station from the quay at Port Isaac in carts and wagons, nearly all the farmers in the neighbourhood being employed in the work. The event provided striking proof of the benefit resulting from the advent of the railway to the district. [34]

Before fresh fish became an item of mass consumption and few varieties were in demand, many varieties had no interest for the dealers, or even the boat owners. At Polperro, for example, these were known as 'rabble fish', and consisted of dogfish, ray, skate, gurnard, and scadd, and were regarded as a perquisite of the crew. At Brixham these and other varieties such as conger, monk, pollack and hake along with fish livers, were known as 'stocker' and in the 1880s there was a strike by the crews when the smack owners first began to claim a share in the pro-

Trawling – hoisting in the fish.

ceeds of their sale. A demand for some of these fish had developed with the national spread of fish and chip shops of which there were estimated to be 25,000 by 1913. At Plymouth prime varieties had never made up a high proportion of the catch, and it was the new market for coarser fish which encouraged the adoption there of steam trawlers. Varieties, which still would not repay the transit cost to Billingsgate might do so to nearer urban centres like Bristol, Exeter or Taunton, while Plymouth itself with nearby Devonport had a large and growing working class population. [35]

The extent to which fishermen were victimized by buying rings is hard to establish. Given the inevitable fluctuation in catches, it would have been difficult to know even from one day to another what constituted a fair price. In the 1880s mackerel sold on the quays from as much as 1s to as little as 4d a fish. When the latter price prevailed boats might throw catches overboard, rather than bring them in for a price, which hardly met their harbour dues. Even within a single day prices fluctuated as the boats did not all arrive at the same time and the dealers had to speculate on the early arrivals. Those coming in late might find their catches eagerly awaited or simply not wanted. The advantage lay with the buyer. He could limit his buying so that a glut at the port did not become a glut at the destined market. Sufficient writers commented on the large profits taken by the dealers for the complaints of the fishermen to be taken seriously. Dealers' margins were traditionally large for they covered the risk of fish reaching markets in unsaleable condition. But the speed of the railway and use of ice minimized these risks, while the margins do not seem to have come down. In the 1870s dealers' profits were said to have increased three or even four fold. At the same time fishermen were becoming more price conscious. Many who had previously largely fed their own families from their catch, were increasingly interested in the purchasing power of their income in the context of a more varied diet. [36]

The period of railway-related prosperity for the South-Wests' fishermen was ending by the beginning of the twentieth century, just as the railway opened new possibilities for the local fishermen, it also suggested to others that the fishing grounds of the South West had become worth exploiting. East coast drifters began to follow migrating shoals westwards, reversing the movements earlier in the century of the Devonshire and Cornish boats. By 1905 they were spending sixteen or seventeen weeks fishing from Mounts Bay and landing their catches there. Although one writer described them as mingling with the Cornishmen in 'more or less friendly rivalry', there was considerable underlying tension, which could burst out as it did at Newlyn in the Sunday fishing riots of 1896, the seriousness of which can be gauged from the fact that three hundred soldiers went to the port to restore order. They had been provoked by Methodist scruples against fishing on Sundays. The East Anglian fleet had no such tradition and thus supplied the early week market at Billingsgate, with no Cornish-caught fish arriving before Tuesdays. By the 1890s steam drifters were fishing for mackerel on days when the local luggers were ineffective. Around 1905 even Brixham trawlers began to trawl the mackerel grounds. Heavy fishing played its part, but there seems also to have been a natural decline in the herrings and pilchard shoals and changes in their pattern of movement. At Brixham the smacks were surviving only by fishing away from home for eight months of the year. The chairman of the Cornwall Executive Committee for Fisheries complained in 1896 that, 'Up-country boats come here, clear our seas, sweep our bays clean'. It was a local aspect of a national change. North Sea stocks were themselves beginning to show worrying signs of decline. Public taste in white fish had moved strongly towards cod. Landings of white fish from the North Sea decreased from 260,00 tonnes in 1903 to 170,00 in 1913. Although total landings increased from 330,000 to 420,000 tonnes as a new generation of steam trawlers brought in cod from Iceland or the White Sea. [37]

1 *Quarterly Review*, IX, 1813, pp. 166, 275-277.
2 W. Stern, 'The Fish Supply to Billingsgate from the Nineteenth Century to the Second World War', in T. Barker and J. Yudkin, (eds.), *Fish in Britain*, 1971, pp. 30-82; W. Chaloner, 'Trends in Fish Consumption', in T. Barker, J. Mackenzie and J. Yudkin, (eds.), *Our Changing Fare: two hundred years of British food habits*, 1966,

p. 111; *Quarterly Review*, 1813, p. 277. A nineteenth century account of the Brighton fishing industry does provide descriptions of Cornish drifters and their catching methods, but this familiarity came from the fact that both fleets fished together off Plymouth in the early part of the mackerel season. See: C. Fleet, *The Brighton Fishery in the mid-Nineteenth Century*, (reprinted edition), A. Durr, (ed.), *Brighton*, 1994. That the Cornish fleet did not follow the mackerel beyond Plymouth is confirmed in an authoritative account in the *Royal Cornwall Gazette*, 1 March 1850.

3 *Quarterly Review*, LXIX, 1842, pp. 231-232.

4 ibid, p. 232; W. Chaloner, 'Trends in Fish Consumption', p. 111.

5 S. Walpole, 'The British Fish Trade', in *Fisheries Exhibition Literature*, 14 vols, 1884, 1, pp. 9-10; G. Aflalo, *The Sea Fishing Industry of England and Wales*, 1904, pp. 100, 209; W. Stern, 'Fish Supply to Billingsgate from the Nineteenth Century to the Second World War', p. 99.

6 On the Devon fishery generally see A. Northway, 'The Devon Fishing Industry in the Eighteenth and Nineteenth Centuries', in M. Duffy, (ed), *The New Maritime History of Devon, Vol. II, From the Late Eighteenth Century to the Present Day*, 1994, pp. 126-135. See also Northway, 'Devon Fishing Vessels and their Ownership, 1760-1880', in H. Fisher and W. Minchinton, (eds.), *Transport and Shipowning in the West Country*, Exeter, 1973, pp. 23-31. Other statistics in this paragraph come from E. Holdsworth, *Deep-Sea Fishing and Fishing Boats*, 1874, pp. 117-118, 120, 197-199; G. Aflalo, *Sea Fishing*, pp. 293, 297-298; E. March, Sailing Trawlers, 1953, pp. 45-53.

7 E. March, *Trawlers*, pp. 45, 53; G. Aflalo, *Sea Fishing*, pp. 40-41; E. Holdsworth, *Deep-Sea Fishing*, p. 82.

8 J. Couch, *The History of Polperro*, Truro, 1971, (reprinted), Newcastle, 1965, p. 44; T. Cornish, 'Mackerel and Pilchard Fisheries' in *Fisheries Exhibition Literature*, VII, pp. 10, 13; G. Aflalo, *Sea Fishing*, p. 311; *Morning Chronicle*, 21 November 1849; *Royal Cornwall Gazette*, 1 March 1850; *West Briton*, 2 April 1856; K. Johns and M. Rule, *Portloe: an illustrated history*, Redruth, 2004, p. 35.

9 Although Stern, 'Fish Supply', p. 38, suggests some fresh pilchards were sold in London, sale was insignificant outside Cornwall. On the local sale of pilchards see Report of the Commissioners appointed to inquire into the Sea Fisheries of the United Kingdom, *British Parliamentary Papers*, 1866, XVIII, Minutes of Evidence pp. 21474, 21972, 22116, 23918, 24229-24233. The two cited examples are from 21474 and 21972.

10 The account of the Brixham migrations is based on G. Alward, *The Sea Fisheries of Great Britain and Ireland*, Grimsby, 1932, pp. 19-30; E. Holdsworth, *Deep-Sea Fishing*, p. 208; E. Holdsworth, Sea Fisheries of Great Britain and Ireland, 1883, p. 107 and G. Aflalo, *Sea Fishing*, pp. 290-291.

11 The account of the Cornish seasonal pattern of fishing is based on *The Morning Chronicle*, 21 November 1849: G. Afalo, *Sea Fishing*, p. 310; *Royal Cornwall Gazette*, 1 March 1850; *West Briton*, 7 July 1865; J. Bertram, 'The Unappreciated Fisher Folk, Their Round of Life and Labour', in *Fisheries Exhibition Literature*, II, p. 229; Cornish, 'Mackerel and Pilchard Fisheries', p. 13; N. Pender, Mousehole, *Mousehole*, 1970, pp. 40-42.

12 The poem was written by Robert Maybee in 1883 and titled: 'On the Mounts Bay

Fishing Boats driving around the Scilly Islands for Mackerel and landing them at St Mary's every morning then two Steamers took them to Penzance'. *Robert Maybee: the Scillonian Poet*, Isles of Scilly Museum Publication, No. 9, 1973, pp. 61-62.

13 *West Briton*, 21 October 1836.

14 Report of the Royal Commission on Child Employment, *BPP*, 1842, XVI, Minutes of Evidence, p. 847; E. March, *Soiling Drifters*, 1952, p. 107; *West Briton*, 26 December 1834; *Morning Chronicle*, 21 November 1849; *Royal Cornwall Gazette*, 1 March 1850; *Royal Cornwall Gazette*, 29 March 1834.

15 *BPP*, 1817, III, Minutes of Evidence, p. 114; W. Chaloner, 'Trends in Fish Consumption', p. 101; *BPP*, 1866, XVIII, Minutes of Evidence, p. 18799.

16 W. Chaloner, 'Trends in Fish Consumption', p. 101; *Penny Magazine*, 1837, p. 292; *BPP*, 1866, XVIII, Minutes of Evidence, pp. 9165, 18787-18792; *BPP*, 1817, III, Minutes of Evidence, p. 116.

17 *Cornwall Gazette*, 13 March 1802; *BPP*, 1817, III, Minutes of Evidence, pp.116-118.

18 *West Briton*, 6 April, I June 1827, 26 March 1830; *Cornwall Gazette*, 8 April 1836, 14 April 1837, 18 May 1838.

19 *West Briton*, 26 May 1843; *Cornwall Gazette*, 1 March 1850.

20 P. Pool, (ed.), *Reminiscences of Penzance*, Penzance, 1976, pp. 52-53, a collection of articles by G. Boase contributed to the *Cornishman*, 1883-1884.

21 *Royal Cornwall Gazette*, 8 April 1859.

22 E. Holdsworth, *Deep-Sea Fishing*, p. 66.

23 E. Holdsworth, *Sea Fisheries*, p. 6; E. March, *Sailing Trawlers*, p. 195.

24 C. Gregory, *Brixham in Devonia*, Torquay, n.d., p. 33.

25 Report of the Board of Trade Inquiry into the Relations between the owners, Masters and Crews of Fishing Vessels, *BPP*, 1882, XVII, Minutes of Evidence, p. 6243; E. Holdsworth, *Deep-Sea Fishing*, p. 208.

26 Stern, 'Fish Supply', pp. 35, 41; *BPP*, 1866, XVII1, Minutes of Evidence, p. 8172; 13225; G. Aflalo, *Sea Fishing*, pp. 340-341.

27 *BPP*, 1866, XV111, Minutes of Evidence, pp. 18800, 19171-19172, 21361; W. Chaloner, 'Trends in Fish Consumption', p. 107.

28 D. St Thomas, *A Regional History of The Railways of Great Britain, 1, The West Country*, 1963, p. 100; *West Briton*, 26 October 1866 and 23 April 1968.

29 D. St Thomas, *Regional History of Railways*, p. 100; C. Noall, *Cornish Fishermen*, Truro, 1970, p. 13; J. Simmons, 'The Railway in Cornwall', in *Journal of the Royal Institution of Cornwall*, IX, 1982, p. 19; Cornwall County Council, *Report of the Executive Committee for Fisheries to the Technical Instruction Committee for 1896*, pp. 22, 30.

30 *Cornwall Gazette*, 1 March 1850. The figure was given in numbers of fish, but has been converted using Mayhew's ratio of 1 lb per fish; Cornwall County Council, *Report of the Executive Committee for Fisheries*, 1896, p. 47; Stern, 'Fish Supply', p. 99.

31 E. Holdsworth, *Sea Fisheries*, p. 6. See also Alward, *Sea Fisheries of Great Britain*, p. 44.

32 *BPP*, 1866, XVIII, Minutes of Evidence, pp. 19492-19495, 21361, 22240.

33 J. Hammond, *A Cornish Parish, being an account of St Austell*, 1897, p. 58; *BPP*, 1882, XVII, Minutes of Evidence, p. 6243; G. Aflalo, *Sea Fishing*, pp. 97, 313-315; Simmons, 'Railway in Cornwall', p. 19; G. Boase, *Reminiscences*, p. 22.

34 *West Briton*, 28 October 1897.

35 J. Couch, *Polperro*, p. 45; C. Cutting, *Fish Saving*, 1955, pp. 239-241; G. Aflalo, *Sea Fishing*, pp. 294-295; *BPP*, 1866, XVIII, Minutes of Evidence, pp. 21358-21359.

36 Cornish, 'Mackerel and Pilchard fisheries', p. 10; W. Rowe, *Cornwall in the Age of the Industrial Revolution*, Liverpool, 1953, p. 299; A. Hamilton Jenkin, *Cornish Seafarers*, 1932, pp. 139-140, 202; M. Herubel, *Sea Fisheries: Their Treasures and Toilers* (translated B. Miall), 1912, translator's footnote to p. 14. The preserving value of ice had long been known of course, but it added very considerably to the weight of the fish being freighted. North Sea trawlers started taking ice to sea at the end of the 1850s. A trawler needed between two and four tonnes for its catch. C. Cutting, *Fish Saving*, pp. 231-234. At Brixham the trawler men resisted the taking of ice to sea, fearing that its use would lead to their being required to spend longer spells away. J. Horsley, 'The Shipping of the port of Dartmouth in the Nineteenth Century', in H. Fisher, (ed.), *The South West and the Sea*, Exeter, 1968, p. 57. In any case in their home season, like the Cornish drift fishermen in theirs, they were not fishing at such large distances from port. In the railway era huge quantities of ice were used. In Cornwall it was supplied in the 1870s from local ice works, by a supply of compressed natural ice from the Bodmin Moor and by imports from Norway.

37 G. Aflalo, *Sea Fishing*, pp. 322, 327-328, 342-343; N. Pender, *Mousehole*, pp. 45-46; Cornwall County Council, *Report of the Executive Committee for Fisheries for 1896*, p 1.

12 Gender and Feasting in Nineteenth Century Cornwall

At the beginning of the seventeenth century Richard Carew observed that the Cornish tinners kept more holidays than were warranted by 'the Church, our laws or their own profit'. He conceded that this had some justification in the arduous nature of their labour. A hundred years later, his editor did not agree:

> *Their toil is not so extreme as Mr Carew represents it, that few labourers I believe work so little; except when they draw water, for which their are so many new engines now invented that that this labour is in a good measure taken off. For what between their numerous holidays, holiday eves, feasts, account days (once a month), YeuWiddens or one way or another they invent to loiter away their time, they do not work one half of the month for the owners and employers. Several gentlemen have endeavoured to break through their customs, but it has been hitherto to little purpose.* [1]

The county's historian William Borlase echoed this in 1758 stating that the tinners still kept 'some holidays peculiar to themselves including St Piran's day, their patron saint on 5 March'. Many still kept Midsummer's Day and each parish had its Feast Day, which as well as the Sunday when the supposed dedication of the parish church was celebrated, typically lasted through until Monday and at times till Tuesday. [2] On some of these occasions the miners were allowed small amounts of money to enable the celebrations. This donation was still being made in the 1780s, but by the 1790s an attack on the miners' calendar was being implemented as management practices in the principal mines began to change. In 1802 a mine steward complained of 'those so-called Holydays,' and three years later of 'so many holydays, as people call them, but in fact they are idle feasting days', which he estimated cost each time, a £100 loss to the adventurers. [3] The early nineteenth century brought a marked shift away from tolerance as the 'managerial revolution' of the early industrial era began to contest traditional and customary notions of time-use. Cornwall was a typical example as deeper mining with its higher capital costs, came to dominate the copper and tin mining industries bringing 'industrial time' to the mines was a two-dimensional task. The first involved the definition and enforcement of the working day, while the second involved taking tighter control of the calendar and stamping or squeezing out the time-losing holidays. [4]

It is hard to be specific in assessing how and when this double task was achieved. It certainly did not happen quickly or uniformly; that it was happening, however, is firmly indicated in several diverse sources. In 1808, a travelling cleric observed that 'the riotous revelling held on particular days', when the 'gains of labour were always dissipated in the most brutal debauchery', had become so rare, that in a few years they would be 'only remembered in tradition'. While nine years later another observer was pleased to report that 'riotous revellings' and the associated cruel and barbaric sports had become of rare occurrence: 'The spirit of sport has evaporated, and that of industry has supplied its place'. Mining filled up the time of the miners too effectively to allow, 'leisure for prolonged revels or frequent festivities'. In 1824 tinners' holidays were said to be regarded with such little veneration that many knew little about them and cared less. [5]

The process of erosion was gradual, but by the time the Parliamentary inquiry into child labour in the mines reported in 1842, the evidence from the larger mines suggests that it was substantially complete. In general no holidays were then kept except Christmas Day and Good Friday, although an exception was the Levant Mine in St Just where six days were still allowed, the captain describing this as an 'old established custom in the mine', which was acknowledged to be a very hot one. A vestige of the older pattern could be found too, in the at least partial survival of the time allowed for the Parish Feast. It was allowed, for example for St Austell Feast by United Tin Mines, while at Wheal Vor, the young surface workers were allowed to have time off for the Parish Feast at the expense of a day's wages, which option they unhesitatingly took. Particularly in the Redruth district Whitsuntide was still allowed to the extent of being 'generally very nearly a holiday', the large mining parish of Gwennap with its several villages including St Day and Lanner kept its feast at Whitsun. [6]

For more than two centuries the Parish Feast was for most mining communities the high day of the year, more so than Good Friday or even Christmas Day. It was still being kept up almost universally at the end of the nineteenth century, as Charles Lee, noted soon after his arrival at Newlyn in 1892:

The Churchtowns hereabouts, have each an annual "feast day" when all friends and relations from neighbouring villages are invited to sup, and merrymaking is the rule.

The late A. L. Rowse described St Austell Feast as still being observed in his boyhood up to the Great War. The description by Borlase writing a century-and-a-half before Lee is almost identical:

Every parish has its annual feast. And at such time (however poor at other times of the year) everyone will make a shift to entertain his friends and relations on the Sunday, and on the Monday and Tuesday all business is suspended: and the young men assemble and hurl or wrestle, or both, in some part of the parish of the most public resort. [7]

Borlase on the whole approved of the Feasts and thought it a great pity that 'frolicking and drinking immoderately' should have led to them being attacked by those who, 'distinguish not as they ought, between the institution, and the disorderly observation of it'. A visitor to West Cornwall in 1750 noted that parish feasts were celebrated with 'great profaneness and debauchery', while the vicar of St Erme preached against wrestling and hurling in 1755 and for a time at least, removed them from the feast agenda. [8] Hurling in particular ceased to be a general feature by the 1820s, its opposers included Methodists from John and Charles Wesley on, and, especially in the 1840s, tee-totallers. Critically too it lost much of its gentry patronage by the early nineteenth century. [9] Richard Polwhele, staunchly paternalist, regretted in 1833, that sports among the common people were declining in no small measure due to the increasing detachment of the upper classes:

...gentlemen used to entertain a numerous peasantry at their mansions and castles in celebration of the two great festivals, or the parish feast or harvest home; when at the same time when our halls echoed to the voice of festal merriment, our lawns and downs and woodlands were enlivened by the shouts of wrestling and of hurling. Hospitality is now banished from among us; and so are its attendant sports. [10]

As one aspect of parish feasting declined so others came to be seen as more important and there may well have been a shift which made Sunday's Feast meal in the homes of the entertaining households the most important component of the festival. Such a shift implies a movement away from patronage and towards self-provision on the part of the parishioners, and also one towards domesticity. In tales that were told of the parish feast and its celebration in the nineteenth century, the main successes, and the failures, are usually those of women. The processes of change within what was an enduring institution can be best understood by looking at an example. St Just Feast was one of the most strongly kept and the best described and will serve us as a case study.

St Just was the most westerly of the mining centres and a district where rocky ground, wild Atlantic winds and thin soils combined to provide little work in agriculture. It was the mining town par excellence and that occupation was the main material support of its growing population, while its 'very large and stately Wesleyan chapel' which, 'surprised the stranger by its proportions', saw to its spiritual needs. The parish feast was celebrated at the beginning of November on the nearest Sunday and Monday to All Saints, known locally as 'Allantide'. It was said in the mid-nineteenth century when mining was at its full, to have been kept up, 'with more revelry than almost any other'. [11] On the Monday, games like quoits and skittles were played and for the younger men there were wrestling contests. Once the men of St Just had been distinguished for their strength and skill at hurling, so good, that neighbouring parishes had to combine to play them, but none of the accounts, examined from the 1830s mention that sport as being still played. Surviving accounts of the feast make it seem innocent enough, apart from the suggestion that the level of drinking was perhaps high and removed restraint from the St Just men who were in any case 'proverbially pugnacious', so that games which were played often ended in a free fight. Looking back at these earlier times, a local journalist remembered the feast as a 'hubble, a squabble and a hubbadullian altogether'. [12] In this manner the feast fits well enough into the general nineteenth century narrative of contestation between the rougher forms of popular amusement and the civilizing, improving and soul-saving forces of Methodism and its offshoots. There are however, other accounts to be considered. Rich and poor, we are told, kept open house for friends and relatives, while families were re-united by the short release of girls and young women from their places in domestic service from Saturday to Tuesday morning. On the Monday evening a fair was held in the streets, at which the young men were expected to treat their sweethearts liberally, 'so that a good deal of foolish money that can be ill-afforded is often spent'. [13]

Clearly there were more purposes than revelry met by the parish feast and it can be reasonably suggested that the importance of these social functions varied according to age, relative wealth and gender. The maleness of the associated sports is evident as is the man-thing of drunken brawling. Dancing involved both sexes of all ages, but keeping open house had implications for relative well-being and especially defined what the parish feast had become for the married women. The fair had its attractions for most people, but it had a special place in the courtship pattern of the young men and women. Overall from the over-extension of hospitality, through spending on drink and even on 'fairings' for sweethearts, from this account hangs a faint but definite imputation of improvidence: a lingering prejudice that the parish feast, although its excesses had been moderated was still a thoughtless waste of time and money. [14]

Evidence for a multi-layered investigation of the parish feasts which hears internal as well as external voices is not plentiful, but a reading of the collected Cornish drolls proved unexpectedly valuable. Both of the two major collectors William Bottrell and Robert Hunt, insistently claimed that the folktales which they included were presented as told to them, with the only changes being the making of extreme dialect passages more comprehensible and, especially to be regretted, the toning down of not infrequent passages where the droll tellers 'indulge in a plainness of speech which the fastidious might regard as indelicate'. They also entered their drolls as they heard them and it is this, which gives them real value, for they made no attempt to reduce the material into original 'pure' forms. Instead they stressed the teller's practice of embellishing their stories; one tinner took four evenings to complete a tale about a giant because he included great detail about the tin found in the giant's castle. [15]

These wanderers perpetuated the traditions of the old inhabitants but they modified the stories according to the activity of their fancy, to please their auditors. Not merely this: they without doubt introduced the names of people remembered by the villagers and when they knew that a man had incurred the hatred of his neighbours, they made him do duty as a demon, or placed him in no very enviable relation with the devil. [16]

An indentation in the rock illustrates changing explanations. It was known as a giant's footprint, the devil's hoof mark and as a mark made by the devil as he jumped for joy at carrying off a miller who had lost his soul, by mixing china clay with his flour. Wide publicity was given to just such a fraud in 1814 when miners in Truro burned the effigy of a miller. [17]

Bottrell in the Preface to his third series in 1880 was eager to place his work within the folklore movement that was then manifesting itself in the setting up of societies, journals, and lectures. In the justified belief that his writings brought learned recognition as well as local appreciation, he made a bold claim:

...the folklore student, in collecting the myths, the proverbs, the traditions, the customs of the peasants of many lands, is doing an important work in accumulating facts bearing on the history of mankind; not the mere records of the wars and doings of kings and generals, but of the beliefs, aspirations, thoughts and feelings of the working classes of various nations. [18]

The importance attached to their feast by the people of St Just is indicated by their pattern of pig killing. Several stories on this theme are included in the folk tales collected by William Bottrell. In his first story the household concerned is that of a prosperous miner, who also had a small-holding of a few acres. He and his wife have gone to Penzance on the eve of the feast to purchase meat and other provisions. But significantly they were not there to sell their pig. That animal, fed opportunely from household and other scraps was a symbol for many of the advantages of self-helping providence on the part of the working people. It was desirable not to kill it until it had been fattened to its peak, and that was not reached by the beginning of November. Bottrell explained:

They did not want to kill their pig for winter's store before it was fat, and sell one side of it on the Thursday before the Feast, as many did that they might buy beef and other good things for the Tide. [19]

In two further tales on how poorer mining households committed themselves to the upkeep of the Feast, he again draws attention to pig killing:

Bill killed his pig which wasn't half fat - not so good to kill as many running the lanes. He took one side to market and left the other hanging in the kitchen. Now Hallen Market is the worst in the year for selling pork; so many San tusters' poor lean trash are there that they keep down the price and people who want good pork seldom come to that market. Bill made a few shillings, laid out a trifle on a bit of beef, and kept the rest to pay off a little of his long score at the shop in Churchtown, that he might be trusted again. [20]

The social imperative to have beef for the feast dinner had driven Bill to this transaction. He is represented as one of many acting similarly in exchanging pork for a lesser quantity of beef and the settlement of his outstanding shop debt. A fatter pig in a less over supplied market, and he would have done better. Only the coming feast forced him to go too early to market. A further example reinforces the need for a pig/beef strategy:

A poor tinner was determined to keep his parish feast as well as he could, that he might not be looked down on, and sneered at by his comrades. He killed his pig before it was as fat as it should be, sold one side at Hallantide Market, left the other home to be put in the 'kool' against winter. A piece of beef and other things were bought to keep a decent feast. [21]

If the poor behaved in this ill-considered and improvident manner then the importance of keeping a 'decent feast' even if it involved hardship for some families is clearly revealed. The more affluent could manage things with relative ease. Bottrell's prosperous miner and his wife, who were not forced to sell their pig at the worst time, were able to manage this calendrical demand by following it with a period of frugality. They had spent on the feast more money than usually kept them for a month, and 'Christmas being near, with its bills to be paid, they lived very carefully in the interval, buying the few groceries they wanted in Church town'. In short they avoided shopping visits to Penzance with its seductive wares. [22]

Jackey and Mary, as the story names them, managed the demands of the feast. Managed is an appropriate verb, for the outcome depended on the domestic and housekeeping skills of the wife. Mary is presented as a very good wife. What had Feast Sunday been like for her? Her house was full. The couple had six children and also present was an elderly spinster cousin from the parish who played a helping role. The guests were not only from other households they were also invitees from other parishes, who needed to be impressed by the very best of St Just hospitality. There was a warehouseman from Madron (Penzance), who had issued a reciprocal invitation to the Madron Feast. There were two 'damsels', sisters of courting age. They were bal maidens from Morvah, whose sweethearts were to come later to walk them home. No suggestion of their relationship to the hosting couple is offered, but it can be surmised since Jackey spoke to them familiarly about a named mine captain at their mine, that work was the link. Completing the group was an elderly couple from Sancreed, whose relationship to Jackey and Mary is not indicated, but whose main intention was to say very little, but to eat and drink as much as they could. [23]

Mary's first chore had been to provide a breakfast for the warehouse-man who had been persuaded to arrive early enough to attend the first church service of the Sunday. When one had out of parish guests, pride demanded that they be displayed before the parish - that was part of the theatre of the feast. Mary herself did not go to the church. When all the guests had arrived, she announced:

Jackey my son, tes time for you to take our feasters to Church, for I and Cousin Gracie want all the room to cook dinner. You'll stop a spell at the Public House as usual, and all will be ready in place on the board by the time you come in.

There was no suggestion of only the men going to the church and pub. The female guests did not miss out.

Three hours later at two o'clock the feasters returned. What awaited them was a huge crock containing boiled beef, a couple of fowls, a piece of pork and the usual vegetables, with a rabbit pie and a sugar-coated figgy pudding to follow. And a separate crock full of steamed potatoes: 'Choice red apply potatoes'. This crock is described as being one-tenth the size of the other. Ale was served from pewter flagons, which 'shone like silver'. The honour of the wife, of the house, and that of the par-ish were not let down for all declared, 'they were choke full and ready to burst'. Hot toddy was then brought, which had probably been made from the finest smuggled spirits, and pipes of tobacco for the men, while the fire of furze and turf was stoked to a fuller glow. The men made themselves comfortable before it, while the women went upstairs for 'women's talk' about:

...the births and marriages that had lately taken place, or were likely soon to occur amongst their acquaintances; the new dresses seen in Church; and scores of other matters dear to female hearts.

After a while Mary's pride was further enlarged when the young women asked to see the 'treasures' in the parlour. This hardly used room housed the ornaments and artefacts that a cousin of Mary's, who was a seaman, had brought back from his voyages. Admiration and wonderment were expressed and Mary, presumably well pleased with the way the day had so far gone, went back to the kitchen to bake a cake to be served hot for tea, as the centrepiece of a meal, which also included other cakes, bread and honey and cream.

This couple generally lived carefully, but were essentially comfortable, the husband's wages being supplemented by the possession of a small-holding. Such relatively advantaged households could indeed offer a groaning board of meat dishes. The miner poet John Harris's family at Troon, for example, could serve up a repast, which indicates that St Just was not an exceptional case.

> *All hail, once more the smoking platter.*
> *The sirloin rich and sweet fowl pie*
> *On Friday eve they kill the lamb*
> *Which in the summer miss'd its dam?*
> *And Jem's grey duck, too lost its head,*
> *It hung up in the pantry dead*
> *A well-fed drake which, bye and bye;*
> *Would make a sweet delicious pie.* [24]

At St Just, Mary's preparations for the feast had begun days earlier, for in addition to the marketing and baking there was the cleaning: the extra presentation of a house that to most eyes was always clean. Mary judged it of sufficient importance to send Jackey to a particular beach to fetch sand and grit that she esteemed for its quality as an abrasive. 'None else will please Mary,' he said proudly, 'she's a capital wife she is'.

Feasten Sunday did not go so well for poorer households. Bottrell includes in his collection two drolls, told interestingly by a female story teller, which colourfully draw humour from the experiences of two poorer mining households. In one the wife is represented as competent enough, but a victim of misfortune and of the impositions of out-of-parish feasters. Things began hopefully enough. Although her husband had killed their pig too soon and consequently sold one half at too low a price in the spoiled Hallantide market, the wife dealt sensibly and carefully enough with the retained half. She carefully salted it all, except for a few choice pieces from which she made a special pie for the feast, while for the days remaining she frugally made use of the liver and like bits. Only one guest was expected, a former mine comrade from Zennor, so serving the small piece of beef together with the special pork pie and finishing with the traditional figgy pudding seemed to take care well enough of the meal which was main event of Feasten Sunday. Things however went badly from the start. The Zennor miner had been invited on his own, but he brought a wife and six children, some of whom were actually his sister's. Then the grandparents turned up, one of whom was sharp-eyed enough to notice the last remaining feasten item, a special cake which the wife had hidden behind the pantry door. To cut a long and humorously told droll short:

When they had sat eat, drink and squat [stuff] till they were ready to burst, they all straddled away as fast as they were able with the heavy loads they bore in their stomachs and without as much as once asking the tinner to their own feast in return.

This was, as indeed was the overall behaviour of the 'guests', a fairly common representation of Zennor folk as notorious free-loaders. It seems the men of that parish, esteeming themselves to be the very best of singers, considered that this in itself justified their attendance at any feast or for that matter funeral! [25]

The second of the poorer wives whose feast day meal turned into a disaster, was in part at least also a victim of Zennor imposition, but her own improvidence and lack of domestic skill is represented as making a strong contribution to the sad outcome. Her husband too had sold half of his pig at the lowered market price, but she was less than provident with the other half. Even before her husband returned from his shift at the mine, she was already cutting off prime slices for herself and her sons, who had finished work sooner. They ate the rare treat with gusto, so that by the time her husband returned, she was starting on the leg for his supper. By the Saturday all that was left were 'thin flaps of belly pieces, one shoulder and a pile of bones'. Her husband had invited a miner from Zennor for the Feast Sunday. She was puzzled how she could contrive a dinner out of that for a hungry Zennor man, who would eat the bit of beef and look over his shoulder for more. She made up a poor sort of pie from the scraps and skin and made sure that there were plenty of potatoes. The problem was compounded; in fact it was doubled, for the Zennor man had brought along an uninvited cousin, confidently assert-ing that his singing would be reciprocation enough! Things went from bad to worse. The beef lasted no time at all, but the pie proved inedible even for Zennor folk, whose diet when home, according to the female story teller, 'es fish and potatoes every day of the week and conger pie of a Sunday for a change' and who, being used to 'nothing but conger-fat for their cakes and pastry', could usually be relied on to eat anything. Bill was left with his shame. Even the two insensitive guests sympathized with his plight and took him to the pub for a consolation pint or two. The teller concluded her homily for that is what in effect it was, by laying the blame on 'his wife's bad management'. [26]

For St Just folk to fail before Zennor folk was bad indeed, for eve-rybody knew 'that ef a San Juster don't keep up the feast in some way jest as a can, he's looked down on and jeered at'. The domestic events described are said by the droll collector to have taken place in the 1830s or 1840s, but another droll in the collection is said to have taken place at the end of the eighteenth century, when fears of a French invasion were at a height. Betty Toddy an unmarried young woman lived with and kept house for her brother, a miner. They lived parsimoniously until they in-herited a small holding on which they kept a cow or two as well as grow-ing a useful amount of oats and barley for their own use. For cash Betty marketed eggs and butter. Used to wearing 'all sorts of worn-out finery' handed down and made over, she nourished a dream that one day she would save enough for a dress which would be the smartest in the par-ish and the only day fit for its first outing was the parish feast. This time duly came. The material was purchased, and by Feasten Eve the mantua

maker had made up the gown. The launch of the gown of course demanded a feast dinner of comparable magnificence to which 'not a few;
cousins and old acquaintances were invited'. Jacob killed the pig and
also a calf, beef had been purchased and to these were added geese and
ducks, hares and rabbits. On feast Sunday, Betty rose early to fill the great
crock with the beef, the calf's head and dumplings. Just covering the con-
tents with water, for she had no intention of making a dishwash for Feasten broth. She then made rabbit and veal pies and the traditional figgy
puddings. The village simpleton was brought in to watch over things, so
that Betty could go to the church and display her new gown. She even
managed a theatrical entrance, by arriving after the sermon had begun.
Causing the parson to stop while the congregation turned to gaze upon
'such a gay gown which has never been seen in Church-town from that
day to this'. [27]

Most of the afternoon was spent in eating and in the evening, the men
sought out their old comrades and went as a group to the pub. The women
remained at home to talk over sweethearts past, present and hoped for,
until the men rejoined them for a supper, 'as substantial a meal as they
had for dinner'. About midnight the older guests went home, while the
young folks stayed over to watch and participate in Feast Monday and
Tuesday's games, dancing and singing. The droll continues to describe
wrestling and hurling, making the point that in those times at the end
of the eighteenth century, those sports were still being played under the
patronage of the gentry. This wonderful droll, surely one of the funniest
in Bottrell's collection, ends in high farce. On the Wednesday, known as
'servy day' when the odds and ends of the feast were served at mid-day
before the remaining guests departed. On the Thursday Jacob and his
fellow miners returned to work, although they didn't labour very hard
as it took time to 'tell all the news about the feast [and] the news brought
into the parish by the strangers'. That night Betty served Jacob a meal of
pease-porridge. In the early hours Betty heard a strange noise. Panicking
she thought the French had landed and, not recognising a noise produced
by her brother's indigestion from the undercooked peas, roused the parish, including the man responsible for lighting the warning beacon. He

duly performed his duty and from his signal the beacons were lit all the way up the coast to Plymouth, from where, some say, a troop of soldiers set out and were well into Cornwall before they were turned back. [28]

A fifth droll involved legends of giants. The young giant Tom, who was small by giant standards measuring only four feet across the shoulders, nevertheless slew the giant Blunderbuss in so fair a contest that the latter left him his castle and all his possessions. When Tom entered the castle he found there something the old giant had not mentioned: his wife. She having learned of the outcome of the fight had quickly come to the conclusion that it 'was the wisest course to "take up" at once with Tom; and she being a tidy body, Tom was by no means unwilling'. Jane was a good wife, 'a wonderfully cleanly body - the castle seemed to be always fresh swept and sanded, while all the pewter plates and platters shone like silver'. She never quarrelled with Tom except when he came in covered in mud, when in temper she would threaten to go home to her mother. They had plenty of children. Indeed, they were contented in that unambitious way that so many giants are if they are not interfered with. She was also noted for her butter and cheese. All went well enough until Jack the Tinkeard came on the scene. He and Tom fought to a standstill, Jack using his special blackthorn stick and Tom swinging a broken gate. Suffice it to say that a fair contest ended in mutual admiration and with Tom inviting his opponent for dinner. Jane was somewhat put out, she had already called her husband three times. She was vexed that she had not had warning enough to set something better before them than just peas and beef. The amount, however, was more than sufficient with 'huge pieces of beef and mountains of pease-pudding'. The droll then tells at length of the growing friendship between the three. Jack taught the rusticated giant and his wife many things, including how to grow vegetables, thus starting one of the industries for which that part of Cornwall became famous. Time passed in alternate feasting and fighting, until Tom became jealous. There was a row and Jane went home to her mother, Jenny, with whom she soon quarrelled because the older lady said bad things about Tom, and only Jane was allowed to do that. Reunited again Jack succeeds in what had always been his intent. He persuaded Tom to allow the exploitation of the large amounts of tin ore, which he had always known to be under his land. Reluctantly, and with small understanding, the giant's seclusion broke down and he became a part of the local economy. After a period of travelling the road again Jack came back and married Tom's daughter, with a celebration in nearby Morvah with such revelry and rejoicing on a Sunday that from that day forth, its date was annually celebrated as Morvah feast. [29]

Five drolls have now been examined. Three are directly concerned with the Parish Feast and the ways of keeping it; a fourth is partly so, although its main purpose is to unfold into a splendidly Chaucerian finale. It is the only one to date its occurrence precisely, but a feature of the droll is its presently relevant detail on habits and expectations, attached to a narrative that is timeless. In short, the same things were feasted on in the long-ago time of the giants as were in more recent remembered times. It follows that the 'goodwife' at all times needed to posses the same virtues of domesticity, for it is these values, which the tellers of drolls were 'approving' as they related their embellished stories to their village audiences.

Parish feasting, then involved little of the carnivalesque for the parish wives. It offered no temporary reversal of roles, hardly much in the way of licence. It seems that by the middle decades of the nineteenth century the Sunday Feast meal had become the domestic centre of its celebration. The droll seems to judge the women in the same way as did middle-class witnesses on the mining population for parliamentary and other official bodies:

You will find two men, and one has got a clean, decent, wholesome, industrious wife and that man's children will be kept as clean and comfortable as possible. You will then see one of the same 'pare' who has got a dirty careless wife and that family will be in rags, and yet that man will have the same earnings. One man will be well off and the other always in misery.

There is a woman living about four or five miles from Penzance, she has a husband and four or five boys who are all working in the mine, and I calculate that they are earning from £11 to £13 or £14 a month, and yet they have not got a chair to sit down upon; there is scarcely a cup or saucer in the place, and as for a bed what they have would disgrace the poorest persons in the kingdom. [30]

The Wesleyan minister at St Just added the voice of the chapel to the chorus of concern over women's house-keeping competence, resulting, he believed from girls and young women working at the mines rather than learning and experiencing in the home the skills of domesticity and as a consequence were 'unable to make and mend'. Medical opinion, concerned with the prevalence of stomach disorders among the working miners, blamed a deficiency in 'culinary knowledge of the young women' which led to a crude and course preparation of the miner's food. [31]

Dr Schwartz has analyzed the changing attitudes towards employment of women at the Cornish mines produced by the rise of the middle-class ideology of 'separate spheres':

Women were urged to return to their natural position in life - the domestic realm - to become an "angel in the home", grounding their lives in domesticity, housewifery, childrearing and nurturing'. [32]

It is at least possible that an indication of the rapid colouring of the views of many working class people, which Dr Schwartz suggests, is the ease with which women were judged by this assumption and expectation even in the most vernacular form of communication: the droll.

Lack of domestic skills was closely associated with 'want of management in the outlay of earnings'. Even those who did not see the feast as harmful expressed some concern that it of its nature teetered on the edge of improvidence. The fables of pig-killing at St Just convey this problem by inverting a cliché. Pig keeping was in the discourses of the time, the very cornerstone of the self-providing cottage economy. In William Corbett's huge volume of writing, pigs seem at times to be only outweighed by politics in the space they are afforded. It is true that it was the husband's decision to sell half the pig at the worst moment in marketing terms, but it was what the wife did with the other half and with whatever beef the unfavourable exchange had procured which determined the adequacy of the Feast Day meal. Did keeping the feast amount to a careless outburst of unnecessary, irrational and, to many, unaffordable conspicuous consumption? [33] Hans Medick has argued that conventional accounts of such behaviour miss the point. Faced with long-term uncertainties and low expectations, the peasant household deciding to indulge with whatever resources it can put to that end, is not behaving irrationally, but exhibiting preferences, which were profoundly different from those of the middle class advocates of thrift and saving. [34]

According, however, to one account of St Just Feast written at the end of the 1850s, the extravagance versus saving argument was somewhat more complicated. George Henwood began his account with the apothegm: 'It is a faint heart that never rejoices', and continued that it was to be applied, 'as the watchword and palliative for the exuberant glee, riotous festivity, and (for them) lavish expenditure indulged in on the ancient annual festival'.

The everyday diet of the St Just cottagers was based on fish and potatoes with 'flesh' on Sundays. Christmas with its goose was one exception. The other was feast day 'when roast beef and plum pudding grace the board, with a drop of "moonshine" to wash it down'. That:

...the habits of these poor people being, of necessity, very economical, their lavish expenditure renders the contrast more striking, and the zest with which they enjoy their festival the more keen. To many who fare luxuriously every day,

Woman collecting 'furze and turf'.

*it may appear trifling and silly; to them it is a high day - indeed the highest in
the calendar, all parish gossip taking its date from its golden letter.* [35]

The account continues to describe the saving that took place prior to
the Feast. Here is perhaps another inversion. Saving was approved as a
means of forgoing some measure of present gratification to increase independence and guard against future need. In St Just according to Henwood things began to happen six months before the feast, from the bal
boys, demanding sixpence a month back from the wages they handed
their mother, to the miners working extra hours to put by a few shillings, which they kept secret from their wives. The 'frugal housewife' too
put by all that she could spare for 'nackins' (trifling luxuries). By Tuesday the feast was winding down following Monday's sports, dances and
evening's convivial drinking. A few remained to see that the savings of
six months were 'reduced to mere dribblets'. By the end of the week little more was thought of the feast until six months passed and the saving
process began again. [36]

Mary, the wife in the droll of the prosperous miner, did in fact get
some reward for her efforts, apart from that is a hard-earned sense of
pride. One of her guests, the store man from Madron invited her and
Jackey to that parish's feast due to be held soon after. Had it been from
a poorer neighbouring parish like Zennor, it would not in the eyes of
St Just people have carried much credit, but Madron was Penzance, the
nearest place which offered urban civilization, style and politeness. Mary
had some apprehension. She would be paraded as visiting feaster not in
some village church, but in a grander town one, with a proper organ. The
family was being honoured, and her cousin eagerly offered the help one
might expect from a kinswoman at such a time:

*I'll come and see that you are all smart and tidy to go to Penzance Church
and hear the organ. I'll come over very early and titivate ee off, for the credit of
the parish. Before you go to Penzance Feast to see grand people and things.* [37]

A sequel droll follows Mary and Jackey to Madron. Their host was
a bachelor and much of this droll is concerned with how he, without a

wife, managed the meal. At one point, Jackey, cheerfully and proudly made an offer to his host: 'Sit thee down, mate' said Jackey, 'and touch pipe a bit, lev Mary do the rest about dinner'.

The visit to Penzance would provide a talking point for neighbours for some time to come what had been worn, how the hair had been styled for instance doubtless provided much material for female gossip. The Madron host had, in an ill-tempered early morning outburst, claimed as much:

"Ask'd 'e to feast, ded I? Perhaps I ded", replied Dick; "I've asked scores, I bla, mainly for the sake of asking, and that they might have it to say they feel proud to tell their neighbours how they have been invited to Penzance to feast"[38].

It was, however, the particular thing about Feast Day's women's talk that it centred, filled with reminiscences, on courtship and marriage. The fair was ideal for couple's to walk out together, and for sweethearts to be treated. Quiller Couch commented on the feast:

The maids of the village know this is the recognised day for courtship and frankly array themselves for it, to attract the young swains who also recognise Feasten Day as the proper date for choosing. [39]

The distinguished scholar and writer wrote this in an introduction to Charles Lee's novella *Dorinda's Birthday* that captures this aspect of Feast Day well:

"Finished up your cake, my dear? Dragging to be off, shouldn't be frightened. Off with 'e then, fitty maid as soon's you've a mind to. Didn' come up to do the polite to fat old women, did 'e? Found a chap yet?"

"Maybe I have, maybe I haven't", said Dorinda.

"Well no time like feast time for that. Maid's harvest I call en. I catched mine 'pon a feast-day, and so did your ma here".[40]

Folklorists and cultural theorists attach great importance to the feast considering it to be one of the strongest manifestations of popular culture, although the several functions are recognised; for the people making up the crowd may be there for different reasons. There is a strong tendency to see village feasts as forms of 'carnival'. Understanding by this not only extravagant eating, and dress display, but also a challenge to the usual lines of authority and the taking of a broad license in drinking, sexual behaviour, and general revelry. The Oxford English Dictionary defines 'revelry' as 'riotous and noisy merrymaking' but allows 'revel,' as a transitive verb to mean 'to spend or waste time in revelry'. The date of the parish feast was supposedly the anniversary of the dedication of the parish church. This was in most cases lost in the mists of time. As John Harris asked in his mid-nineteenth century poem:

> I know not how this custom came
> Which all my clansmen love to name.
> They've told me by the embers seated,
> Our parish church was then completed;
> And since that time, when comes the day
> A feast awaits both old and gay.
> Vague tradition may be true;
> I've seen no record, - pray have you? [41]

The Church remained associated with the feast, as we have seen attending its service on the Sunday morning was part of the programme, even for some of those who usually worshiped at the chapel. In the North and Midlands the same commemorating role was played by the Wakes, and there too were complaints that the devotional aspect was forgotten and the festivity turned into riot, drunkenness and mischief. It has been argued that the Wakes can be better understood through applying the idea of 'carnival'. [42] There are Cornish cases when the concept seems applicable. Ludgvan feast in 1839 was said to have been 'one scene of revelry and drunkenness' so that it 'seemed as if destruction had taken hold of the four corners of it'. [43] There is a case too for wondering what forms of behaviour characterized eighteenth century feasting, but the evidence which survives for the nineteenth century, especially the folkloric, indicates a tradition of feasting which served several significant social functions, and cannot be simply generalised as 'carnival'.

1 The comment was made by Thomas Tonkin whose eighteenth century marginal notes to Richard Carew, *Survey of Cornwall*, 1602, were included in the edition edited by Lord de Dunstanville (Sir Francis Bassett) in 1811, p. 35. YeuWhidden was held in honour of the discovery of tin smelting.

2 W. Borlase, *Natural History of Cornwall*, Oxford, 1758, p. 302.

3 Jenkin MSS, William Jenkin to H. Britton, 4 April 1802 and to J. Cole, 9 Jan 1805.

4 For an international perspective on 'industrial time' see my contribution 'Keeping Industrial Time', in T. Murray, ed., *Time and Archaeology*, 1999, pp. 61-79.

5 R. Warner, *A Tour Through Cornwall in the Autumn of 1808*, 1809, pp. 300-301; C. Gilbert, *An Historical Survey of the County of Cornwall*, 1817, I, p. 104; F. Hitchens, and S. Drew, History of Cornwall, 1824, I, p. 725.

6 *British Parliamentary Publications*, 1842, xvi, *Employment of Children*, Minutes of Evidence, pp. 935, 848, 783, 850, 841, 832, 844, 836, 838, 839, 842.

7 K. Phillipps, ed., *The Cornish Journal of Charles Lee 1892-1898*, Padstow, 1995, pp. 1-2; A. Rowse, *A Cornish Childhood*, 1962 ed, pp. 15-16; W. Borlase, *Natural History of Cornwall*, p. 301.

8 ibid, p. 300; R. Pococke, *Travels through England*, ed., J. Cartwright, 1888, reprinted 1965, p. 136; Anon MSS, 'Account of a Tour in Cornwall in 1755', CRO, Pendarves Papers.

9 The Methodist and tee-total attack on popular amusements is fully discussed in Chapter 7 above.

10 R. Polwhele, ed., *Lavington's Enthusiasm of Methodists and Papists Compared*, 1833, pp. cxxi-cxxii.

11 G. Henwood, ' 'St Just Feast', Cornwall's Mines and Miners', (Articles from the *Mining Journal* edited R. Burt, Truro, 1972), p. 71; M. Courtney, *Cornish Feasts and Folklore*, 1890, reprint 1973, p. 3.

12 ibid, p. 4.

13 A. Hamilton Jenkin, *Cornish Homes and Customs*, 1934, p.238; M. Courtney, *Cornish Feasts*, p. 4.

14 For example the brief account by Courtney pp. 3-4

15 The collections are those of R. Hunt, *Popular Romances of the West of England, or the Drolls, Traditions and Superstitions of Old Cornwall*, (3rd edition), 1881; W. Bottrell, *Traditions and Hearthside Stories of West Cornwall*, three volumes 1870, 1873, 1880. The third is entitled *Stories and Folklore of West Cornwall*. I have used the facsimile reprint by Llanerch Publishers, Felinfach, 1996; Hunt, pp. 31; Bottrell, pp iv-v.

16 R. Hunt, p. 28.

17 ibid, p. 43; *West Briton*, 10 November 1817.

18 W. Bottrell, 3rd Series, *Preface*.

19 ibid, p. 50.

20 ibid, p. 62.

21 ibid, p. 69.

22 ibid, p. 73.

23 The account given here is based on Bottrell, pp. 50-50.

24 John Harris, poem entitled 'The Parochial Festival' in *Shakespeare's Shrine*, 1866, pp. 303-306.

25 W. Bottrell, 3rd Series, pp. 69-71.

26 ibid, pp. 69-71.

27 W. Bottrell, 1st Series, pp. 143-145. The passing reference to the village simpleton adds nothing to the narrative directly. I suggest it is a skilled teller's device to provide a peg for some comic digression.

28 ibid, pp. 145-151.

29 I have based this summary on Hunt, pp. 55-72 in preference to a slightly different version in Bottrell, 1st Series, pp. 1-40.

30 *BPP*, 1864, xxiv, *Condition of Mines in Great Britain*, pp. 43, 146.

31 *BPP*, 1842, xvi, *Employment of Children*, pp. 848, 834.

32 S. Schwartz, 'No Place for a Woman': Gender at Work in Cornwall's Metalliferous Mining Industry', *Cornish Studies*, 8, 2000, pp.ibid, 81-82.

33 See I. Dyck, *William Cobbett and Rural Popular Culture*, 1992, pp. 115-116.

34 See Hans Medick, 'Plebeian Culture in the Transition to Capitalism' in R. Samuel and G. Stedman Jones, eds., *Culture, Ideology and Politics*, 1982, pp. 84-112.

35 G. Henwood, 'St Just Feast' pp. 71-73.

36 ibid p. 73.

37 W. Bottrell, 3rd Series, p. 58. Dialect spelling as in original.

38 ibid, pp. 74-75.

39 Sir Arthur Quiller Couch, introduction to Charles Lee, *Cornish Tales*, 1941, p. 8. The late A.L. Rowse also admired Lee's ability to capture Cornish ways and dialect.

40 Charles Lee, *Dorinda's Birthday*, 1911, reprinted in *Cornish Tales*, 1945, p. 255.

41 J. Harris, loc cit.

42 See D. Reid, 'Interpreting the Festival Calendar: Wakes and Fairs as Carnivals', in R. Storch, ed., *Popular Culture and Custom in Nineteenth Century England*, Croom Helm, 1982, pp. 125-133.

43 *Cornwall Gazette*, 1 Feb 1839. Of course some of the old traditional rituals of 'misrule' can be found in Cornwall, for example 'mock mayors', were elected at Mylor (Penryn), St Germans and by the inhabitants of Bodmin on Halgaver Moor. Of the first Hunt wrote 'The popular opinion is that there is a clause in the borough charter compelling the legitimate mayor to surrender his power to the Mayor of Mylor, on the night in question and to lend the town sergeant's paraphernalia to the gentlemen of the shears', pp. 401-403. The 'gentlemen' were the journeymen tailors who took the lead in the proceedings.

Bibliographical and Historiographical Notes

The text has been fully referenced in respect of both primary and secondary sources and the purpose of these notes is mainly to draw attention to some new, general contexting or comparative works.

Introduction: So far as general histories of Cornwall are concerned , Philip Payton's masterfully composed and superbly illustrated *Cornwall*, (Alexander Associates, Fowey, 1996) is challengingly argued as well as being extraordinarily comprehensive. It has a complementary volume, *The Cornish Overseas*, (1999). The 'New Cornish History' is well presented in the essays which make up *Cornish Studies, X*, edited by Philip Payton, (Exeter University Press, 2002). Publication of Bernard Deacon's important Ph.D thesis 'The Reformation of Territorial Identity Cornwall in the Late Eighteenth and Nineteenth Centuries' (Open University, 2001) is promised soon.

Britain has been especially fortunate in the number of monographs on regional and particular industries, which have been produced since the beginning of the last century, many the products of a long tradition of teaching and researching economic and social history. Well able to hold their place in this distinguished tradition are A. K. Hamilton Jenkin, *The Cornish Miner. An Account of his Life Above and Underground from Early Times*, (First published, Allen and Unwin, 1927; third edition 1962) and John Rowe, *Cornwall in the Age of the Industrial Revolution* (Liverpool University Press, 1953; reprinted St Austell, 1997). More recently a general history of Cornish mining has appeared: Allen Buckley, *The Story of Mining in Cornwall*, (Cornwall Editions, Fowey, 2005), while S. Schwartz and R. Parker, *Lanner: a Cornish Mining Parish* (Halsgrove, Tiverton, 1998) is a major local history. Lead was less important than tin or copper in

Cornwall, but its mining was still significant employing 2500 males in 1851. It is well covered in Roger Burt's national study, *The British Lead Mining Industry* (Dyllansow Truran, Redruth, 1984). Of the British coal-fields, that of the North East offers perhaps the most intriguing comparisons with Cornish mining communities. See R. Colls, *The Pitmen of the Northern Coalfield. Work, Culture and Protest, 1790-1850*, (Manchester University Press, 1987) and D. Levine and K. Wrightson, *The Making of an Industrial Society: Whickham 1560-1765*, (Oxford University Press, 1991).

For a balanced assessment of E. P. Thompson's influence in the 1960s and 1970s on the writing of social history see: D. Eastwood, 'History, Politics and Reputation. E. P. Thompson Reconsidered', (*History*, 85, 2000, pp. 34-54). Thompson produced little history in the 1980s committing his energies to the Peace Movement. When he began writing again his main concern was with the popular culture of the eighteenth century, and several important essays were brought together in *Customs in Common*, (Merlin Press, 1991). The 'social history project' of those years came under attack from various strands of post-modernism in the 1980s. Concerns for gender, ethnicity and place, demanded and rightly received attention while class, in terms of experience-derived consciousness as well as materialist determination, has given room to the accommodation of other identities. Some of the new historians have been strident in their wholesale rejection of the 'modernist', approach to historical thinking, researching and writing. 'History' according to some of them is not only ceasing to be, it never really was! Its claim to a distinct epistemology have been denied. Marxism has been a special target but has not been alone - the social history project's most influential input seems to have come from a humanized Marxism which allowed social consciousness to develop from social being, that is from lived experience. Following Thompson 'making' became one of the most active words in the historian's vocabulary. When, as it often did, it appeared in the title of historical productions it was an indication of the author's belief that people made their own histories, though not in circumstances entirely of their own choosing. To many post-modernists this thinking is a late example of Enlightenment delusion. They have found all grand narratives wanting, and have no greater appreciation of the slower ambiance of the *longue durée* of the Annalistes. One reason for this unaccommodating approach is as a reaction to what is viewed as only slow progress being made in the re-structuring of history generally, either in its practice by academic historians or in its acceptance by the wider population. An example of an unrelenting dismissal of what he calls the 'old social histories' characterises Patrick Joyce's 'The End of Social History', (*Past and Present*, No. 133, 1992). In an effective response, Geoffrey Eley and Keith Neild 'Starting Over: the Present, the Post-modern and the Moment of Social History', *Social History*, 21, 1, 1996) responded that to advocate the simple abandonment of a body of work which only recently was the dominant and most advanced of history's fields of inquiry is as misguided as it is unnecessary. Joyce, they argue, fails to address 'the substantial and honourable and concrete, historiographical achievements of the field'.

Migration Studies have been brought to a new level by the work of historians at the Institute of Cornish Studies. This contribution has been acknowledged in a recent national study of the importance to the economy of emigrant remittances: G. B. Magee and A. S. Thompson, 'Lines of Credit, Debts of Obligation: migrant remittances to Britain, c. 1875-1913', *Economic History Review*, LIX, 3, 2006.

Food Riots: His original 'moral economy' article and response to his critics can now be found in Thompson's *Customs in Common*. An important in depth study is Roger Wells, *Wretched Faces. Famine in Wartime Britain 1793-1803*, (Gloucester 1988) which contains important Cornish data in its Appendices. A. Charlesworth, *An Atlas of Rural Protest in Britain 1548-1900*, (Croom Helm, 1983) provides an essential mapping. A. Charlesworth and A. Randall provide a useful introduction to their edited collection *Moral Economy and Popular Protest. Crowds, Conflict and Authority*, (Macmillan, 2000).

Mortality and Morbidity: See Cyril Noall, *Cornish Mine Disasters*, with introduction by Philip Payton, (Dyllansow Truran, Redruth, 1989). The subject is covered well in R. Burt, *Lead Mining*. On the Levant episode of 1920 when the main engine collapsed see 'Jack Penhale' (Raymond Williams) *The Mine under the Sea*, (Lake, Falmouth, 1962).

Methodism: The most authoritative voice in recent years has been that of David Hempton see *Methodism and Politics in British Society 1750-1850,* (Heinemann, 1984) and the essay collection, *The Religion of the People. Methodism and Popular Religion c. 1750-1850,* (Routledge, 1996). For Cornwall the data collected and sorted by J. C. C. Probert has been an invaluable resource see especially *The Sociology of Cornish Methodism,* (Cornish Methodist Historical Association, 1971). An ongoing oral history project is presently producing interesting results. See for example Kayleigh Milden, "Are you Church or Chapel?" Perceptions of Spatial and Spiritual Identity within Cornish Methodism', (*Cornish Studies*, 12, 2004, pp. 144-165).

Tribute System and Trade Unionism: Roger Burt, (ed), *Cornish Mining: Essays on the Organization of Cornish Mines and the Cornish Mining Economy* (Newton Abbot, Croom Helm, 1969), remains an essential source reprinting six nineteenth century articles. Burt's very recent comparative article, 'Industrial Relations in the British Non-Ferrous Mining Industry in the Nineteenth Century' (*Labour History Review*, 71, No 1, 2006) is an important addition to the literature. James Jaffe, *The Struggle for Market Power: Industrial Relations in the British Coal Industry, 1800-1840,* (Cambridge University Press, 1991) is a strongly argued account of wage bargaining on the North Eastern coalfield.

Deep-Sea Fishing: The fishing industry has been rather neglected by modern historians. A listing of older works on British deep-sea fishing can be found in John Rule, 'The British Fisherman: 1840-1914', (*Bulletin of the Society for the Study of Labour History*), No. 27, 1973). An important and original essay by Bernard Deacon is 'Imagining the Fishing: Artists and Fishermen in Late-Nineteenth Century Cornwall', (*Rural History, 12, 2, 2001*). For a remarkable account of inshore fishing from Sidmouth in Devon see the classic *A Poorman's House* by Stephen Reynolds, (1908 and subsequent editions).

Folklore, Custom and Culture: Although now twenty-five years old, R. W. Bushaway, *By Rite: Custom, Ceremony and Community in England 1700-1880,* (Junction Books, 1982) is still the leader in its field. In addition to the classic Cornish collections of William Botrell, Robert Hunt and, to a lesser extent, Margaret Courtney, there is the more recent book by T. Deane and T. Shaw, *The Folklore of Cornwall*, (Batsford, 1975). This volume has a long introduction by Venetia Newall, the Secretary of the Folklore Society. For popular recreations see: R. W. Malcolmson, *Popular Recreations in English Society, 1700-1850*, (Cambridge University Press, 1973). Concern with popular culture has led to a growing interest in social anthropology among historians. Keith Thomas, *Religion and the Decline of Magic* (Weidenfeld and Nicholson, 1971) was a pioneering work and E. P. Thompson, 'Anthropology and the Discipline of Historical Context', (*Midland History*, 1, 1972) is an appreciative review. Anthropologists like Mary Douglas and Clifford Geertz are among the prominent influences on present day social historians. See Aletta Biersack, 'Local Knowledge, Local History: Geertz and Beyond', in Lynn Hunt, (ed.), *The New Cultural History*, (University of California Press, 1989). Amy Hale, an anthologist and folklorist has recently suggested that ethnography has been under-stressed in the medley of disciplines which have made up the new Cornish studies: See Amy Hale, 'Cornish Studies and Cornish Culture(s): Evaluations and Directions', (*Cornish Studies*, 10, 2002). In an introduction to a reprint of Salome Hocking's *Some Old Cornish Folk. Characters from St Stephen-in-Brannel*, (1903; reprinted Cornish Hillside Publications, St Austell, 2002), she presents it as a work of great anthropological value as an account of the Cornish in the later nineteenth century from the pen of an insider, particularly able to offer insight into the role and nature of Methodism. The quality of Salome Hocking's insights may be exceptional, although as the many and varied references to other accounts of the Cornish people made throughout this book, suggest the sources from which an ethnographic history could derive, if problematic, are not insubstantial. It all depends, I suppose on how imaginatively historians approach them. Historians of the period about which I mainly write can hardly live among those whose culture they seek to understand, but empathy, attention to the possibility of several readings of sources and immersion in them so that 'voices' can be heard suggest that the practice of what might fairly called 'ethnographic history' is an attractive agenda.

Clio Publishing is a young company with a growing reputation for providing bespoke publishing solutions for authors and researchers in the arts and humanities. The incredible flexibility, speed, and cost-efficiency of print-on-demand technology combined with the marketing opportunities of the internet and direct mail, now offer authors a powerful new way of exploiting their intellectual property.

If you are an author in the arts and humanities that would like to take charge of your publishing destiny, please contact in the first instance Dr Susan England at info@cliopublishing.co.uk or telephone +44 (0) 23 8058 4460. You can also view the Clio Publishing website at www.cliopublishing.co.uk